THEY'LL NEVER PUT THAT ON THE AIR

AN ORAL HISTORY OF TABOO-BREAKING TV COMEDY

ALLAN NEUWIRTH

Illustrations by Glen Hanson

ALLWORTH PRESS
NEW YORK

10   09   08   07   06   5   4   3   2   1

Published by Allworth Press
An imprint of Allworth Communications
10 East 23rd Street, New York, NY 10010

Cover design by Allan Neuwirth
Cover illustration by Chris Boyd
Interior design by Mary Belibasakis
Interior Illustrations by Glen Hanson
Typography by Integra Software Services

ISBN: 1-58115-417-8

Library of Congress Cataloging-in-Publication Data:

Neuwirth, Allan.
    They'll never put that on the air: an oral history of taboo-breaking TV comedy/Allan Neuwirth; interior illustrations by Glen Hanson.
        p.   cm.
    Includes bibliographical references and index.
    1. Television comedies—United States.   I. Title.

PN1992.8.C66N48 2006
791.45'617—dc22   2005035239

Printed in Canada

Contents

Acknowledgments

What an adventure this book has been! As you read it, you'll understand—as I do—that I could never have created it without the brilliant legendary television and comedy talents who so generously agreed to share their experiences and thoughts with me. They are as much the authors of *They'll Never Put That on the Air* as I am.

Our credit roll includes interviewees Chris Bearde, Allan Blye, Allan Burns, Pat Carroll, Ernie Chambers, Larry Charles, Tom Cherones, Stephen Cox, Mike Dann, Sam Denoff, Larry Gelbart, Leonard Goldberg, Barry Harman, Valerie Harper, Susan Harris, Charlie Hauck, Arte Johnson, Coslough Johnson, Ken Kragen, Perry Lafferty, Norman Lear, Rick Ludwin, Dick Martin, Peter Mehlman, Burt Metcalfe, Gary Owens, Glenn Padnick, Rod Parker, Bill Persky, Joyce Randolph, Carl Reiner, Gene Reynolds, Mickey Ross, Jay Sandrich, Bob Schiller, George Schlatter, Alfred Schneider, George Shapiro, Elliot Shoenman, Fred Silverman, Treva Silverman, Tommy Smothers, Martin Starger, David Steinberg, Leonard Stern, Don Taffner, Bill Tankersley, Grant Tinker, Alan Wagner, Mason Williams, Paul Junger Witt, and Bud Yorkin.

Deepest appreciation to my good friend Peter Winter, for egging me on to write this book when it was still a mere whim. Very special thanks to Glen Hanson for his gorgeous and distinctive illustrations, which appear at the head of each chapter, to TV historian and author Stephen Cox, who graciously provided many vintage photographs from his own personal collection, and to Karen L. Herman, a director of the Academy of Television Arts and Sciences' Archive of American Television, for sharing the great Carroll O'Connor, Jean Stapleton, and Beatrice Arthur testimonies. Without her help, their voices could not have been part of this.

And before I run out of ways to say *thank you*, heartfelt huzzahs to the many delightful production people, colleagues, friends, and family members who encouraged, aided, and abetted me (including one or two who probably abetted I'd never finish this book): Cherie Simon, Marilyn Pessin, and Jean Anderson at Act III Communications, Aimee Hyatt at Shapiro/West and Associates, Ed Zimmerman at Columbia Tri-Star, Bess Scher at Clear Productions, and Ellen Benjamin, Wendy Blair, Tony Cacciotti, Jim Colucci, Steve Daly, Angelo DeCesare, Glen Hanson, Linsey Hubbard, Duncan McInnes, Rowan McInnes, Risa Neuwirth, John Olson, Tanya Oskanian, Kathy Reese, Jaime Toporovich, Robyn Steinberg, and Elliot Wax. On a sad note, talented director/producer and longtime TV exec Perry Lafferty passed away at 88, some months after our conversations. He was a true gentleman and a television pioneer, already missed by many.

Finally, my deepest gratitude and respects to publisher Tad Crawford and senior editor Nicole Potter-Talling at Allworth Press, who gave the greenlight to this project almost immediately and then creatively challenged me, offering their guidance and wisdom; to my savvy assistant editor, Monica Lugo, who patiently helped me whip the book into shape; and to artist Chris Boyd for his wonderful 3-D cover illustration. I honestly couldn't have done this without all of you!

But First, a Word from Our Author

Over the last few decades, we've watched television grow up.

Back in the 1960s, gimmicky programming ruled the airwaves. Series like *Bewitched, The Beverly Hillbillies, Green Acres, The Munsters, I Dream of Jeannie, My Favorite Martian, Mr. Ed, The Flying Nun*, and *Gilligan's Island* happened to be some of the most popular shows on TV. Were they funny? Sometimes they were hilarious . . . other times downright stupid. Of course, most of them were not exactly what you'd call highbrow entertainment. By then, TV sets had become pretty much affordable to everyone, so the networks homogenized their creative output until it appealed (presumably) to all. Shows about nose-twitching witches, country bumpkins, goofy monsters, genial genies, avuncular aliens, talking horses, airborne nuns, and moronic castaways were perfect fodder for children. But it wasn't just kids watching—the whole country seemed to be.

Later that same decade, television finally entered puberty, and its voice grew deeper . . . more politically aware, more concerned with the social issues of the day. And though viewers weren't privy to it at the time, some of the same conflicts and rebellions that so many of us were living through were being played out behind the scenes in the TV industry.

Since the very beginnings of the medium, commercial sponsors have determined what programs audiences will get to choose from on network TV. And let's face it, if you're a salesman and your goal is to sell as many cans of dog food or tubes of toothpaste as you possibly can, the last thing you want to do is offend any potential customers. All language or content deemed remotely offensive—no matter how trifling—was expunged from television. Can't show this, can't say that. No jokes about God or religion. Swearing was out, of course. But so were words like "sex," "pregnant," "damn," and "hell." No married couples shown sleeping in the same bed together (they might be touching each other's naughty bits), or people

Cartoonish sitcoms like The Beverly Hillbillies *ruled the ratings roost throughout much of the 1960s. Pictured (l-r): Jed (Buddy Ebsen), Granny (Irene Ryan), Jethro (Max Baer, Jr.), and Elly May (Donna Douglas).* © *CBS Television Network*

with different colored skin (gasp!) showing affection to one another. Skin? You couldn't even show a belly button. Political humor was verboten: no jokes about government policy, the president of the United States, or the atom bomb. Interestingly, violence was okay—at "acceptable levels," whatever those are.

America was still immersed in an irrationally overheated *red scare*: There might be Commies lurking behind every corner, hatching their devious plans to bring down our society. Too many talented men and women—Communist sympathizers or not—found themselves blacklisted and unable to work, their names popping up in *Red Channels*, an insidious publication widely distributed to film studios and TV networks.

Once that crimson cloud finally lifted, the country soon found itself deeply divided again—mired in a conflict in Vietnam that we couldn't possibly win, dealing head-on with issues of poverty and hunger, racial and sexual equality, fighting to preserve our environment, dealing with a growing drug culture, and rapidly changing tastes in art and music. They were turbulent years, and TV both reflected these controversies and was engulfed by them.

In the 1960s and 1970s, a small handful of television series—*That Was the Week That Was, The Smothers Brothers Comedy Hour, Rowan & Martin's Laugh-In, The Mary Tyler Moore Show, All in the Family, M*A*S*H, Maude*, and *Soap*—began dramatically changing the face of prime-time broadcasting. It was no mere coincidence that these were *comedy shows* breaking the mold—make your point with humor, and people don't feel they're being preached to. These series' creators often didn't have the easiest time of it, facing opposition from network censors, fearful executives on high, and even political pressure from Washington.

The late 1980s and 1990s saw a second explosion occur, and its fallout continues to be felt in the new millennium. Fueled by basic cable TV's looser restrictions on content, the landscape changed forever suddenly. Television characters could say or do almost anything within the boundaries of taste . . . and often beyond those previously established boundaries, most especially on pay cablers like HBO and Showtime that answer only to their subscribers. The big three networks, CBS, NBC, and ABC, lost their stranglehold on viewership to all these upstarts and began scrambling to keep pace. With younger networks like Fox and CW (the merger of UPN and the WB) and basic cablers like MTV, Bravo, FX, Spike, Logo, and Cartoon Network's "Adult Swim" in the game, the playing field has grown broader than ever, presenting show content more unshackled than anyone could have dreamt of just a few decades earlier.

The Cosby Show featured an affluent, educated African-American family, and changed the way this country (and the world) perceived black people . . . *Roseanne* showed us working class, overweight Middle America more honestly than ever before . . . *The Simpsons* brought subversive, razor-sharp satire back to primetime . . . *Seinfeld* merely turned the sitcom form upside down and inside out, rewriting the rules along the way . . . *Friends, Cheers, Frasier, Everybody Loves Raymond, Will & Grace, Arrested Development* and *My Name is Earl* were born, along with cable comedy series like *South Park, Ren & Stimpy, The Larry Sanders Show, Sex and the City, Tracey*

Takes On . . ., Curb Your Enthusiasm, Entourage, and so many others that continue to enrich television.

As you read this book, you'll find that some make a reasonably convincing argument that censorship isn't entirely a bad thing; that it forces creative minds to find ways around whatever obstacles are placed before them—to be funny in *spite* of them. Indeed, scholars and students of comedy have long held that humor derives much of its power from *pushing against* limits. If there were no limits, would there be comedy? Isn't the tension between boundaries and how the comic dances around them, or transgresses them, the thing that makes comedy edgy? Absolutely. But deft comedic minds don't need repression to be funny. They need nurturing freedom to create. There are enough inherent obstacles and conflicts in our everyday lives that artists do not require artificial barriers to spur the creative process. Most of us instinctively know, by listening to our inner voice, how far to go in our work . . . and when to draw the line.

Look no further than the output of today's pay cable TV channels—most notably HBO, which has produced some of the most innovative and best-written programming to hit television in decades, and which the broadcast networks have been doing their best to emulate for several years now. HBO places no restrictions and no limits on their creatives. If anything, they're encouraged to go further, wilder, and darker, since that's what the channel's subscribers are presumably paying for. They may not be to everyone's taste, but comedies such as *The Larry Sanders Show, Sex and the City,* and *Curb Your Enthusiasm,* and dramas like *The Sopranos, Oz,* and *Deadwood* have blazed a new trail, standing head and shoulders above the pack creatively.

When asked point blank if they would have preferred to conceive programming for the likes of today's pay cable channels, some of the most celebrated minds in television history—the creators and writers sprinkled liberally across these pages, who are justifiably proud of what they were able to accomplish on network TV in spite of the restraints—unhesitatingly said they would have welcomed the freedom.

It must be noted that, despite so many of the advances celebrated throughout this book, there are some among us today who'd like to turn back the hands of time: politicians mostly, and self-appointed moral judges, who have decreed themselves the arbiters of what constitutes decency and acceptable language or behavior in our media, and try to tell us what we can or cannot watch or read or say. I fervently believe that we've come too far to usher the Dark Ages in again, and that, in the long run—despite whatever temporary political setbacks the next few years may or may not offer—we'll continue to move forward.

My goal here from the very beginning was to not inject my own voice into the narrative any more than necessary, but rather to let the stories tell themselves. Throughout the pages of *They'll Never Put That on the Air*, you'll hear from creators, writers, producers, directors, actors, and network executives who forced the medium to grow up—and a few who tried to resist it. Many of them are famous, others not so famous, but all played an important role in TV's evolution. More than a few have been interviewed countless times before, and asked to tell and retell their tales. Since we're attempting to cover some new ground here, the best thing I could possibly hear in the course of a conversation was, "Gee, I've never been asked that question!" Which, thankfully, happened often.

Best of all, between television networks like TV Land and Nick at Nite, and boxed DVD sets offering entire shows season by season, these classic series are out there again, just waiting to be rediscovered—or experienced for the first time by a new generation. You'll find that most of them are timeless, and will still be brilliant in the *next* millennium.

Finally, I hope you enjoy learning what went on behind the scenes as much as I did while researching, assembling, and writing this oral history. Because this is how it happened—from the people who made it happen—in their own words.

ALLAN NEUWIRTH

Setting the Table . . . . and Girding for Battle

1

Woody Allen once famously noted that comedy writers and comedians are often relegated to the "children's table"—never taken as seriously or accorded the same respect as creators of dramatic material, despite the fact that it's much harder to make people laugh. Inspiring large groups to guffaw or even chuckle at the same thing is no easy task. While TV was still in its youth and early adolescence (yes, actually sitting at the children's table), a small herd of geniuses defined popular television comedy—making *millions* laugh all at once—before branching out in the 1960s, 1970s, and beyond to spawn or inspire some of the funniest, finest shows the medium has ever known.

Four American television networks ruled the roost in the early days: Columbia Broadcasting System, National Broadcasting Company, American Broadcasting Company, and the DuMont Television Network. DuMont disappeared in September 1955, leaving just the *big three* to dominate what we could watch for decades. Limitations on content and language were tight, controlled by networks and their commercial sponsors who hoped to avoid offending viewers at all costs. Interestingly, many of these shows were products of their less politically correct times—so while certain words, phrases, and images may have been strictly forbidden, Milton Berle mincing in drag was perfectly fine. Even the suggestion of physical violence against one's wife, in a comedic context, was acceptable, as in Ralph Kramden's, "One of these days, Alice, one of these days . . . POW! Right in the kisser!"

Although viewers knew that Jackie Gleason's lovable, bumbling bus driver in *The Honeymooners* was all bluster and no bite, his bullying taunts toward Alice would never be seen in a modern situation comedy. There've been many Ralph Kramdenesque shlubs, both live and animated, populating the world of TV since that day, but none that threaten to beat women.

Sitcoms can trace their beginnings on the radio, where they thrived for years on the airwaves. Eventually they emerged on television as the new medium began to take over. The first half-hour, domestic family sitcom, *The Goldbergs* (running on CBS, then NBC, and then DuMont), appeared in 1949. The genre soon began appearing as regular sketches on live musical variety shows, which were then the most popular form of entertainment on TV. *Your Show of Shows* featured Sid Caesar and Imogene Coca as Charlie and Doris Hickenlooper, a middle-class couple who bickered about everything. When that show eventually gave way to the less music/more comedy–oriented *Caesar's Hour*, a series of sitcom sketches called "The Commuters" presented three suburban couples coping with upward mobility, as well as life's general ups and downs. *Cavalcade of Stars* first introduced Jackie Gleason and Audrey Meadows as Ralph and Alice Kramden, and Art Carney and Joyce Randolph as their neighbors, Ed and Trixie Norton, well before *Honeymooners* was spun off into its own half hour series in 1956.

Yoo hoo! The mother of all sitcom moms, Molly Goldberg (Gertrude Berg), in the mother of all sitcoms, The Goldbergs. *© CBS Television Network*

Throughout the 1950s and early 1960s, some smartly written, well-produced comedy series found their way onto the screen—shows that are now deservedly considered classics, including *The Honeymooners, I Love Lucy, The Phil Silvers Show, The Danny Thomas Show, The Andy Griffith Show,* and *The Dick Van Dyke Show*. Despite the stricter broadcast standards imposed on their creators and stars, they still resonate with audiences decades later. Some are still laugh-out-loud funny. Since it was all so new, they were figuring out how to do it day by day, basically on the fly—setting the table for what we've come to know as TV's modern situation comedies.

But, dear reader, this book is an oral history, and the writers, producers, directors, performers, and network execs themselves can paint a far more vivid picture of what it was like to be creating television in those years. So I'm going to now swing the camera away from me, and squarely onto them. (Not to worry—as your host and author, I promise to stick around and throw in my two cents whenever the need arises.)

There Was Nothing You Couldn't Do!

LEONARD STERN, writer and producer:
New York was the mecca for comedy. First of all, all television then was live—and as a result, immediate. It was opening night each week for *The Sid Caesar Show*, *The Colgate Comedy Hour*, *The Jackie Gleason Show*, and *The Phil Silvers Show*. Oh, and *The Steve Allen Show*. All of us were happening simultaneously. I started with *The Honeymooners*.

JOYCE RANDOLPH, performer, *The Honeymooners*:
It was the most wonderful time here. The city seemed nice and clean and peaceful . . . Everybody seemed kind of happy, with jobs—and you could act on television! I think there were always shows coming out of L.A., but we had plenty here. And I didn't feel a lot of competition, though by the 1960s, some friends were moving out there. There was quite a migration. My husband's work was here, so we never *thought* of going out there.

ALAN WAGNER, former V.P. of Program Development at CBS:
At that point, anyway, New York was still the locus of the intelligentsia as far as California was concerned—the smart guys. Gelbart was a New York writer, and Norman Lear was a New York guy. All the New York guys, if you will, seemed to have this aura, and so I had a kind of buzz about me for a while, too.

LARRY GELBART, writer and producer:
It was magical, 'cause I was young. Everything's magical when you're young. And I happened to be young in a place that was very vibrant. First of all, it was the early days of television. There weren't so many footprints in the snow. You could do something, reasonably sure that somebody didn't do it the night before. And there was a period there where television had been energized. First of all, the product was very urban—you can see how long I've been in Hollywood, 'cause I'm calling it the *product*.

Dramatic shows were fueled by wanna-be playwrights: Paddy Chayefsky, Reggie Rose . . . directors who came from the theater, actors who came from the theater . . . it was a time of discovery. It was a time when, really, people were experimenting, finding out what was this *thing*—what was television? What was different about it other than being visual radio or being tiny movies? So, it was exciting in that way.

PERRY LAFFERTY, director, producer, and network executive:
My most wonderful time in the entertainment industry was the period between 1950 and 1958, when live television was flourishing in New York. To direct live television was the most challenging thing that could happen to a director, because it was opening night and closing night! And great things went on.

I finally got a television set over my wife's strenuous objections—because she was a radio actress—around 1950. She said, "It'll never stay, it's just a fad."

CARL REINER, performer, writer, and director:
We were not pioneers—we were actors looking for work, and we were just doing our act. It so happened that they put cameras in front of us. I mean, we were all theater people originally. When the movies came, they put a camera in front of *those* people! The pioneer was Farnsworth, the guy who invented the tube. We were the workers who worked in front of the machine that somebody had built at the time. But we were mainly doing what we would have done either in nightclubs or on the Broadway stage . . . we didn't say, "Hey, let's find out if there's a new thing we can stand in front of so we can send our image overseas!"

You know you're pioneering when you say, "Let's go out. There must be another ocean out there!" *Those* guys were pioneers.

PAT CARROLL, performer:
Television—nobody knew about it. I mean, was this a new baby or what in the entertainment field? And because it was so new, you had the sense from everybody that it was the gold-rush days of entertainment. It was all so vivid . . . every day was full, and you were learning all the time. You were learning, learning, learning. I knew nothing about cameras. And to have three cameras pointing at you, the first thing you'd learn was to watch for the red light. And then finding yourself *looking* for the red light! Nobody had a rulebook. Everybody was doing it off the cuff.

It was a new medium that captured all of us . . . those of us who were beginning to work in it, and the audiences who were beginning to receive this silly thing with all those moving figures on that little tube in your living room. And the excitement of the writers—the creative writers. Weren't they in heaven! Nobody could say, "Oh, we don't do that here." Who knew? You could do anything. And they proved it—you *could* do anything.

MICHAEL DANN, former V.P. of Programming at CBS:

Remember this: Comedy is king. There never was a time in the history of radio, and most of television—in series—that the top shows were not comedies. Basically, comedy was at 8:00, and it led off the evening. I remember even from the radio days, that it was *Amos 'n' Andy*, and then of course, *Jack Benny*, and *Fibber McGee & Molly*, *Life of Riley*—they were all comedies.

When Caesar Ruled from on High

PAT CARROLL:

People were staying home on Saturday nights to watch *Your Show of Shows*. They weren't going out to films. They wouldn't miss it—in *bars* they were showing *Your Show of Shows*.

CARL REINER:

When I was on *Your Show of Shows*, I always wrote things for myself—but I wasn't hired as a writer. And I was excluded from the writing room. The writing room was either Max Liebman's office, or the male toilet where the fellas would go. There was one female writer, she couldn't go in there. It was Mel Tolkin, Mel Brooks, and Lucille Kallen . . . and then maybe Joe Stein came in 1952, and Neil Simon came in 1954.

What happened in the third week was, I disliked waiting to get inside the room to hear the sketch . . . so I came up with the idea for foreign movie parodies. I could do double talk, and so could Sid—I knew that I'd never use my double talk on the air, because Sid Caesar was the master—but I'd done it in my act in the army.

So, I said, "We all love foreign movies. Why don't we do a foreign movie?"

The great comedian Sid Caesar, whose Your Show of Shows *and* Caesar's Hour *set the standard for sketch comedy on TV.* © *CBS Television Network*

5

I went over to Sid and in double talk I started selling him a pack of cigarettes that was lying around. And they said, "Oh, yeah!" That became the beginning of the foreign movies. We did one every three, four weeks. But they also actually said, "Oh, let him stay in the room."

So, I was in the room for five years, without portfolio. But I was allowed to contribute.

LARRY GELBART:

Caesar's Hour was mostly comedy. It's not just that *Show of Shows* had an extra half hour. First of all, there was lots of time to give to a show in those days. You weren't looking to put shows bumper to bumper. And Max Liebman was very skilled at doing a show that had broad elements and artistic elements, or higher—opera, even . . . ballet, modern dance, and much more music. *Caesar's Hour*, once in a while, had just a kind of musical relief, but it was basically comedy.

CARL REINER:

We thought some of it was the best stuff we'd done. On *Your Show of Shows*, sketches were not allowed to breathe . . . now sometimes we let 'em breathe *too* long! Because it was, "Now we don't have to worry about dancers jumping in." But for the most part, I think there were some awfully great things that happened in *Caesar's Hour* and *Caesar Presents*.

LARRY GELBART:

It was really like being called up by the Yankees, you know, from the minors. This was the Show. Literally. And so the first week of my employment there—actually for the first two weeks—it was routine for live shows to get together maybe two weeks before the first show went on the air, 'cause you just had more time to prepare. So, during that time, I was not suffering from any lack of confidence, but I couldn't help noticing that Sid Caesar, who sat in the room with the writers, was . . . not *ignoring* me, he just didn't *look* at me. And I knew I was carrying my weight, 'cause I was there to do that. And I didn't weigh that much anyway then.

I thought, "Jeez, am I bombing here? Is he sorry that I'm here, that he made this deal?"

Then, after the first show aired—as I found was going to be the custom—we went to dinner at Danny's Hideaway in New York, which was a favorite hangout of a lot of people in the business. And I found myself on the sidewalk afterwards, standing up, waiting for a taxi while Sid Caesar waited for his limousine . . . and he looked at me, and I thought, "Oh, he's going to say

Two of Caesar's second bananas almost make a bunch: funny-men Howard Morris and Carl Reiner clowning in a publicity shot. © CBS Television Network

something!" But instead of saying anything, he bent me back as though I was Theda Bara and he was Rudolph Valentino, and kissed me smack on the lips and said, "You're too young to be smashed." Whatever that meant.

But I got the idea that he loved me, that I'd made the grade.

PAT CARROLL:

All of those gentlemen came from that same old school. Making you laugh was the goal of their lives. And I learned from watching them what actors can do when they know each other so well. It's like musicians when they're playing jazz—they know when to riff. When you play straight to great comics, you'd better be a damn good actor or actress—because they are the musician and they play on *you.*

You have to listen very intently. Carl Reiner was marvelous about listening to Sid. He didn't let him get away with an idea that he had started, because he *repeated* it for him. You take any great comedy team: study the straight man. I watched Howie Morris and Carl work with Sid . . . It was a year of comedy schooling for me. I learned so much from them, and from the writers, of course. For me, *Caesar's Hour* was heaven.

We had the women's auxiliary there. You know, the guys were all in on writing sessions with Sid. Carl Reiner, Howie Morris . . . all of the guys who were actors on the show were also in the writing sessions. The women on the show—Shirl Conway, Janet Blair, me—we sat and knitted or read the paper while the guys were creative. We were used as the wives in "The Commuters" sketches, and any other things that came up in musical numbers or some other kind of sketch. The guys really predominated as far as the humor was concerned. And that was mostly because of Sid, because that was the way his humor went.

The girls were played off as the femme fobs. That was the standard of the 1950s anyway, so why wouldn't television reflect that? I was so happy to have a job that I didn't care, and I thought, "They know what they're doing." I guess Selma Diamond and Lucille Kallen were the only women writers in comedy at that time. At one point or another, those two gals were in there, slugging it out with the boys. They were totally different women, and they both had totally different viewpoints in humor . . . but it was so exciting to know that there were women contributing to this. **(See chapter 4 for much more on this subject.)**

Brought to You by . . . the Advertising Agencies

ALAN WAGNER:

When I started in the business, my first job was at Benton & Bowles, and at that time, it was one of the few ad agencies—along with Y&R and BBD&O—that actually produced shows, physically produced them. And owned them on behalf of the clients. I figured the place to be, if I wanted to be in some kind of creative part of television, was an ad agency. And I started writing to them alphabetically. Benton & Bowles answered earliest, before anybody else did, and at that time, when I went there, I guess they had *Danny Thomas* on the air, and they had *Andy Griffith*, and pretty much owned Monday night on CBS. They *told* CBS where they were going to put the programs.

BILL PERSKY, writer, producer, and director:

In the days of *The Dick Van Dyke Show* and *That Girl*, the shows were sponsored by *one* sponsor—so you were more involved with the sensibilities of the sponsor than you were with the network's! You'd get a note: We've gotta change so and so. That was about it. Sometimes you fought it, even though it didn't matter, just because it pissed you off.

GENE REYNOLDS, producer and director:

I had one run-in with them on my show, *Room 222*, in which I had a character that was challenging the food in the cafeteria, the junk food, and he'd leave notes around the school. Kurt Russell played the part—he was an environmental terrorist, in a way, threatening to throw a stink bomb in the room . . . but he was basically an ecologist and environmentalist.

And two guys from the ad agency came by and said, "You made some remark about too much white flour and too much fattening food. This is what we're selling!"

They always looked over your stuff, and they always called.

GRANT TINKER, producer and former chairman/CEO of NBC:

I was offered a job at McCann Erickson as a program development guy . . . and I was there for three or four years, making judgments about programs. In those days, programs were bought by agencies for specific clients. So, it was GE this, or the Hallmark that. But I learned a lot, and managed to become sort of a good television executive there. And then I went over to Benton & Bowles, and became head of the whole program department, which was then swallowed up by the media department.

We had Procter & Gamble, General Foods, Johnson & Johnson . . . people who bought a *lot* of television. Because we had so many shows, I was the agency guy who hung around and got to know the producers and writers—you didn't supervise them, at least I certainly never presumed to— and generally made sure they didn't do something Procter & Gamble wouldn't want them to do.

So, I went out to L.A., and I met Mary Tyler Moore, as a matter of fact, when they shot the *Dick Van Dyke Show* pilot. I wouldn't even have known who she was—she was an aspiring, somewhat working actress and a dancer. And I was very struck by her immediately. So, when she came to New York some time later to do promotion stuff, I took her to dinner a couple of times, and that started our relationship.

One night I was at a backyard barbeque thing thrown by one of the General Foods executives, and I ran into a guy named Mort Werner who I knew slightly, because he had been at Young & Rubicam, competing with Benton & Bowles on many of the same accounts—and he had just gone back to NBC as the head of programs. He said, "How would you like to come back to NBC?" and I said, "I'd like to!"

So, I went back—that was the second of three times—in, I guess, 1961. Mort knew I was seeing Mary Tyler Moore in California, and I think he just very cleverly knew that I would like to go there for good. So, he sent me out to Burbank to be in charge of NBC programs on the West Coast, and that was probably the first important network job I had. I was running Burbank and Mary was working over in Hollywood . . . I would go over on Tuesday nights—that's when they shot the thing in front of an audience, every Tuesday night—I'd just drive over from Burbank. So we had a double life in a way . . . we were a two-network family.

ALAN WAGNER:

There was one kind of comedy that was around for a long time . . . bland, sweet, amusing, warm, gemütlich, unable to press any corners. One foot on the floor at all times, married couples in twin beds, all that stuff. There was a sameness overall to everything . . . the pot needed to be stirred. Some of them were very funny—*The Dick Van Dyke Show* was hilarious. I mean, it was fall-down funny sometimes. It was because Carl Reiner and Shelly Leonard hired so much talent—and the cast was brilliant . . . and John Rich, who directed most of them—they were all just drop-dead brilliant.

The *Bleep* Van *Bleep* Show . . . Starring *Bleep* Van *Bleep*

Okay, perhaps that's a bit of an exaggeration. But *dick* and *dyke,* words that we hear today on primetime commercial TV in pretty much any context, would never have been uttered back in the early 1960s. Despite airing during television's most prohibitive era regarding content and language, few sitcoms have consistently aimed as high or achieved the excellence of *The Dick Van Dyke Show.* Though Carl Reiner originally created the series as a starring vehicle for himself—fresh off the success of his glory years with Sid Caesar—he couldn't sell the project. Reiner was convinced the show was dead . . . until performer Danny Thomas's producing partner, Sheldon Leonard, convinced him it merely needed "a better actor" in the lead role. Rather than take umbrage, Reiner embraced the idea.

"I really wasn't insulted," he muses today. "As a matter of fact, I had

The Petrie family: Moore, Van Dyke, and Mathews as Laura, Rob, and Ritchie. © *CBS Television Network*

already been writing. I hadn't directed yet—but I don't know, I just felt it was time to *move*." So, Carl Reiner stepped back behind the camera, and the series sold.

The hallmarks of *The Dick Van Dyke Show* were brilliant scripting—much of it by Reiner himself, who later entrusted Sam Denoff and Bill Persky to write and story edit—and a dream cast starring Dick Van Dyke as comedy writer Rob Petrie; Mary Tyler Moore as his wife, Laura; Larry Mathews as their young son, Ritchie; showbiz veterans Morey Amsterdam and Rose Marie as Rob's co-writers, Buddy Sorrell and Sally Rogers at "The Alan Brady Show," the fictional hit comedy series within the series; and Richard Deacon as Mel Cooley, the show's stuffy producer. (Reiner amusingly cast himself in the occasional supporting role of star Alan Brady, whose face was never seen by viewers till *The Dick Van Dyke Show's* fourth season.)

But the road to "classic series" status was not easy. The show struggled to find a buyer, its cast, and even an audience to watch it.

GRANT TINKER:

Danny Thomas, Sheldon Leonard, and Carl Reiner couldn't find a Rob Petrie. And I remember when Sheldon was in New York, despairing about finding anybody . . . and he went to the theater one night and saw *Bye Bye Birdie*. He came in the next morning and said, "I found him!"

So, Dick was cast. And then they tried to find *Mrs.* Petrie, who was not going to be quite as prominent in the show as she became, because of the things Mary could do. And the home wasn't going to be as featured. It was going to be mostly an office comedy. So, Danny Thomas stuck his head into Sheldon's office one day when they were trying to figure out who they'd get, and said, "Why don't you try that girl with the three names?" It turned out Mary had read to play a part as his daughter on his own show, and she'd done a good job—so good that he remembered it—but he said, "Nobody would believe that was my daughter with *that* nose!"

So, they brought her in, and ultimately cast her.

ALAN WAGNER:

When CBS first hired me, they asked me one question: "We've got two pilots here. One you developed at Benton & Bowles, and one that we think is really very funny. We've developed this thing with Carl Reiner with Dick Van Dyke. Have you seen it?"

I said I had, that it's maybe the funniest pilot I'd ever seen in my life. I thought it was brilliant. The other show was *Car 54, Where Are You?*—and *that* was screamingly funny. It was done by the same genius who did *Bilko*, Nat Hiken. This was Carl's first show, alone. The first pilot for *The Dick Van Dyke Show* was not *The Dick Van Dyke Show*. It was Carl Reiner playing that part, called *Head of the Family*. Based on the pilot, the noise in the room was clearly much louder for *Car 54*. And their question was, "Which one do you think we should schedule?"

Of course, a year afterward I looked like an idiot, 'cause *The Dick Van Dyke Show* had failed. It did not get numbers at first . . . but a lot of us had faith in it. And the second year, it exploded. *Car 54* did okay for a year or two on NBC, like it should have, and then it failed. 'Cause it was a one-joke show.

CARL REINER:

Procter & Gamble, who were our sponsors, went on a train ride with us some-place, and the guy who was the head of it gave me the thumbs up. He said, "You guys'll be on [again]." And his wife was there nodding. And they *did* pick us up for the second year, but only for 50 percent of the show. If it wasn't for Sheldon getting Kent cigarettes to pick up the other 50 percent . . . CBS had a show called *Howie* that they owned themselves—so they would've preferred that. But we were saved in the nick of time.

And the other thing that saved it in the second year was the fact that somebody suggested that we put it on in the summer. Perry Como was our competition; he was killing us. And there was an argument about how there was not enough money for it . . . sixty-five hundred dollars, that's what you'd get! They said, "No."

I screamed and I said, "Put it on! At least somebody will give us a look-see!"

Y'know, Como wasn't on then. At least take a shot! And that's what I think did it for us. But we knew we had something special. The actors were so good. They grooved. And the audiences told us! When you're sit-ting in an audience, and they're not told to laugh—they're laughing for real—you can tell.

GRANT TINKER:

It started with the writing. Those shows, shows that you shoot in front of an audience, they develop over five days. They're written, and then they're rewritten during the week to get better and better. They weren't just turning out forgettable witless comedy. It was well written, and they cared to do it as best they could. And they worked hard to polish it to a bright shine before they put it in front of an audience.

CARL REINER:

I used to fight for fifteen seconds sometimes because a show was a little long, and it had a great joke or something I wanted to save. I actually went into an editing room once and took a frame out of each scene—a *frame*—to get the thirty-two seconds or twelve seconds I needed. I mean, it was back-breaking. But that's how much time meant to us.

ERNEST CHAMBERS, writer and producer:

I wrote four *Dick Van Dyke*s . . . that was when I was getting started. It was smart writing. But I think you need casting—in television series, casting is most important. And second is writing. After that, what else is there? I mean, *Dick Van Dyke* was going to be cancelled at the end of the first season. And they kept it on because it was so smart, it took time for its audience to find it.

One of the problems with television is that you have a television audience. And if your show doesn't appeal to that television audience, it's going to get low ratings. But there is *another* audience out there, if they can just keep you on the air long enough till they *hear* about you.

CARL REINER:

All I knew was, whoever *was* watching was giving us wonderful feedback. Nobody ever called us and said the show was no good. As a matter of fact, there was only one review that was questioning . . . it was Cecil Smith in the *L.A. Times*. He didn't smash it, but it was just very mild. And *he* was the one, when we finished after five years, who wrote the most glowing review. It's the

Laura and Rob Petrie laughing it up at home with Rob's fellow comedy writing cutups, Buddy Sorrell (Morey Amsterdam, on guitar) and Sally Rogers (Rose Marie). © CBS Television Network

only review I ever put in a frame, because of the fact that it took him five years to say there'll never be another show like it!

GEORGE SHAPIRO, agent and manager:

When Carl first started writing it, Sam Weisbord[1] advised strongly against doing it, because the subject matter was too elite. It was about work in the office . . . working with writers, working with producers. So, he said it would not have broad enough appeal, especially in the Midwest and in the South, because people don't care about show business outside of New York and L.A.

CARL REINER:

I was writing about what I *knew*. And I crept into an area . . . I didn't even know I was doing something groundbreaking, which was seeing both sides in a situation comedy. Seeing what the guy did for a living! Until then, we knew that *Father Knows Best* worked in the insurance business. But we never saw. The only one that was close to it was *Danny Thomas*. You knew what he did because you once in a while saw his nightclub act . . . but most of it was in the house.

So, I mean, that was accidental, because I was just writing about what I did in the old *Show of Shows*. I was breaking ground without knowing I was doing it. But that's why it probably worked, because it was one person's reality. And if you do one person's reality, there's a pureness about it. When you talk to one person and start telling him about yourself, they say, "Oh, yeah, I've got an uncle like that" or something. But they know there's an honesty about it.

SAM DENOFF, television writer and producer:

Carl was our mentor in teaching us how to write, and tell the truth with no bullshit. We learned the difference from Carl about writing stupid, and writing *real*. One time we wrote something, and he wrote "R.R." on the page—meaning "rotten 'riting"!

And he said, "Okay, you guys, listen. How many funny cops do you know? How many funny firemen do you know? How many funny bank presidents do you know? How many funny complaint department people, in department stores, do you know? None of those people are funny. What they *do* makes your star funny. Tell the truth. Be real."

Then we wrote another thing where we had Rob doing something . . . and he said, "Okay, fellas. Now I wanna ask you a question: Do you guys agree that you're two of the most insane people who ever lived? And if you didn't do this for a living, you'd probably be in a home somewhere?"

---

[1] *Then president of the William Morris Agency.*

"Well . . . yeah."

He said, "Okay. Taking into consideration that you're crazy, never let Rob Petrie do anything you wouldn't do." So, that's why that show was so different from all the others. Because it was never stupid. Kids never did jokes, and all of that crap that goes on now.

CARL REINER:

They were wonderful . . . the thing that I did was, I gave them an office, and they were right down the hall from me. So, they were able to come in my office and chat with me about everything we were doing. And they saved my life. I was *alone* on the *Van Dyke Show* for the first few years— I was the producer, and story editor, and writer. I wrote the first forty out of the first sixty! If they hadn't showed up, I don't know if I could have done it. But in the fourth year, they became the story editors. That helped me breathe. And in the fifth year, the last twelve shows were when I did [the feature film] *The Russians Are Coming, The Russians Are Coming*. Anyway, I owe them a lot. We owe each other. It's symbiotic. We really helped each other.

SAM DENOFF:

Carl had a certain talent and a certain taste. And he had the unqualified support of Sheldon and Danny Thomas . . . but primarily Sheldon, because Sheldon was really on the line most of the time. Danny was off doing club dates, as well as his own show.

CARL REINER:

Well, Sheldon was the main producer. Danny Thomas put the money up! Forty-seven thousand dollars. He got quite a good run for it. I think that's the best investment anybody ever made in show business . . . one of the better ones, anyway.

Sheldon was a hands-on executive producer. But he had five or six shows that he was executive producing . . . so he very carefully and quickly gave you his take on every script, and let you go about your business. He and I didn't agree a lot on substance, because he had a different attitude about situation comedy. But he was wonderful. If we had a disagreement, a *major* disagreement, he'd say, "It's your show. You show me." He was also wonderful on stories . . . and he did bring in some good writers, like Jerry Belson and Garry Marshall and a few others. So, he was a real good executive producer—one of the best ever.

Good Lord—You Can't Say That!

SAM DENOFF:

The censors would get the script to make sure that you did not use the name of the Deity in vain. And many other rules. You couldn't say "for God's sake" or "darn." We thought it was hard, but it made us write better. Once in a while, Carl would have a fight, or we would have a little argument, and you'd trade off things.

WILLIAM TANKERSLEY, former Director of Program Practices at CBS:

Once we did something that I'm not really very proud of. This was from the movies, I guess, we inherited it. The Code said that "any reference to the Deity should be reverent, and all clergymen should be treated with respect."

The editor came back one day from *Dick Van Dyke*, and said, "They filmed a show over there with a young priest who's kind of a smart-aleck, y'know, all the way through . . . and if we follow the Code, he's not treated with much respect."

I said, "Well, I guess we'll check."

So, I called Monsignor Devlin's office. He represented the Catholic Church in movies, and, by extension, television. I asked Devlin if he'd send somebody over to look at this film—and he did. He sent the most conservative young priest who'd just come from Ireland, if you can imagine . . . and he went over, looked at it, and said it ought to be changed. He didn't like it at all.

Dick Van Dyke as Rob Petrie, trying to explain the facts of life to young son Ritchie (Larry Mathews) in the then-controversial episode, "Where Do I Come From?" © CBS Television Network

So, they re-shot the scene, and he sat on stage. And Carl Reiner, whom I love, called over and said, "Y'know, Bill, you're the most civilized man I know—but you're driving me to the *movies!*" And he was right. That was interpreting the Code much too strictly. Carl didn't do anything in bad taste, ever.

CARL REINER:

I very vaguely remember that. I had written a show called "The Life and Love of Joe Coogan." And at the end, he didn't give up his love for another girl, he gave her up because he married God, y'know . . . and it was very acceptable to everybody.

As a matter of fact, the only thing I remember was that Loretta Young was in the audience, and she was a real *Catholic* Catholic. At the end, when the audience really accepted this premise so well, a smiling Loretta Young said, "Very good. Now you must do one for *us.*"

I don't know what she meant by that. A pro-Catholic story? This wasn't an anti-Catholic thing. But the fact that a Catholic could love somebody at one time—maybe *that* was it, I don't know . . .

BILL PERSKY:

You pretty well knew what you could and couldn't do. Sometimes you would bump into something *so* outlandish—that you couldn't say the word "pregnant" was a surprise. It happened on the *Van Dyke Show*. We had the word "pregnant," and they said, "You can't say that, because some people don't tell their children that there's such a thing. They think that children come from under cabbages—and we don't want to impose upon them to have to deal with it."

CARL REINER:

That was the one I wrote, "Where Do I Come From?" They wouldn't accept the fact that when the son asked, "Where did I come from?" they actually told him, "You come from Mama's belly."

And I heard: "No, no, no, no." I argued for days, and if I'd had *fuck you money* I would've left, I was so mad. I said, "It's not an opinion!"

They said, "A lot of people don't wanna tell their children that."

I said, "Little kids, when they hear it, it won't mean anything. Older kids will ask, 'What does he mean?' And then the parents can say as much or as little as they want. And if they want to go back and say, 'No, that's not true, you come from a cabbage,' they have their option. But at least the truth is out, and that's what we should be doing. Telling people the truth!"

I was screaming at them. And they wouldn't accept it. So, I let the audience know that that's what I was talking about by saying, "Let's see what Dr. Spock has to say." At least telling the audience to go to Dr. Spock to get the good answer.

And then the kid said, "Oh, I know where I *come* from . . . I mean, do I come from New York or New Jersey?" In other words, the kid already knew.

How the F—k Did Network Censorship Begin, Anyway?

Before television came along, radio networks had put a system in place of monitoring the language and content of their programs. Editors would routinely comb through the material and flag anything deemed indecent, questionable, or potentially offensive to listeners. Radio's censors largely adhered to the same strictures imposed by Hollywood's Production Code (also known as the Hays Code). The Code was a set of standards that the studio chiefs—in the hopes of avoiding government censorship—had adopted voluntarily in 1930, and strengthened in 1934, to regulate just exactly what made it onto the big screen.

The Code was broad and draconian, filled with rules like: "Passion should so be treated that these scenes do not stimulate the lower and baser element." It specifically banned "excessive and lustful kissing, lustful embraces, suggestive postures and gestures" and "miscegenation" (sexual relationships between the white and black races) as well as bluntly decreeing that scenes of seduction "are never the proper subject for comedy." It further instructed that "pointed profanity (including 'God,' 'Lord,' 'Jesus,' 'Christ'—unless used reverently—'hell,' 'S.O.B.,' 'damn,' 'gawd'), or every other profane or vulgar expression, however used, is forbidden."

The power of the Code's administrators to censor scripts angered and frustrated many in the creative community. In the mid-1950s, several producers began to openly challenge it, and by the mid-1960s, it had become virtually unenforceable. The Production Code was abandoned in 1967 and replaced, in 1968, with the MPAA film rating system. Television, however, was still being beamed out into people's living rooms where anyone might see it, driving networks to continue their tight controls over program content.

WILLIAM TANKERSLEY:

I worked for twenty-two years at CBS—sixteen in Hollywood, and about seven in New York. In 1950, we were putting cameras on the radio shows, like Jack Benny and Edgar Bergen and George Burns, and Lord knows who else. And they became television hits right off the bat.

Not too long after, they called and said, "Would you consider taking over Program Practices?" It didn't have that name yet—it was just called editing. In radio days they felt they had to have somebody go over the scripts. I didn't know anything *about* that department in radio. It was over there someplace and there were two or three people, including John Meston, who came up with the idea of *Gunsmoke*, incidentally. He was manager of editing.

But these people called and asked if I would take that over. There'd just been a hearing in Washington by Kefauver,[2] who was screaming about juvenile delinquency and too much violence on television. So, I took over that job, and reorganized it . . . I set up a system that was unique in the industry, but worked very well.

First of all, I went to New York. NBC and ABC had handbooks. We didn't have those—just a compilation of memos, and the evolving policies that came from that. The fellow in New York wasn't anxious to give up all those secrets. New York didn't believe in giving Hollywood anything. So, on a Sunday, with my wife and daughter in New York, I went through a huge file . . . and made quick notes on all the precedents, compiled that, and went back to Hollywood.

Then I devised forms. Very formal things, for every script submitted— even script ideas—saying whether they were approved, or what changes should be made . . . considering the theme and the treatment of that theme. The thesis, really. And they all had my name at the bottom in big black letters, in the center. [laughs] I mean, there was no pity. The editors would sign them—I didn't sign them, but my name was there.

And they would ask, "Where can we appeal?" The editors wanted to know. I told 'em, "There *is* no damn appeal. You just *do* it, you know?"

We had no set standards. We took each situation and looked at it in its context. Every show had its own character, and we thought that blanket rules wouldn't be too good. But there was a common understanding of what was in accepted taste . . . and profanity, naturally, was out. We worked to keep down violence—to violence that was absolutely essential to the plot.

Then I set up a system of *measuring* everything: reduce it to numbers.

How many acts of violence in this show? How many suspected paid plugs for different products? Put all those things down . . . you list them all. But violence, primarily, because we had people saying, "They have five thousand acts of violence" or something. So, I could answer them—and *did*.

In short order, television was still very new, but we established ourselves. I had a director in New York, I had a director in Hollywood, and each had

[2] *Senator Estes Kefauver was a vocal crusader for consumer protection laws, antitrust legislation, and civil rights.*

a staff. We had forty-some-odd people. They were all editors. And then the department was strengthened at that time by bringing back Joe Ream to CBS. Joe Ream was executive vice president way back when CBS was formed. He was head of the law department . . . a brilliant man from Harvard. Then he became our representative in Washington.

And then, when the quiz scandals came along[3], they pulled Joe Ream back from Washington and put him in charge of this department—and in typical Washington style, he called it the "Department of Program Practices."

ALFRED SCHNEIDER, former V.P. of Policy and Standards at ABC:

There was always "Continuity Acceptance." When I took over in the 1960s, we changed it to Standards and Practices. Standards and Practices came in effect, really, after the quiz scandals. At that time, the networks started to take control of their programming.

Because of the violence hearings, we got involved in the preparation of two documents, one with the major assistance of a forensic psychiatrist, Dr. Mel Heller. We used him for putting together a handbook on how to deal with violence, and an incident classification analysis form—which was the document that tried to analyze how you will eliminate gratuitous violence.

And then we did a book on sexuality.

There was one incident where we went out to a city in Utah . . . we were responding to a request by an affiliate station to come talk to a leadership group about violence, and the treatment of violence on television. It was during the time of those hearings. And we explained what we do with guidelines, and how we review all material, whereupon we said, "Are there any questions?"

The first question was, "Why do you show a man and a woman in bed together? And why do you show teenage sex? And why do you show adultery?"

Mel looked at me and said, "Isn't this supposed to be about violence?" I said, "Yes, it is." So then he said to the people in the audience, "Let me ask you a question. How many of you have guns?"

Everybody raised their hands! So, it all depends. In the major cities, there was a great concern about the degree to which violence was affecting children . . . and in suburban areas, they were more worried about sexuality.

---

[3] *In the late 1950s, it came to light that the outcome of several popular big money TV quiz shows had been rigged, most notoriously* Twenty-One. *The House Subcommittee on Legislative Oversight held a series of sensational public hearings on the scandals that rocked the TV industry to its core, with Congress following suit by declaring it a federal crime to rig a game show.*

LEONARD STERN:

The censors had many names. We originally thought of them as censors, then they became Continuity Acceptance . . . and Broadcast Standards . . . now editors. They've gone under many transitions of identity, but they were all equally nondescript. They were usually empathetic . . . but then again, you know, I was in a position where they *would* be. I don't know how they would've taken an innocent, or somebody unestablished at that time, and dealt with them.

There was a woman who was head of the department for a long time at NBC, and when we were doing shows, she had sort of signature complaints. It was, "Oops. We're gonna get a memo from Jean Messerschmitt." And then Don Bays was the man assigned by the network to *Get Smart*. He was empathetic. He tried to find some way, if there was an objection, that we could circumvent it. So, we had a tendency to be respectful of whatever he said to us. I guess others operated on a negotiation theory: put in five, we'll have to take out two.

We entered a period in time where there was a whole debate as to what was obscene. Justice Potter Stewart had said, "I know it when I see it." And then we got into the question of: Is it obscene or is it indecent? And what's the difference? Who knows indecency when they see it?

When I started as a young screenwriter, you couldn't have a couple in bed together . . . and you couldn't say "I'm pregnant," but you *could* say "We're having a baby." What happened was, we found ways of being inventive. We were forced to . . . imply things. And as a result, we got clever at it. And entertaining. We knew how to get around that, and be better because of it.

DON TAFFNER, producer:

Restricted or not, these were the writers that came out of burlesque, so by *innuendo*—if you wanted to have *fucking around* going on—the writers were good enough that you knew there was fucking around going on but you didn't have to say "fucking around going on"!

CARL REINER:

Well, you *tried*. A little double entendre . . . but they didn't go very far. Today, they do *no* entendre, you know? They call an asshole an asshole! But I remember the first time [on *Your Show of Shows*]—we were doing a war thing, and we were in the trenches. And somebody said, "War is hell."

They said, "You can't say that. Can't say *hell*."

So, the line was, "Oh, war is heck!" We actually said that. We knew we were making a comment, though, on the stupidity of it.

WILLIAM TANKERSLEY:

All that came from the motion picture industry. That was theirs, not ours. But it was followed by our people just automatically, because so many of our producers were from the movies. The Hays Code was deeply embedded in the minds of all the motion picture people. And those that came over to TV, they just followed that automatically. It was very stringent—put together by the church, primarily, I guess. A great influence.

But CBS was a little different. Each show had its own character. And people could never understand that. They always *wanted* blanket rules. If you allowed *Playhouse 90* to do it, then John Mantley at *Gunsmoke* would say, "Why can't we do the same thing?" I'd say, "Well, you're not the same show!"

ERNEST CHAMBERS:

I got into the business in the mid-1960s. I wrote for Sid Caesar. His last series was called *As Caesar Sees It*, and Mel Brooks was the head writer. At that time, there was an English actor, Edward Everett Horton, who used to go out every

Jackie Gleason, Art Carney, Audrey Meadows, and Joyce Randolph in their always clean and funny classic sitcom, The Honeymooners . . . *which still featured humorous threats of domestic violence!* © *CBS Television Network*

summer in a play called *Springtime for Henry*, and Mel used to joke, "I'm going to do a show called *Springtime for Hitler.*" This was 1964, something like that.

Then I was on *Danny Kaye* for three years, became his head writer. But on *The Danny Kaye Show*, there *were* no censorship issues, because Danny was Mr. Clean. He was totally apolitical . . . It was like Jackie Gleason. Gleason never dealt with issues of that sort. Gleason's subjects were the working class, the rich, and the glamour of show business.

JOYCE RANDOLPH:
Nobody used any dirty words on *Honeymooners*. Jackie felt it had to be clean, and it had to be funny! Trixie was supposed to be an ex-burlesque dancer . . . but if they mentioned it, Trixie just acted very annoyed, and they didn't go into it in any depth. Jackie didn't want to explore the other characters so much. He once said, "This show is about the bus driver, his wife, and his friend"—leaving me *out*. Which was not very nice of him, but that's the way he thought of it. You were glad to be working, and you wished for more . . . but you didn't make waves.

Network censors were careful when dealing with stars of great magnitude like Lucille Ball, seen here with husband and business partner Desi Arnaz (as Ricky) on their beloved hit sitcom I Love Lucy. *© CBS Television Network*

LEONARD STERN:
I must say, in terms of Jackie Gleason, and it was probably true of Sid Caesar, and *Bilko*—which would be Nat Hiken and Phil Silvers in tandem—and *I Love Lucy*, there was a great reluctance to send them any disparaging comments. Because they were so powerful.

It always depended upon the attitude of the star or the person who created the show. Steve Allen was relatively impervious to that, and if they were insistent, he would then make *fun* of it—incorporate it into the program! So, they had to weigh the messages they sent. Beware of what you write . . . or never put it in writing!

Later, we no longer had a shield: the protection of a major talent. So, they actually exerted more and more influence. Also, anxieties. There were a lot of nose-to-nose conflicts between creators and the network censors. Most of the time you could negotiate your way through almost anything . . . but there were adamant moments.

ERNEST CHAMBERS:

The stuff we wrote, you wouldn't think of doing anything. What would you do? I got a memo—I can't remember what show it was, but it was in the 1960s—from a network censor. And their only comment on that particular program was, "Please obscure nipples." Because apparently, with the girls' bras, you could see their nipples showing through the costume.

Mel Brooks and Buck Henry's nutty secret agent send-up, Get Smart, *was originally rejected by the ABC network—who found the show distasteful and "un-American." Pictured here are stars Maxwell Smart (Don Adams) and Agent 99 (Barbara Feldon).* © *NBC Television Network*

Some riotously inane memos from network censors have been preserved for the ages.[4] We assume that these were the exception and not the rule, but they are works of art nonetheless. Witness these notes to The Honeymooners creatives from CBS, requesting that "When Ralph says, 'You're going to the moon, Alice,' it may be the wrong destination. The moon is generally regarded as romantic. Could Ralph send her to Mars?" and "The license fee for the use of 'Happy Birthday' is prohibitively expensive. Could Ralph celebrate Alice's birthday by singing 'For He's a Jolly Good Woman'?" Some years later, while producing NBC's hit spy spoof sitcom Get Smart, Leonard Stern received a note asking that the show "Please avoid anything morbid, inappropriate, or detrimental to his image in the display of the dead, gay midget lying under the toilet."

---

[4] *"A Martian Wouldn't Say That," compiled by Leonard Stern and Diane Robison, from Tallfellow Press.*

LEONARD STERN:

Jack Hurdle, the *Honeymooners* producer, would receive the memos and then they filtered down to us writers. I think that note about Mars was not in response to a specific script—in other words, "Let's not keep saying you're going to the moon."

By *Get Smart*, I was an established personality behind the scenes. And they were always careful in their wording . . . or sympathetic. So, it was never a dictate— it was always a suggestion or a viable alternate. We got absurd memos from time to time . . . like that *Get Smart* memo about a midget under the toilet. I don't know how he became gay. That was their own supposition. I looked at that film a number of times . . . and maybe they meant something else, but it came out "gay" in the memo.

We didn't get the notes until after they were discussed. They never came to us unannounced. They would call us—there was a rapport. They *had* to do certain things, but I will say this to their credit: Whenever they disagreed, the note always had a reluctant preface to it.

ALFRED SCHNEIDER:

In over-the-air broadcasting, the broadcaster has the responsibility to operate in the public interest. As such, he has the obligation to maintain a responsibility with respect to the portrayal of violence, to telling the truth, to the control of sensationalization of sexuality. *Taste*—questions of taste.

So, the role of the censor is to try to balance what is respectable and acceptable to the general audience, with the needs of his company to prosper in order to be in the business of producing television. It's a judgmental role.

It was a *very* delicate balancing act. The balancing act was between your own management, the affiliated stations, who were much stronger than they are today in terms of their voice, and what may or may not be broadcast because of what they would accept or not accept, and the advertisers, who said, "I'm going to pull my advertising!"

STEPHEN COX, television historian:

By the mid-1960s, sex was creeping in a little bit more. A little bit more blatant. *The Flintstones*, with Wilma and Fred sleeping on the same slab together, attempted to correct that 1950s wholesome nonsense. There were terrifically funny scenes with Lily and Herman Munster in bed together, having arguments or dueling dreams . . . and there were certain innuendos that they'd throw around in *Green Acres* between Eddie Albert and Eva Gabor. Of course, they were a very sensual couple.

But I wouldn't even call them as sensual a couple as Gomez and Morticia on *The Addams Family*—there's one, in a sense, if you don't look at them as monsters but as a couple, even though they'd been supposedly married for a while, they were constantly slobbering over each other. Much more so than any other couple on television at that time, really. I remember John Astin once told me that some psychologists dubbed them the most healthy couple on television. He and Carolyn Jones were proud of that.

Paul Henning would touch on some topics that he felt were taboo. For instance, a drug reference on *The Beverly Hillbillies* . . . it was an episode

where Jethro dresses up as Robin Hood in green tights, and leads this band of *beatniks* into the forest. And when Granny stumbles across this group of beatniks, she wants to make some food for all of them, and says that she wants to smoke some crawdads that she plucked out of some stream—and they think this is the code word for smoking marijuana.

She says, "I wanna smoke these crawdads, but first I gotta get me a little pot!"

And of course she's talking about a kettle, and they're talking about dope. It was a funny gag that worked really well.

Gomez (John Astin) perpetually hungered for his wife Morticia (Carolyn Jones) on The Addams Family, *which certainly flaunted the Hollywood Production Code's firm stance against excessively lustful kissing. © ABC Television Network*

But we're talking about 1967 or so. So, pot references—even on *The Beverly Hillbillies*—started creeping in, and the censors were either looking the other way or they happened to slip past. Paul used to complain about what they *did* bother him about. Simple things, like at the very beginning, one of the jokes was Elly May mistaking a bra for a slingshot. He had to say, "No, that stays in there." It was a funny gag, and just harmless. Even the pilot of *The Beverly Hillbillies* makes reference to Donna Douglas popping the buttons off of her shirts.

Jed says, "She throws her shoulders back with pride."

And Granny says, "It ain't her shoulders that're poppin' those buttons!"

ALFRED SCHNEIDER:

Well, certainly for the production community, it was an interference with their freedom of expression. It was an interference with their economic viability, because of things that they could not do. I mean, to the production community—writers, directors, producers, performers—*censor* is a bad word. From those who felt that there had to be more control over television offerings, the censor was encouraged and lauded. So, there was both sides.

DON TAFFNER:

If there was one thing that I learned in that period of time, it's that mores change. From our first go with Program Practices, they would never have a show on where a guy was living with two girls . . . to two years later, our pilot of *Three's Company* was made. And I could just see the mores changing each time.

ALFRED SCHNEIDER:

It becomes evolutionary. And change took place as viewer expectations changed, as television grew in prominence . . . and then, cable came along. The major distinction that exists today is between the fact that there were three dominant networks—*really* dominant, in terms of thirty shares and thirty-five shares for television programs—and five hundred cable opportunities today, where an eight or a nine share is a major success!

So, you have the fragmentation of audiences. And the concerns dissipate and are varied. And the choices are so much different. Cable is just starting to launch, for the first time, promotions saying that parents should control your television set. There's the V-Chip, there's technology, so that you can *control* what your children are seeing.

That shift took place over thirty years, gradually, as network dominance declined, as cable began to increase in acceptance, and as Congress could not grab three guys by their necks and shake their heads anymore—because there are now a *hundred* guys to deal with!

Of Course, You Realize, This Means War!

2

The late 1960s and early 1970s might be the most combative years America experienced within its borders since the Civil War. Women and people of color struggled for equality, an idealistic younger generation rebelled fiercely against the old ways of the establishment, the Stonewall riots kicked off a gay and lesbian revolution, and protests raged on against what was widely regarded as an unjust and unwinnable war in Southeast Asia. Change was spreading rapidly throughout the country.

Television took a little while to notice.

It mollified us with a seemingly endless parade of popular escapist entertainment shows in primetime, with feel-good sitcoms like *The Lucy Show, The Andy Griffith Show, The Beverly Hillbillies*, and *Bewitched* leading the fray, along with westerns like *Bonanza* and *Gunsmoke*, and musical-comedy-variety shows like *The Ed Sullivan Show* and *The Jackie Gleason Show* drawing the largest audiences. Aside from the news reports, there was nary a mention of what was actually going on in the real world, and a case can be made that many people just didn't want to hear about it when they sat down in front of their TV sets, anyway. The assassination of JFK in 1963 was devastating, the pain of its aftermath still all too fresh in people's minds . . . the war in Vietnam continued to escalate, seemingly with no end in sight . . . and the Cold War with the Soviet Union remained on low boil, threatening to blow up at any time. Not unlike Nero fiddling on while Rome burned, network executives and commercial sponsors just kept the diversions coming.

The groundbreaking satiric show also spawned a record album featuring songs and comedy excerpts. © 1981, The Radiola Co., and NBC Television Network

But change was inevitable, and TV finally reacted with not one, but *three* groundbreaking comedy series: the short-lived *That Was the Week That Was*, and the wildly popular and successful *The Smothers Brothers Comedy Hour* and *Rowan & Martin's Laugh-In*, both of which—unbeknownst to the millions who tuned in each week—waged their very own wars with the networks that aired them.

In the midst of all the unrest, viewers witnessed something they'd never experienced before: On November 10, 1963, American TV's very first topical political satire show was born in primetime. *That Was the Week That Was* began that night as a one-hour special, based on an already successful British television show of the same name created by producer/director Ned Sherrin.

TW3, as it has been affectionately (and thankfully) dubbed, launched as a weekly series on NBC in January of 1964. It featured a semi-regular cast of players that included Sir David Frost (the lone star to also appear in the original Brit version), Nancy Ames, Elliott Reid, Alan Alda, Buck Henry, Bob Dishy, Tom Bosley, Burr Tillstrom's puppets, and satirist/composer Tom Lehrer (author of the riotously offensive "Vatican Rag," among others), who all performed barbed comedy sketches, mock news reports, and musical production numbers. *TW3* also boasted a collection of guest stars amounting to a *who's who* of comedy and showbiz, including Woody Allen, Steve Allen, Art Carney, Bill Cosby, Mike Nichols, Elaine May, Henry Fonda, Margaret Hamilton, Gene Hackman, Mort Sahl, and many, many others.

Each show was not unlike a musical comedy revue, filled with the kinds of songs and satiric sketches that were so popular in urban coffeehouses of the late 1950s and early 1960s. On the very first regular episode, there were repeated digs at both political parties; faux news reports taking aim at leaders like Castro, Khrushchev, de Gaulle, Barry Goldwater, and George

Wallace; a Gilbert & Sullivan song parody about a young page with enough dirt on his bosses to blow the roof off the Senate; an arty "hand ballet" by puppeteer Burr Tillstrom to dramatize the closing of the Berlin Wall; a sketch lampooning the world of society and high fashion; and guest star Audrey Meadows singing a sarcastic ditty skewering President Lyndon Johnson.

Week after week, *TW3* presented clever material aimed at a sophisticated and educated audience. A regular sketch on season two, "Surrealism in Everyday Life," was penned by none other than Gloria Steinem, one of the founding mothers of the women's movement. Although the series only lasted for a year and a half, it attracted a lot of attention in the press (both loving it and hating it), won an Emmy Award (for Tillstrom's "hand ballet"), and ultimately kicked off what were to become traditions on shows like CBS's *The Smothers Brothers Comedy Hour* and NBC's *Saturday Night Live*.

Smothering the Brothers

The Smothers Brothers Comedy Hour came in like a lamb and went out like a lion. It started quietly in 1967, without any particular expectations from CBS, quickly became a breakthrough hit, and—just a few seasons later, following countless knockdown, drag-out battles with network censors and executives over content—went out with a deafening roar; perhaps the noisiest cancellation of any series in the history of television.

Since that day, much has been written and spoken of the brothers' firing, and of their show's brilliance.

Fingers have been pointed in every direction, and blame assessed: Some are convinced it was political pressure exerted on CBS by the White House of beleaguered President Johnson, followed by a newly elected, ultraconservative Nixon administration, neither of whom took kindly to being mercilessly, satirically poked and prodded over America's involvement in Vietnam. Some claim great ambition was the culprit, as CBS chairman Bill Paley and president Frank Stanton, both seeking ambassadorial appointment to the Court of St. James—which neither ultimately attained—conspired to curry favor in Washington by extracting the irritating Smothers' thorn from President Nixon's paw.

Others put the blame squarely on the shoulders of Tommy Smothers, a talented *enfant terrible* who bit the hand that fed him once too often.

Were they sacrificial lambs—as an incensed *New York Times* article claimed shortly after their dismissal—victims of behind-the-scenes political maneuvering? Or did they do themselves in by displaying a mixture of bravado, immaturity, and youthful rebellion intolerable to their network and sponsors? However their war ended, while it raged it was indisputably a clash of two generations, with TV's old guard being challenged to put up their dukes for the first time.

It began with the unlikeliest of catalysts: fresh scrubbed brothers, comedians and folk singers by trade, whose wholesome white-bread act couldn't possibly have been expected to kick off a counter-cultural revolution on American television. When CBS bought *The Smothers Brothers Comedy Hour*, they expected a pleasant, hour-long variety show with some laughs and a few songs, hosted by Tom and Dick Smothers. There was nothing remotely controversial about them.

Their popular stage act consisted of funnyman Tommy on guitar and straight man Dickie on bass, harmonizing folk songs that would break down in the middle for comedy riffs—Tommy's gripe, "Mom always liked you best!" was a frequent lament—before going on to finish off each number. Tommy's persona was that of the simple son prone to inane comments, which invariably exasperated his calmer, smarter, more worldly brother. The show's supporting cast included Pat Paulsen, a droopy-faced comedian with a deadpan delivery, cerebral comic Bob Einstein, hippie comedienne Leigh French, an astoundingly varied array of guest artists, and a brilliant writing staff that occasionally appeared as characters on-air.

An earlier attempt to capitalize on the brothers' popularity resulted in their first network TV show, an undistinguished primetime sitcom called *The Smothers Brothers Show*.

ALLAN BURNS, writer and producer:
I had been working with a partner named Chris Hayward. He and I had started together at Jay Ward Productions, where they did *Rocky & His Friends*. And Chris and I ended up leaving Jay Ward when the Smothers Brothers were looking to do a sitcom. Not their famous variety show . . . this turned out to be a sort of embarrassing sitcom I'm not proud of.

But it was a time when people were doing *My Favorite Martian*, and *Bewitched*, and all those kinds of very gimmicky shows . . . and so we were just going along with the trend, and coming up with these terrible concepts. This was one in which Tommy Smothers played an angel—a brother who was dead—who comes back to bedevil his brother who's still alive. It was Aaron Spelling's concept that I thought we made palatable by fairly funny writing.

KEN KRAGEN, manager and producer:

In those days, the attitude was that Tom and Dick were the hired actors. They were not allowed to see dailies or to have any input in the show. And Tommy, who's very creative, had wanted to do a show that was essentially the concept that *The Monkees* then hit with. Tommy had this idea, but no one would listen to him.

And their show, as a result, was rather trite. At times it was good, at times it was bad, but generally it wasn't anything earth-shattering or groundbreaking. In those days you got twenty-six episodes—I think we lasted a whole year. Because they just didn't put things on, like they do now, and take 'em off three weeks later.

But that show went off the air.

What happened after that was, George Shapiro was the Smothers' agent at William Morris, and he also represented Carl Reiner. And we decided— [management partner] Ken Fritz and I—that we needed advice about what to do next. So, we went over, George, Ken, and I, to what was Desilu at the time, to meet with Carl.

We got there and his secretary said, "He's in the gym." So we went over to the gym . . . and he started to give us advice while he was doing pushups. Then he was on the *rowing machine*, still talking, still telling us ideas . . . and after about three or four of these things—he never stopped working out the whole time he was talking—he said, "Take off your clothes." Here we were, in suits and ties, right? So, we all undressed and went in the sauna with him.

We're now in the sauna, buck-naked. And Carl says something that we realize is the breakthrough idea. And George Shapiro turns to me and says, "Ken, that's great! Write that down!" I said, "George, with what? Sweat!?"

Then what happened was, the Smothers' success was continuing, in terms of concerts and everything . . . and Abe Lastfogel of the William Morris Agency went to [CBS chairman] Bill Paley and said to him, "Look at the age of your stars. They're all in their fifties and sixties, they're all getting older. They're not going to be around—you've *gotta* develop some younger talent. You should do something with the Smothers Brothers."

Well, at the time, *Bonanza* was number one—and CBS had been throwing shows up against it constantly. So, they decided to do the Smothers Brothers' show.

MICHAEL DANN, former V.P. of Programming at CBS:

Nine o'clock on Sunday night is the highest viewing public on all of television. He who wins Sunday night at nine, wins the battle. And I couldn't lick

Bonanza. I had Garry Moore on the air, the third show against *Bonanza* in just over two years.

Paley called me up one day and said, "What've you got in place of Garry Moore? Get it off the air by the first of the year."

He was calling me on December 5! What the hell could I do? I knew I had to go with a variety show—it was an *hour*, wasn't just a half hour. So, I said to [William Morris agent] Lou Weiss, "Have you got anything you could be ready for?" He started telling me about this show, and that show . . . and then he said, "I've got a show with the Smothers Brothers."

I said, "What do they do?"

"They sing, they dance, they do sketches. They can do everything."

And I said, "Do you have any film on them?"

"Yeah, they did a short series, but it wasn't so good. They should be in their own variety hour."

And I remember I said to him, "Can it be ready January 12?" It was about five weeks then till January 12.

KEN KRAGEN:

We had a big meeting at the William Morris offices. *We* were planning to go on with a show in the fall . . . but CBS wanted to throw us into the breach in January to fill a hole they now had—and not ever expecting us to do well.

So, we were hit with this quandary: Should we go on in January up against *Bonanza*, and take all those risks? Or should we wait until September? Tommy finally said, "I think we should go on *now*, because if we fail against *Bonanza*, everybody's gonna say, 'Hey, they were just a victim of the juggernaut that's been beating back every show everybody's tried to throw against it.' But if we *succeed*, it'll be huge. It'll be news." He really, really understood that idea.

ERNEST CHAMBERS, writer and producer:

My partner Saul Ilson and I wanted to create the *right show* for the Smothers Brothers . . . they had just come off their failed situation comedy. But they were really wonderful entertainers. Saul and I did a summer series for a singer named John Gary, and the Smothers Brothers were guests . . . and we wrote material for them. So, when the subject of doing a series together came up, Perry Lafferty at CBS had seen what we did with the Smothers Brothers, thought we really had the right sensibility to create a show for them, and hired us to produce the show.

Tommy, when we started, knew nothing about any social issues . . . he was a pothead folksinger, you know? But he began to get educated through all of us.

KEN KRAGEN:
The Smothers weren't candidates for the edgy activist role that they were later portrayed as. They really weren't. They were the *antithesis* of that.

TOMMY SMOTHERS, performer and producer:
We didn't become politically conscious until that show happened, during the mid 1960s . . . we started to hear other voices. When we got the greenlight for the variety show, we wanted to be *relevant*. After the experience with the sitcom—which was so vacuous—we wanted creative control, and we wanted to have something at least relevant. We didn't know what that would be, but we knew that the humor would not be the stupid sitcom type of stuff.

PERRY LAFFERTY, former V.P. of Programs at CBS:
We didn't set out to do the kind of show that they did. They were very attractive young guys doing a comedy act. And then, when it came time to start production, they had quite a fresh view of things. It had a youthful point of view . . . there was no variety show at the time that I can think of that was doing skits that bordered on y'know, taking a little *whack* at people. It started out pretty tame, but with freshness to it.

TOMMY SMOTHERS:
They put us with an audience. With the sitcom, we had no audience—it was a huge difference. They'd put us on a sitcom, and took away the guitar and the bass, and made us actors. When we got the variety show, here it was: We had our guitar and our bass, and we had a live audience, and it was working.

KEN KRAGEN:
We went on, and *hit*—and the show became hot. I don't think right away, but it did okay, because we had some pretty interesting guests and a well-written show. It was a very traditional variety program, with the exception that it was fronted by two guys whose material was wonderfully funny, and accessible to all ages. Little children loved it cause Tommy is like a little kid being the bad boy, or misunderstanding, playing really a childlike character. Adults loved it because of the interplay between Dick and Tom. I mean, Dick's role in this is so critical, because there wouldn't be anything for Tom to play off of if Dick wasn't so brilliant a straight man.

They don't look like rebels: Wholesome brother act Tommy and Dickie in clean-cut blazers, performing on their trademark acoustic guitar and stand-up bass. © *Smothers Brothers and CBS Television Network*

What made it *stand out*, first and foremost, was the absolute delight and across-all-demographic appeal of the Smothers Brothers. College kids liked it because Tom and Dick were a big act on college campuses at that point . . . and until the show got controversial, even older conservatives liked it.

PERRY LAFFERTY:
Tommy had a special font of energy, and point of view. And he was a young man. He didn't really have a big overall picture, nor did he give a damn. He just wanted to do what he wanted to do . . . which is usually when you get something good.

ERNEST CHAMBERS:
I had already had this background writing topical material in revues . . . and Saul had come out of little revues in Canada. Both of us had experience at what makes a variety show work. So, one of the things we did was we put

together a staff. We were the head writers, but our two major writers were two of Jack Benny's writers. Jack Benny was, in my mind, the greatest comedy talent of my life . . . just a brilliant performer, and his writing was phenomenal. He'd had four writers, and we hired two, Hal Goldman and Al Gordon, to be our senior writers.

KEN KRAGEN:
Thanks to Ilson and Chambers, we got George Burns and Jack Benny to come on and "be" the Smothers Brothers—in the red coats with the guitar and bass. And it's a classic moment, where Benny is Tommy. Because Tommy's material, Tommy's whole persona, has a huge amount of Jack Benny in it.

ERNEST CHAMBERS:
Every show began with the silhouette of Tom and Dick, and then we'd bump the lights and there they were in their red blazers, with their guitar and bass. The second show, you saw the silhouette—and when we bumped the lights, it was Jack Benny and George Burns. I thought that was emblematic of what we accomplished, because if Jack and George were out there saying these guys are the funniest, and the most wonderful guys, then you at home—who don't know who we are—*you* can accept us in your living rooms.

KEN KRAGEN:
That appeal, getting Burns and Benny on our show, probably opened the door for the incredible star lineup that we brought. We had Bette Davis playing Queen Elizabeth . . . all of the hottest people in the country suddenly wanted to do our show. And the biggest names were traditional—they weren't Elvis Presley or the Beatles, not initially. That was *later*, when the show became hipper as time went on, and as the writing staff started to feel its muscle, and the younger guys took over.

ERNEST CHAMBERS:
We booked stars who had acceptance with the public. We booked Kate Smith, for example. In those days, Kate Smith and Roy Rogers were the two guests that if you put them on, you would see an up-tick in your ratings that week. She was so important in this country at that time. So she did stuff with Tommy . . .

Mason Williams was a buddy of Tom and Dick. They wanted us to hire Mason, so we did . . . and I remember the big piece, which Mason wrote, was "Sergeant Pepper's Lonely Hearts Club Band" with Kate Smith as a Salvation Army lady. And the fact that she was singing the Beatles was a big thing in 1967.

MASON WILLIAMS, writer and composer:

We said to her, "Come on and sing something from *your* world, and then you're gonna step into something from *ours*." We tried to present everybody in a broader duality: "Here's what you do, but now here's you in the context of something you're not known for, or you've never done, or whatever."

You didn't see Kate Smith in too many comedy sketches. She had a great time.

TOMMY SMOTHERS:

Well, Mason Williams was our guy. *My* guy. I got him a writing position on the show. He was a good friend of mine, a guitar player . . . we'd recorded some of his songs, and he was a creative guy. I tried to always bring someone. I brought Pat Paulsen in right away—I brought in as many people as I knew that I trusted, that had a different viewpoint.

MASON WILLIAMS:

Ernie and Saul didn't want to hire me. But anyway, Tom insisted that they take me on. I didn't get an office of my own . . . I ended up in an office with Allan Blye, and we just sat across two desks from each other. Allan's a great guy, and very pleasant to be with, and funny and a good writer. So, it just happened that I ended up in a situation that was workable.

ALLAN BLYE, writer and producer:

We were two kids, relatively speaking, and they didn't have room anywhere else—so we ended up in the music room. I had a little desk there, and Mason had a little desk. That's how it started . . . and because of geography, we started to work a little bit *together*—and found that we worked wonderfully together! It was just one of those natural things.

ERNEST CHAMBERS:

I think at that time I was thirty-eight, and the Smothers were like thirty . . . but there was a huge difference because they were the pot generation, and I was before that. I think Mason was the youngest, and certainly the least experienced, but on the other hand the most offbeat and imaginative. So, for the real solid comedy material, you had Ilson, Chambers, Gordon, and Goldman . . . and for the really offbeat, ingenious stuff, you had Mason.

MASON WILLIAMS:

The staff was actually put together in a very hip way. You had Mike Marmer and Stan Burns, who were writers for Steve Allen. So, they came from that sort of hip side of television. They were writers on *The Tonight Show* with him. And then we had Hal and Al . . . and I believe they were thinking of Allan Blye as someone who might be involved in musical comedy, 'cause he was quite knowledgeable about music, and sang, and knew the repertoire.

And the great thing about it was, when Allan and I got together, he had a whole repertoire that *I* didn't know about, and I had a whole one *he* didn't know about . . . but we still knew about a lot in the middle, together, folk music in particular. So, that was one of the things that we became, the source of most of the musical routines.

But when I started moving over to the philosophical comedy stuff, Allan picked right up on it. And we all moved into it, just because Tommy was open to exploring this idea of these little comments on the times. It's things that are on everybody's mind, but nobody's saying anything about it . . . so the minute you even bring it up, it's kind of electrifying.

ERNEST CHAMBERS:

Mason and Tommy were extremely close from the beginning. And Mason would write these wonderful things . . . but you couldn't rely on Mason to do a show, because Mason is more of an artist. I mean, Gordon and Goldman, having worked for Jack Benny, were used to turning out a funny script on schedule every week. As we were. Mason would bring something in every three weeks—one sketch. Because he didn't know how to work the other way. He couldn't write a joke. But when Mason brought in his material, it was fully developed and very unique. There was nothing to be done to it by the joke writers, 'cause it was a different kind of writing.

MASON WILLIAMS:

Tommy liked these oddball, arty things. I did one called "Leg Man." I had all the dancers on the show stick their legs through a velvet thing, so all you saw was their legs, you couldn't see any of the rest of their body. And they were in a circle, and Tommy was in the middle of them, singing, "Hello, I Love Your Legs," surrounded by these faceless, beautiful legs. Kind of like a June Taylor Dancers number. It was kind of salacious, because these girls were doing those star things, and he was right in the center of them looking up, right into their crotches. I mean, that's not what was intended . . .

Anyway, when something's really over the line, slyly, it gets passed around to everyone inside the network. And we heard that's one of the tapes that made the rounds.

ERNEST CHAMBERS:
Mason was the kind of creative writer—not what I'd call a *comedy* writer—you'd just have to let him go and do his thing his way. He has a piece in the Museum of Modern Art, and he wrote "Classical Gas," which is a fabulous piece of music . . . he was that kind of a guy.

KEN KRAGEN:
What sustained us was that it morphed into this wonderfully cutting edge show—in every area. We had Jefferson Airplane on, we had the Doors, we did all kinds of things. And it also was a clear-cut alternative to *Bonanza* . . . if you were a woman who didn't wanna watch shoot-em-ups in the West, here was a viable alternative that'd make you laugh, that was entertainment! We were in the middle of the Vietnam War. We needed some escapist entertainment that you could laugh at and enjoy.

ERNEST CHAMBERS:
It was a hit by the end of the first season. It went on the air in January, and by the time we'd finished our first season, which was thirteen shows, we were already discovered by the media. And that alone was enough to keep us on the air. Just like *Saturday Night Live*, which the media discovered before the public did. So by the second season, it really started going well.

PERRY LAFFERTY:
The show succeeded in beating down *Bonanza*, and got bigger and bigger. Tommy and Mason Williams just kept pushing the envelope, kept pushing and wanting to do things that were more and more related to Vietnam. They did stuff that wasn't on the air at the time, and the audience seemed to love it.

ALLAN BLYE:
They were kind of Peck's Bad Boys. And they were so brilliant, because they didn't just do political satire—they satirized the right by *exhibiting* the right. Pat Paulsen was like a right-wing guy. He said things that were obviously very funny, but they were very conservative. And that's how we made fun of that side of the political spectrum.

MASON WILLIAMS:

The whole censorship battle came about because Tom and Dick wanted to be funny, step over the line a little bit, be controversial. The politics kinda started as these little comments. It was along about the eighth or ninth show, somewhere in there—by the eighth show it was doing well, and people were tuning in a lot—and Tommy mentioned the idea that he wanted to say little things here and there that were sort of like . . . we called them *zingers*. I remember the first one I wrote. He walked up and said, "I like that idea. I want you to do some more stuff like this."

It was a Southern sketch, and he was playing a Southern Confederate general. His brother was, of course, in the Union army, and they had come back

On the folksy, stained glass set of their variety show, the Smothers Brothers pose with playfully non-conformist Mason Williams . . . who decided to sport three ties for this early publicity shot. © CBS Television Network

to the house. It was one of those brother against brother things, tying right into their sibling thing . . . and at one point he said something like "Progress is our most impo'tant product."

By saying that in a Southern accent, he got a good laugh. Because everybody mispronounces *impotent*, so it was a funny little joke. And he thought of it as a kind of little zinger, philosophically . . . ' cause he's saying, well, progress is impotent. So, he liked the idea of starting to throw these little comments into the show.

The Censors Censor the Censors

It was in the middle of that initial season that the Smothers Brothers experienced their first major tussle with the network censors. The brouhaha centered around a harmless comedy sketch that had nothing to do with Vietnam, politics, drugs, or even anything blatantly sexual in nature. It was a simple piece written by Elaine May and Tommy Smothers that dared to poke fun at censors themselves, by having May and Smothers portray two movie censors combing through a script and replacing supposedly offensive words or phrases. By today's standards, it was mild stuff . . . but back then, such things were never mentioned on primetime television, let alone lampooned. It was just the beginning of what would eventually escalate into a continuing tug of war between CBS and the passionate creators of the show.

KEN KRAGEN:

The silliest thing was not being able to say the word "breast" in the Elaine May skit in which they played censors. It was very, very funny, but it never actually saw the light of day. Never got on the air. It was silly, because nowadays it's like, "How can they not say that?" But in England they were saying "fuck" on television at that time. It was a whole different story.

TOMMY SMOTHERS:

It was about two movie censors, a man and a woman, who come in to censor *My heart beats wildly in my breast* . . . "We've got to take the word "breast" out, that's inappropriate." Fuddy duds, you know. And it became: *My heart beats wildly in my wrist*. So, it was two censors, censoring a movie. And it kinda ridiculed censors. It was our first real censorship.

MASON WILLIAMS:

That was Elaine and Tom's creation together. It was funny . . . and sophisticated, too. First of all, it said there *is* a censor. The networks didn't like that at all. It's hard for us to grasp the fact that they liked the idea that the general public didn't *know* that they were being censored—that they thought this was simply what people want to put on. So, by bringing up the concept of a censor, you're actually personifying it: There *is* a censor, he's a guy in a black hat with a twirly moustache. That's the kind of sketch that they could play off-Broadway, and everybody would have fun with it.

So, that's where it really began, I think . . . making the public aware of the fact that censorship is going on, and this may not be *fair* to you, because this is America, land of the free. Where we're free to speak our minds. [cynical laughter]

TOMMY SMOTHERS:

Maybe they were just flexing muscle. *The New York Times* reprinted the entire sketch in the paper . . . and it made CBS look kinda foolish. People couldn't wait for Tommy Smothers to go to the press, because I certainly didn't hold back at all . . . I mean, I just didn't—there's no subtlety, I had no way, I didn't know how to—and people love to *hear* that kind of unfiltered passion!

Well, that certainly got me going. It was the first time the printed media kind of picked up on it. It was pretty exciting. I'd made a big scene about it: "Hey, what's going on?!" And then I realized that there was another court that I could present my case to. It was the first time it really got big attention. We had some little things in *Variety*, but the big one was in the *New York Times*.

MASON WILLIAMS:

It seems like most of the focus before that was on "It isn't working," or "We need to fix this," or "Can you make this funnier?" So you were just kind of dealing with the aspects of production values, and how well-written or performed something was. And this brought that other element into it—of running into the politics of the network. At that point, you were a half-inch away from lawyers.

TOMMY SMOTHERS:

Dickie just said, "Don't make any mistakes and get us fired."

ERNEST CHAMBERS:

I didn't care what they did. If we could get away with it, it was fine with me. Anything in the area of religion was difficult, but the other stuff was political. You couldn't make fun of the president, you couldn't make jokes about the atomic bomb . . . obviously things like sexual references, double entendres . . .

MASON WILLIAMS:

Censorship is one of those things that are useful and also a problem. You know, we may have murderous thoughts, but we don't *kill* people. In other words, you're censoring yourself all the time. And the culture is an extension of the self. We collectively say certain things aren't appropriate, or that we collectively don't like. So, I think that there is a place for censorship, if you *agree* on it. If we say, "These are the parameters, let's obey them."

But when it comes down to suppressing someone for expressing their opinion, then it gets political. So, censorship has these two aspects: Who gets to express themselves, and what do they get to say?

Now, the censorship on *The Smothers Brothers* show . . . we only wanted to be slightly bolder than things had been in the past, and we wanted to link in with what was on the street. Not just what was on television. 'Cause TV had its own world, with all these kinds of *sitcommy* moments. It was juvenile. And we wanted to break away from being so juvenile.

PERRY LAFFERTY:

In those days, if the stations got lots of complaints from their viewers—who could go to their congressmen or the FCC—they wouldn't get their licenses renewed. That was the basis, the fear of upsetting the FCC and not getting re-licensed, which would be the worst thing that could happen to you. So, you're trying to walk this thing where these young men are pushing the envelope. They're funny, they've got a hit show . . . but how far can you let 'em go? It's the public airwaves, and you've gotta keep within a certain parameter.

KEN KRAGEN:

Perry Lafferty and Mike Dann were somewhat caught. I remember that Mike Dann *loved* the controversy, because it brought ratings. I mean, he's the one that went out and got the agreement that we could get [blacklisted folksinger] Pete Seeger.

It was the first taping, or we were in rehearsal, I think, and Kenny Fritz and I were sitting in the audience with Mike Dann. And he said to us, "What can I do for you guys? What do you want?" Ken Fritz, without missing a beat, said, "Get us an agreement that we can put Pete Seeger on." And Dann went and did that.

MASON WILLIAMS:

We didn't have any idea what we wanted him to do, we just wanted him to be a guest. When Pete came to the show, I said, "One of the things we're doing is having people on that just make an entertaining statement—musical, or funny, or whatever it is they do—but then, they can say something about something that's important to them in a different way. We like the idea that you can cover both bases."

ERNEST CHAMBERS:

CBS was reluctant, but by that time we were getting a lot of press . . . and the ratings started to go up, so they let us book Pete Seeger. We were in Vietnam, and Pete had written a song called "Waist Deep in the Big Muddy," about a farmer who kept going out into the river until he was so deep, he could not get out. He never mentioned Vietnam, ever, but the metaphor was clear.

MASON WILLIAMS:

"Waist Deep in the Big Muddy" was the perfect kind of thing for him to address, because it was an artful analogy about Lyndon Johnson, and about the war in Vietnam. And the network didn't want it on because they knew that the Smothers Brothers were making fun of the president and the war. Criticizing him.

ALLAN BLYE:

Literally, before the show aired, we had 5,000 letters. What the hell was that all about? Just because Pete was going to be *on*!? They didn't even know what he was going to do!

MICHAEL DANN:

We got into such trouble . . . we fought over *words* in it, I mean, because this was in the middle of a war. And I thought it was a triumph just to get him on the show! And then I was in the middle of trying to get him to say *some* of the words . . . but you don't exactly tell Pete Seeger how to do his music.

ERNEST CHAMBERS:

When CBS saw it on the tape, they *cut it* out of the tape.

KEN KRAGEN:

From Dann's standpoint, the controversy was a boon because it was getting ratings—and that was Dann's job. And, to some extent, Lafferty's. Lafferty was the West Coast guy, a wonderful, charming, gentle man. He was always the most reasonable, nicest guy to deal with—but couldn't affect what was happening. I think he sided with us to some extent, as well, but his role for the network was: Let's just try to keep everyone calmed down and happy.

ERNEST CHAMBERS:

As the show built more and more, we went to CBS and they said, "Okay, you can bring him back." So, Pete Seeger came back, and did "Waist Deep in the Big Muddy" on the show.

The War of the Words Gets Hotter

KEN KRAGEN:

In the second year, Tommy came up with the idea of a bullpen of young writers who'd work for $150 a week. And he made an agreement with the Writers Guild that we could have six writers in that pool, and two of them every week would get full salary on a rotating basis. Salary for a writer, at that time, was like $1,500. But for $150, we got Steve Martin. It was an *incredible* pool. Those guys went on to be some of the most successful people in town. And that concept allowed us to use some untried, young talent.

MASON WILLIAMS:

Basically, Tommy said, "I want to have a show with younger writers, and people like me." So we went around, looking for different writers. Tommy said, "I want to hire Rob Reiner. He's *gotta* be funny, 'cause his dad is. And he's a young, passionate firebrand about the revolution." And he was. Then he wanted to hire Carl Gottlieb, from the Committee—we admired them 'cause they were really funny. Tommy came to me at one point—they had a list of people they were hiring—Bob Einstein was another one. And he said, "Who would *you* like to hire? I'll just let you pick one person yourself."

I said, "Okay, I'll go for Steve Martin." We'd played together at the Ice House. We were in a lot of shows together . . . I thought his act was unique, so when it came up I said, "I think this guy is pretty interesting." And so he hired him.

KEN KRAGEN:

The other thing about that talent was, they were good performers—so that you look back on that show, and you see the writers in scene after scene. There was a certain amount of *Saturday Night Live* to *The Smothers Brothers* show . . . where you have an ensemble group that comes up with funny skits and things. The only difference is, we didn't have a different host every week. But the writers were very involved.

ERNEST CHAMBERS:

I discovered this comedienne in San Francisco, in a group called The Committee. Leigh French was her name. Tommy liked her, so we put her on the show; and she developed a segment that we did every week called "Tea with Goldie." The character's name was Goldie O'Keefe.

The censors—Bill Tankersley and Charlie Pettijohn—were nice guys, they weren't assholes. They were trying to be helpful, they really were, but they had to answer to the network, and to the advertisers, which was more important. 'Cause the advertisers were scared shitless of the Bible Belt. That was the overwhelming concern . . . as it is suddenly today, again.

So, one of those guys asked me, "Y'know, what is this thing, this 'Tea with Goldie'? Is there anything in there about pot?" I said no, I'd talked to Tommy and asked him about this, and he said, "No, it's just a name. She's having tea, and talking to the viewers."

TOMMY SMOTHERS:

I like that one where she says, "Good evening, ladies. I'd like to welcome you to my show as I always do. *Hi!*"

MASON WILLIAMS:

It was a talk show from San Francisco that had a hippie, counterculture vibe to it. 'Cause the whole hippie world had this kind of secret language of its own—even silly things like "groovy" and "hey, man," and "dig it." So she was basically just going to be a talk-show host that embraced the Haight-Ashbury culture. Drugs, and marijuana, references to "back to Earth," communes, this whole world. And she was a beautiful girl . . . she truly *believed* in that lifestyle and those issues, so she was the perfect person to flesh out that role.

ERNEST CHAMBERS:

About a month later, my wife and I were walking along Sunset Boulevard, and there was a head shop. For some reason, just on impulse, I walked in to see what they had there. And there was a big poster that said: *A puff of keefe makes a man strong as a thousand camels.* [laughing] I never told them that I found out *keefe* was another name for pot.

MASON WILLIAMS:

You could just go under that radar screen so easily; it was unbelievable. We figured if they didn't get it, the general public wouldn't get it, either. It was the idea that they're not tuned in to this world, so they don't know you or what we're talking about. We just thought it bypassed them—and it did.

KEN KRAGEN:

We had two guys who were the censors on the show. Bill Tankersley was this mythical guy in New York . . . he wasn't out there every week, coming in and talking to us about the show. We had his *emissaries*—and the emissaries were these two guys who didn't really like their jobs that much, and would go over and get drunk in the bar across the street. And we'd have to pull 'em out to get 'em back to ask them something. I can remember walking over there to get them one time, when we needed an answer.

The crazy thing was, of course, that they would come in and they'd *miss* a lot of stuff. Which would always get everybody angry after it aired. And we fooled 'em at times . . . we'd put stuff in the scripts that clearly, obviously needed to be thrown out, and they'd miss something on the next page that we'd wanted to get by 'em.

MASON WILLIAMS:

Tommy said, "Let's just be obvious about putting things in that we *know* are gonna get cut." I wrote a piece for Tom and Dick, a Chevalier-esque kind of French production number . . . and at one point Tommy's claiming to be an expert on Paris and France.

First Dick is saying, "Well, what do you know about French wine?"

And Tom says something stupid.

"You don't know *anything* about French wine. What do you know about French cuisine?"

So he spouts off a bunch of stuff.

"You don't know anything about French cuisine! What about French women? What do you know about them?"

Tom and Dick in an early publicity pose on a "two-way bicycle" . . . perhaps a portent of what was to come, as their network wanted to go one way and the Smothers went the other. © *CBS Television Network*

And Tom says, "Ah, French women . . . *Je vous ami, je vous encore, et puis encore*" . . . or something like that.

"Tom, you don't even know anything about French women! You flunked French wine, you flunked French cuisine, you flunked French women."

And Tom goes, "I never *flunked* a French woman in my life."

You know right away that's coming out. But there were more subtle ones, they were the better ones. That was an obvious one, where you were pulling their chain. It was a kind of game we started playing with them: like, what can we get away with? It was fun to—they were like our folks, and we were just getting away with shit. I mean, what could be better?

TOMMY SMOTHERS:

It *was* kind of fun, because we were dealing with people with their feet in their brains a little bit. And they did not have the passion, and I *did*. So, it was an interesting kind of conflict; it was fun to have those conversations. Other times it was quite frustrating, and became emotional baggage for me eventually, but I enjoyed it. I enjoyed the conflict, and making changes, and swapping things for this, swapping things for that.

KEN KRAGEN:

The biggest issue was really that we never were told any clear-cut guidelines. Y'know: *This is what you can do.* And I'm not sure if we had been, if Tom and Dick would have been any more willing. We were in the late 1960s. We were in a period of the hippie movement . . . we were in a period of youthful rebellion . . . and Tom and Dick were feeling empowered and invulnerable.

TOMMY SMOTHERS:

It was scattershot. Sometimes it would be, "You can't say the word 'score,' because it's implying that you might be having some sexual conquest of some woman" . . . and it was the little, typical things—sexual innuendo—that they were set up for. They were never set up for social commentary. That's where they panicked, they didn't know. So, they would revert to trying to repress us . . . we couldn't say the words "sex education" . . . we couldn't say the word "pregnant." I mean, those are the kind of stupid things, and we made an issue of that.

ERNEST CHAMBERS:

What was most difficult was that Tommy, by the middle of the second season, was just throwing his weight around. Saying *this* is what I wanna do, I don't wanna do *that*. The first season—and this is not unusual, by the way, with stars—it was "Anything you want, just make me a star." The second season was, "I'm a star now. I never needed you in the first place." So, by the middle of the second season, Tommy was just so impossible, and so obstructionist.

TOMMY SMOTHERS:

Mason and I would sit and look at the scripts. On a Friday the new script would come out, and we'd go home and read it on the weekend, and say, "That's bullshit . . . that's bullshit . . . that's good . . . that's bullshit . . . that's good . . ." Slowly we started just picking up, throwing out the vacuous things, y'know, trying to make the comedy relevant. And then I'd make those notes and go in for the reading on Monday, and not say that it was just Mason and me sitting there.

MASON WILLIAMS:

It was being extremely *honest*. Tommy would see it from his perspective, and I would see it from mine. Sometimes you'd just fix it right then and there, 'cause maybe you'd think of something . . . but by and large, you were just taking a personal look through it and being very critical. We'd try to pinpoint or flag problems within the pieces . . . but if they had something going for them, we'd try to keep them intact, as well. It worked because it was just two people bouncing around rather than a committee kind of thing. There's always great power in that.

Deadpan comedian Pat Paulsen out on the mock presidential campaign trail. © *CBS Television Network*

ERNEST CHAMBERS:

There was a wonderful comment that one of the censors said to me in the booth one night, during the second season. He said, "Tommy, better be careful. Y'know, the king's jester could say anything he wanted to ridicule the king—as long as the king thought he was just trying to be funny. But if he thought he was serious, it was off with his head."

KEN KRAGEN:

It's the kind of conflict that exists almost in every creative endeavor between the artist and people who are charged with executing their work. I think it came on gradually . . . and I think it was more with Saul, who was kind of tough, more irascible than Ernie, who's kind of mild but charming. Not that Saul's not a nice guy, and very creative, but Saul had more of that New York aggressiveness to him. Which probably meant that Saul was more vocal, and didn't go along with Tommy as much. As we succeeded more and more, and as Tommy identified with the young writing staff, it was the death knell for Ilson and Chambers.

ERNEST CHAMBERS:

Tommy and I just couldn't possibly coexist. There was no way; it just didn't work. He wasn't going to do as he was told, and he was eroding the show. Dickie was a pussycat—but Tommy became much more and more assertive, and in conflict with my partner and me . . . so at the end of the second season, we left the show.

Flying High

As *The Smothers Brothers Comedy Hour* concluded season two, the show was a solid hit. One of their most famous comedic concepts, a bogus independent run for President by series regular Pat Paulsen, began that year and was played to the hilt, drawing much media attention. Paulsen, who never once broke character, ultimately drew about 200,000 write-in votes in the actual election later that year.

Though they never managed to unseat *Bonanza* from its lofty perch atop the ratings heap, *The Smothers Brothers* were consistently finishing in the top twenty, turning a tidy profit for CBS. As a courtesy—extended in those days by the networks to stars of their hit shows—they were allowed to pitch their own summer replacement series. Tom and Dick tapped staff writer Allan Blye to create and produce, and he came up with a country music/comedy variety show (aptly titled *The Summer Smothers Brothers Show*), hosted by rising star Glen Campbell and utilizing Tommy's "special pool" of talented young writers as the series' staff.

The summer show was also a resounding success, which led to Blye taking over producing chores on *The Smothers Brothers Comedy Hour* and the hiring of Steve Martin, Rob Reiner, Carl Gottlieb, Bob Einstein, Lorenzo (Jerry) Music, and the others as full-time writers for the third season. With all this fresh talent in place, and his power base now firmly established, Tommy Smothers pushed the show even further creatively . . . and further into the faces of CBS's wary Standards and Practices editors.

ALLAN BLYE:

Tommy really had an impact now. I thought that the satire—the political stuff that we were doing, and the social stuff we were doing—was wonderful, because it was so nicely disguised. But it hit hard! At one point I said, "God, here we are. We're number one." And Tommy said, "Yeah. Well, now we've gotta start hitting a little harder."

Then, it became less disguised, let's put it that way. And more on the nose . . . and being on the nose was less effective, in my eyes.

TOMMY SMOTHERS:

During the Vietnam protests and the civil-rights legislation going on at the same time, we were very big with African-American people. And we did a lot of stuff. There was one sketch called "The First Integrated Marriage Takes Place in the South." It has an old newspaper clipping that spins, like in the old-fashioned movies. It comes up and stops on me in a clerical collar and a black man and a white lady, and I say to the white lady, "Sally Jean, do you take Billy Joe to be your lawfully wedded husband, till death do you part?"

And she says, "I do."

"Billy Joe, do you take Sally Jean to be your lawfully wedded wife until death do *you* part?"

He says, "I do."

And I turn and say, "The rope, please."

The irony of it, and the cynicism of it, was not lost. It was on the air back then—but these are things you won't see today. That was in 1968, right in the middle of everything. We did a couple of those kind of ironic, cynical little things, and blacks loved it. They saw the cynicism right away.

ALLAN BLYE:

In that third season, we did these little sermonettes with David Steinberg. We were very careful, many weeks in advance, to bring in rabbis and priests and ministers. It wasn't there to be offensive. It was there to have a little fun! And then, five, six weeks later, we actually did them on the air, and the laughter in the audience was incredible.

DAVID STEINBERG, guest performer:

At that time, although it seems quite tame by comparison now, I was doing these sermons as part of my act. I would take any suggestion of an Old Testament personality from the audience, and I would improvise a sermon. If they suggested Moses, I would say, "Moses had a wonderful rapport with God, whom I'm sure you'll all remember from *last* week's sermon." I had lines like, "And God destroyed all of the land with that mystical sense of humor that is only His."

They let the first one run on the air . . . and they got, I'd probably say, the most negative mail on *any* piece of material ever shown on television to that point! And the negative mail was bipartisan. A lot of Jews wrote in that they didn't like it, but mostly it was Bible Belt. Well, I can't say that—because it just was an overwhelmingly negative across-the-board response to it.

ALLAN BLYE:

There was obviously some organized stuff where we got tons of mail: "How dare you do that?!" and, "Such bad taste!"

DAVID STEINBERG:

I was surprised, because I also had done the sermons on *The Tonight Show* prior to that—and the response was overwhelmingly good. But the network said to Tommy, "You can have Steinberg on again, but he can't do another sermon."

All the way along, Tom and Dick were fighting the censors everywhere, on *everything*. Religion is such a controversial subject; to this day you can see how it could ruffle feathers. But their political comments would only ruffle the feathers of the people who the comments were addressed to. The audience was already picking it up. There was a big audience for this that wasn't being tapped into—and the Smothers Brothers got it. They were *huge*! And so they wanted more of their political stuff on the air, and they didn't like that they were being openly censored on these sermons.

So, Tommy had me back on, and I did another character, a psychiatrist character that I play, and . . . I seem to remember Tommy saying, "Why don't you do another sermon?"

KEN KRAGEN:

There was *huge* controversy . . . and Tommy goes and tells him to do it again!

DAVID STEINBERG:

The audience that night gave me Jonah to do . . . and the line that got the biggest laugh was, "They grabbed the Jew by the Old Testaments." That's going a little farther than they liked.

MASON WILLIAMS:

I'd left the show early in 1969 . . . I was playing college concerts and clubs around the country. But while I was out there, I was watching television, and so I would write things for the show and send 'em in from on the road. That's how I got the weird credit, "And sometimes Mason Williams."

I saw the show with David Steinberg on it, and then the next week I was talking to Tommy. He said, "We got in a lot of trouble for that. The sermonette got a lot of hate mail from religious people." So, I wrote this whole thing for Tommy, for the end of the show:

> *We got a lot of mail. People got upset about David Steinberg's sermonette, but we just thought they were funny. Since we have a sense of humor, and since we're supposed to be made in His image, we assume that God has a sense of humor—and so we would think God would think this is funny, too. We've also heard that even if it wasn't funny, God would forgive us, even if the Christians won't.*

ALLAN BLYE:

It started to get difficult just after the sermonettes went on . . . I do recall that they were now really nervous about getting the show. At one point we were a Friday ahead—and it didn't air until a *week* from Sunday, so that there was time for the network to see something on the Wednesday before. Then, as time went by, we started taping on Friday and airing that Sunday.

PERRY LAFFERTY:

I was in the *middle*, between New York who said, "You gotta get these guys straightened out," and Tommy, who was like, "We're gonna do this on Sunday!" It was a constant fight. Then he'd call up the local censor, and then he'd call up Bill Tankersley, who was the head censor in New York.

And it got to the point where he was so out of control, and the show was such a hit, that he would be in the editing room—because of some labor troubles, the schedule was running way behind, and we wouldn't get the show edited till—I don't know, till Friday night, early. And they'd send a courier to New York with it, so they'd have it on Saturday in time to put in the commercials. It was just hair-raisingly tough to finish.

KEN KRAGEN:

Tom and I finally decided that we had to confront these guys—y'know, Tankersley—in New York. So, we flew to New York on the red-eye one night after taping the show. And we got in at 8:00 in the morning, and went to the Drake Hotel where we had a suite with a living room and two bedrooms with the doors facing each other on either side of the suite. We were dressed—as we dressed in those days—with long hair . . . beads and peace medals . . . turtleneck sweaters . . . and leather pants.

So, we go in and we go to sleep for a few hours, 'cause we were meeting at noon. And at 11:30 sharp, when we were ready to leave, we appeared at our doors simultaneously in three-piece suits and ties—without ever having discussed it! And we start laughing. We are on the floor. We can't believe that we both did that.

So, we go to the meeting, and it was nice enough—not that anything was really accomplished. We come back, we change back into our beads and peace medals and turtlenecks, and we fly home. We were trying to look the part for this guy.

What it *did* accomplish was that he sent out a young guy, figuring that a young guy in that role, rather than these older censor guys that he had out there, could maybe relate to everybody. But I don't think it worked. I mean, the guy tried to really hang out with the Smothers and everything, but, y'know, his job was still trying to prevent them from doing the things they wanted to do.

WILLIAM TANKERSLEY, former Director of Program Practices at CBS:

They brought more complaints than any program in history, to that point in time. They were highly entertaining, and highly likable. I liked Tommy very much. I never dealt with Dickie, but I met with Tommy maybe three or four times. And they were wholesome-looking and clean cut. Older people accepted them very well.

But, as I told Tommy one day, "You're double-crossing half your audience, y'know. You appeal to younger people with all your drug jokes, and the Vietnam War." I said, "You have the best of both worlds right now, if you just don't exaggerate it and infuriate the older people."

In any event, they still tossed in stuff that got by. They were pretty cunning. But I got along personally with him very well. He's such a nice person. He's a delight. I talked to him like a father, and lectured him . . . and he would shuffle around.

Once he said, "Well, you just don't understand us kids."

I said, "You're thirty-two years old! When do you grow up?" [laughter]

I always felt if I'd been in Hollywood, working with him face to face, we wouldn't have had nearly so many problems. But I wasn't.

PERRY LAFFERTY:

There're always complaints. But, you see, the network didn't want to *get* to where they were complaining. They were just trying to keep the program within certain boundaries that everybody else was in. Well, that's not true either, because every show has a different set of boundaries . . . I mean, you could do stuff on *The Smothers Brothers* that you couldn't do on *Green Acres*.

They were a comedy show, and they were making jokes. Lyndon Johnson's daughters loved the show, but they read in the paper that the Smothers were after him . . . so they called their dad, who was the president. And the president called Mr. Paley, who was not charmed with hearing about this.

ALLAN BLYE:

In the middle of all of the problems that were going on between the network and Tom and Dick and whatnot—we were doing a television show. For those guys like us, who were on the line, our task was to turn out a funny and entertaining show. We sure made every effort to do that.

And it was wonderful: Steve Martin and Bob Einstein were brilliant comedy writers then, and they're brilliant today. They're each different. I made the mistake for a while that year of putting those two guys together. It was when we ran into trouble with time that I just said, "Steve, you have to write *this* piece. Bob, you have to write *that* piece." And it was incredible what was coming out of those guys! And Carl Gottlieb, and Jerry Music . . . and Cecil Tuck did a lot of terrific work on the political stuff, on Pat Paulsen's stuff.

CBS Drops the Bomb

Behind the scenes, the relationship between Tommy Smothers and the network censors grew even more contentious. Whole segments were now being cut from broadcast, like a musical number featuring guest star Harry Belafonte: an inspired juxtaposition of the singer performing the calypso song, "Don't Stop the Carnival," seen against filmed news footage of the wild rioting around the Chicago Democratic Convention in April of 1968, including graphic images of police beating anti-war protestors with clubs. Joan Baez attempted to dedicate a song to her husband, David Harris, who was being imprisoned for three years. CBS censors allowed some—but not all—of her statement, choosing to clumsily chop her explanation, in mid-sentence, that Harris's jail term was for avoiding the draft as a conscientious objector and rejecting "militarism, in general." Dr. Benjamin Spock, the famous baby doctor also known for his anti-war politics, was banned from appearing on the show. Tommy was ordered to cut David Steinberg's last satiric sermonette entirely, and did so . . . fuming about the network's interference.

PERRY LAFFERTY:

It got to be where at least half my time was devoted to it. Oh, it was endless. And then they'd get people on the air with them, like Richard Pryor or Lily Tomlin, who'd only fan the flame.

Tommy would be sitting in my office at 9:00 in the morning, when I'd come to work. And he'd go over to the bar and pour two shots of scotch, and bring it over to me and say, "Let's talk." I was not going to be outdone by him—I drank it. It was a strange feeling at 9:00 in the morning. There was something that the censors didn't want, and he wanted me to intervene. And then, you know how it is . . . it's like talking at a party about religion or politics. It goes on endlessly, and circuitously. And he didn't give a damn about the network's point of view, he only liked *his* point of view.

KEN KRAGEN:

One of the things that would happen was, as the censorship increased, Tom and Dick got more adamant and vocal. But Ken Fritz and I were able to contain that to the dressing room, or our offices. Tom and Dick might be there saying, "Tell CBS to take the show and stick it up their ass! We're not gonna work this way!"

Ken and I would walk out of there and go first usually to [agent] Stan Kamen, or to Perry Lafferty, and

Singers "Mama" Cass Elliot and Harry Belafonte guest star in a 1969 sketch that poked fun at the Smothers Brothers' ratings rival, Bonanza. © *CBS Television Network*

57

we'd say, "Y'know, we've got a bit of a problem here." Which was *far* different than, "Go take this and stick it up your butt." We would act as the buffer to keeping the network feeling that we were all cooperative, but that we had an issue to work out.

But Tommy got rid of me first, and then he got rid of Ken about a month later. And then he just went one on one with the network, with [CBS President] Bob Wood—and there was no buffer. Now you had a little kid throwing a tantrum, and you had the sort of father figure, the guy in charge, going, "I don't need this."

TOMMY SMOTHERS:

Bob Wood came in as the new guy, and said basically, "You know, Tom, you've got to just kinda relax about this thing, and the Vietnam War. We've got to be a little more cautious about what we say."

And it just escalated into the classic disagreement between the hawks and the doves, and the right wing and the left wing, and pretty soon I was yelling at him. He was probably much more rational. I'd raised my voice a little bit about the disaster that was happening over there. That was the predominant emotion of the time, there were strong opinions there.

It was kind of like, he was going to be the cool dude who knows how to deal with these potheads, and I was the guy who wasn't going to be pushed around.

WILLIAM TANKERSLEY:

Many of the affiliates wanted to withdraw. Cancel the show. And we had a meeting, an affiliates thing in Hawaii once, where we decided that we would close-circuit the show to them in advance. Probably on Friday night, I guess. And if they decided they didn't want the show, they didn't have to run it. We wouldn't let them *tamper* with it—they'd just say, "We don't want to run it." Well, Tommy didn't like that a bit.

DAVID STEINBERG:

Then it became an issue of Tommy and Dick and the producers sending the tape to the network so they could see what was on the show. They were holding it back till the last minute. And the network used that, actually, to get them thrown off the air.

WILLIAM TANKERSLEY:

He refused to turn over a tape once, and sent someone—a young woman—to New York with a tape. Put her in a hotel room while the program department and the engineering department had to put together a substitute show. A repeat. Then, just before air, she got the word to go give them the tape.

That kind of game-playing couldn't continue . . . but it did. Later, he did it again.

PERRY LAFFERTY:

Tommy got to where he was grabbing the master tape off the tape machine and absconding with it. Holding it ransom, so to speak. *That* was the straw that broke the camel's back. Business Affairs stepped in with their big feet and said, "We're not going to pay you."

WILLIAM TANKERSLEY:

They called me at 10:00 one night from the West Coast and said, "Tommy's taken the tape again. He's flown off to San Francisco."

So I called the president, Bob Wood, and said, "Bob, this can't go on. I don't think you want to turn the network over to them—and I certainly don't. But we've tried everything with them. And now, this kid's stuff, this is too much."

Bob called the lawyers the next morning. We met all day long. Mike Dann and I were shouting at each other all day. He didn't want to lose the show. It's understandable.

But I said, "We've *got* to lose the show. They're absolutely out of control. And we've renewed the contract against my objections. So now that will only lead to further defiance, and more of this ingenious circumvention of all the rules . . . and it can't go on. The affiliates won't stand for it. The public is writing letters, advertisers are mad, everybody. It can't continue."

And so Bob listened. And by nightfall, we sent 'em a wire saying, "You're finished."

TOMMY SMOTHERS:

I knew I had to dot my *i's* and cross my *t's*, not to invalidate my contract . . . so I was very careful about that. But I didn't know they were playing that kind of hardball. I didn't realize the level of governmental control that was happening, that the corporate control was that powerful. I didn't believe it. I didn't know it. I was very naïve. So when it happened, I was totally shocked.

ALLAN BLYE:

You know what? Had they just delivered the shows on time, they'd have been on the air another three or four years. I can tell you that CBS really wanted that show to stay on the air. And they were willing to sit down and just talk.

59

DAVID STEINBERG:

To tell you the truth, Tommy will admit this: He *was* out of control. He was the funniest and one of the most talented persons I'd ever worked with in the business. Really, for that time, on the Larry David level now. But he was obstinate. And we were in our twenties and thirties, and we just couldn't understand why we couldn't do what we needed to do.

TOMMY SMOTHERS:

The final season was depressing. I lost my sense of humor, became too involved—and I became the advocate of certain points of view.

WILLIAM TANKERSLEY:

We had to do it. We should have done it at renewal time, when I'd asked, because at renewal time, it'd be routine: "We simply aren't renewing your contract," and that would've been no problem. As it was, we had a lawsuit. I told Bob, when I called him, "They'll *sue* us, Bob, because nothing has changed that much since we re-signed them. Why did we re-sign them if they're so bad? But we did. And now, you have no choice. We'll be sued, and we may lose, but I'll tell you: We can't go forward."

He believed me. And that was that. There was *no way* we could go forward . . . it had to be done, no question.

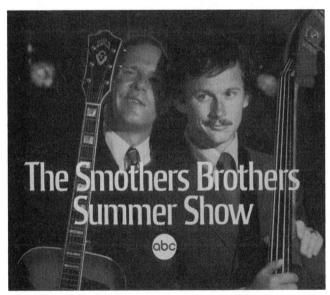

The brothers took their act onto ABC in July of 1970, and then NBC in 1975, but none of their subsequent variety shows ever caught on like the original did. © ABC Television Network

TOMMY SMOTHERS:

I always said that we were kind of at the scene of the accident. We just happened to have a television show at the time when evolution and a lot of stuff was taking place. And we reflected it, which was kind of exciting and fun. It was going to happen anyway, we were just lucky to be there to be part of the scene.

WILLIAM TANKERSLEY:

They had a twentieth anniversary of their firing, and they invited me. The producer called, and Tommy was in the room. I said, "Put Tommy on."

I said, "Tommy, you're now fifty-four years old. Right?"

"Yeah, that's right."

"That's precisely the age I was when you called me an *old man*. How does it feel, Tommy?"

He didn't know what to say! He stammered around . . .

They had intended, I guess, for me to be on stage during the show, and I didn't do that. I arrived for the after-show thing. There were lots of press people there, lining up . . . so the producer told them about the conversation with Tommy, and his being fifty-four, and then they said, "Well, what was the basic problem . . . what didn't you like about them?"

And I said, "Very honestly, I liked them very much. But that had nothing to do with it. Aside from drug jokes, and sexual innuendo, the *main* thing was the Vietnam War. And Tommy was right, in my opinion. Certainly, a terrible war. But we had a policy that shows can't get into politics. They can use politics for jokes, but not jokes used to preach politics. They reversed it, simply. Their humor was written deliberately to get across a point of view, to the point that they'd gotten to be, they thought, headquarters for the whole entertainment industry on the Vietnam War."

TOMMY SMOTHERS:

All the television satire and political things today are on the fringes, on cable or at 11:30 P.M. Nothing is in primetime. We were the last show that had political satire, dealt with public policy, criticizing the United States government in Central America. So that was the end of it. There's a lot of scatological, four letter words, there's more sex, more violence, more word usage being done, but there's been *no* political satire during primetime television.

There's an illusion: Look how much freedom there is . . . but there isn't. They're allowing narcissistic reflections on the crotch, and ego, and cross-dressing. AIDS, homosexuality, all these things that were not discussed before are being discussed. But not a word about politics. That's where people get confused, they think there's more freedom, but it's been less and less and less.

Pat Paulsen said in one of his editorials, "Freedom of speech is a lie. You can get naked, go into a closet, shut the door, say anything you want. No one'll hear you, but *freedom of speech*? It's called *freedom of hearing*. That's what we need in the First Amendment, freedom to hear divergent views. We don't get to hear them."

We get to hear the one or two screeching different voices, and that's it. So, all this great freedom of expression that everyone talks about, it's an illusion.

Sockin' It to Us from Beautiful Downtown Burbank

3

Rowan & Martin's Laugh-In socked it to us, all right. It was nothing short of a cultural phenomenon. The hour-long NBC comedy show was a trailblazer: the first TV series to embrace contemporary editing techniques and lightning-quick pacing—the very same look that would come to define MTV over a decade later. Along the way, it broke taboos and set trends that others would emulate and imitate to this day. Hosted by the popular comedy team of wry, dapper straight man Dan Rowan and his lecherous goofball sidekick, Dick Martin, *Laugh-In* created TV stars out of its previously unknown cast members, *superstars* out of several others—most notably Lily Tomlin and Goldie Hawn—and was literally the number-one show in America for its first two full seasons on the air. Not bad for a modest winter replacement show—a common theme in this book—that few at NBC expected to succeed.

Long before *Saturday Night Live* or *Seinfeld* would do it, *Laugh-In* had millions of viewers parroting its most memorable catch phrases and comedy bits the next day at water coolers all across the country: Judy Carne's "Sock it to me, sock it to me, sock it to me," followed by a torrential splash of water or a boxing glove to the noggin . . . Dewey "Pigmeat" Markham in black robes and powdered wig, announcing, "Here come da judge! Here come da judge!" . . . Arte Johnson's German soldier popping out from behind a bush to slyly observe, "Verrrry interesting" . . . Dick Martin's "You bet your sweet bippy" . . . Lily Tomlin's nasal Ernestine the Phone Operator: "One ringy dingy . . . two ringy dingies," and snorting, "A gracious good afternoon. Have I reached the party to whom I am speaking?"

Strongly influenced by what *The Smothers Brothers Comedy Hour* was doing, it also set out to lampoon sacred cows of the day and poke fun at politics, social mores, and current events, but in an entirely different way than its rival on CBS was going about it. Whereas the Smothers' antics were set within the trappings of a traditional variety show, *Rowan & Martin's Laugh-In* was something else altogether: a dizzying hour-long barrage of loony sight gags, black-out sketches, snappy one-liners, short comedy bits, insane musical production numbers, and swift cameos by famous celebs of the day (Sammy Davis Jr.: "Y'know, my ancestors picked so much cotton that I still hate to open an aspirin bottle!") and politicians (Richard Nixon dolefully intoning: "Sock it to me?"). The show's frenetic insanity and general mayhem was paced more like a madcap Warner Bros. cartoon than a live-action TV show.

Subtle it wasn't. *Laugh-In* was wall-to-wall shtick, from the instant onscreen announcer Gary Owens deadpanned his absurd intros from "beautiful downtown Burbank" with a palm cupped over one ear, right on through the final seconds of the show as the one-liners continued while the end credits rolled up the screen—and even after. The show's naughty creators were always testing, pushing, poking, and prodding further against the boundaries of what NBC's Standards and Practices editors would allow on TV.

One of *Laugh-In's* weekly bits invited us to follow Dan and Dick through some doors into a wild, "mod" cocktail party, where music would blare as regulars and guests gyrated till everything suddenly froze—and the camera zoomed in on someone for a hip one-liner (Sonny Bono: "I only switched to bananas 'cause I couldn't keep my cantaloupe lit"), political barbs (Roddy Maude-Roxby: "Why don't you Americans recognize the Red Chinese?" Dan Rowan: "Because to us, all Chinese look alike"), or bawdy sexual banter, with Dick Martin often hitting on a pretty young thing (Dick: "How about coming up to my place?" Girl: "Are you going to try anything fresh?" Dick: "Nope, same old stuff") before the dancing and music suddenly kicked in again.

While it's an established fact that the landmark series began as a late-summer TV special called *Rowan & Martin's Laugh-In*, some of the subsequent details are a bit fuzzier. Following in the tradition of the old Russian proverb, "Success has many fathers, while failure is an orphan," there are a few different versions of *Laugh-In's* origins, depending upon whom you talk to . . . though the stories do run parallel and eventually dovetail.

Now Here's My—Uh, *Our* Plan . . .

DICK MARTIN, co-star and producer:

Dan and I did the *Dean Martin Summer Show* for [producer] Greg Garrison. We did twelve shows in six weeks, in 1966, when Dean took a twelve-week hiatus. In those days, the performer owned that time slot, so they had summer shows—and that one went through the roof. NBC came to us and said, "Boy, you guys are great. We'd like you to do a show for us."

We said, "Well, we have a show that's just a tad different, and we'd like to do that."

And they said, "We'll try it. We'll do an hour special, with an option for a series. Now go find yourself a producer."

So, we went for Bob Banner, 'cause he was Dinah Shore's person. But he wanted to do a straight variety show, and he was not too thrilled with having Sammy Davis on and not letting him sing. He didn't understand that. So, we went to Greg Garrison, and Greg was tied up. Then we said, "Wait, why don't we get an in-house producer from NBC?" They had George Schlatter . . . so we had a talk with George, and we went ahead and did that.

GEORGE SCHLATTER, executive producer:

I was producing the Grammy Awards. And in the early days, nobody knew what it was . . . it wasn't an award, it was called "The Best on Record." We'd almost give an award to anybody who'd show up, 'cause they didn't have the money to make the awards until after they got the money from the television show! So, for the first six years of the Grammy Awards, every award we gave on the air had Henry Mancini's name on it, y'know?

They wanted me to do it again, and I didn't want to do it anymore . . . so I said I would do it once more if they would let me try a show I wanted to do. I said there's a market out there for an all-comedy show—no music, nothing, just all comedy. And I said the attention span is getting shorter . . . so we'd do a show about just jokes.

They said, "What do you mean about just jokes?"

I said, "Well, it's all different jokes told in different ways . . . it's like this." And I gave 'em a cartoon of two prisoners chained to the wall about two feet off the ground, and they're both hanging. And the one guy says to the other one, "Now here's my plan . . ."

DICK MARTIN:

We had been saving one-, two-, and three-frame cartoons out of *New Yorker*, *Punch*, *Playboy*, whatever was around. *Saturday Evening Post* had 'em. And they were great . . . they were the Peter Arnos, and all the great cartoonists. And I said, "You notice that they can be funny in one frame?" We had just done a sketch on *The Jerry Lewis Show* that took seventeen minutes and went into the shitter. All seventeen minutes. And that's all ego—it's bullshit. So we said no, no, if it's funny, let's get to it, and get out of it.

What we wanted, and fortunately George wanted this, too, was no cohesion. In other words, *fast*. I'll take an example, out of the *New Yorker*: two prisoners in tattered clothes, hanging from a wall. That set-up. And the original line was, "Now here's my plan . . ." One of the great cartoons of all time.

GEORGE SCHLATTER:

I said, "Alright, now you just do that—but you do a couple hundred of 'em."

So, they said, "Well, okay." They agreed to do it and let me do it my way.

From then on, it became a problem, because they wanted to have guest stars. They wanted to have Joey Heatherton do two numbers, they wanted to have Nipsey Russell—I said, "That's not the show, Sparky!"

I said to Herb Schlosser, "You promised me I could do a show my way, and they're buggin' me." So, he said to let me alone. Ed Friendly worked at NBC, in charge of specials. He was one of the ones that said, "Go ahead and do this."

Then Ed went to Timex, and they had what they called Preview Specials. Timex would pay half of the production cost, but NBC could then keep it as a pilot. So, Timex said they would buy it if we got some hosts . . . and of the people they would okay, Rowan and Martin were two guys that I had worked with before. They were kinda crazy and loony, and they were wonderful, y'know? They did the funniest act you ever saw in your life; they were hysterical. The drunk heckler, and all of that. And I'd done stuff with them, and knew them both socially and professionally, so I said they'd be fine.

Originally, the show was going to have no host . . . but it worked out well, because they had a great time.

DICK MARTIN:

George Schlatter wanted Digby Wolfe for head writer. We said, "No, no, no, no. No way." We knew him. We once hired him for a hundred dollars a week to write political humor for us, for nightclubs, but we couldn't use any of it. 'Cause it wasn't funny. So, Digby Wolfe was out right away. He got *credit* . . .

GEORGE SCHLATTER:

Digby Wolfe, who had done David Frost's show, *That Was the Week That Was*, was a famous, famous performer in Australia who had taken on the government . . . and I think they asked him to leave in the middle of the night. He was a real anarchist. And brilliant. A brilliant fuck, man. He and I got together and started working on this show that I'd sold to NBC.

DICK MARTIN:

We brought Paul Keyes from the *Dean Martin Show*, he was the head there. And so we insisted that he be the head writer . . . and then we brought in another element, Ian Bernard. Matter of fact, when we got going, George Schlatter wanted Nelson Riddle.

I said, "I love Nelson Riddle, he's an adorable guy, I know him personally—but he's not right for this. We want someone kooky." Ian Bernard is a writer . . . when we met him, he was a piano player for Vic Damone—but he was funny. So he did all the music.

GEORGE SCHLATTER:

Dan and Dick liked Paul Keyes—and Paul Keyes balanced this politically, 'cause he really leaned pretty heavy to starboard, y'know? He had an office in the White House, for chrissakes! So that gave us the political balance that we needed to survive, because everything Paul wrote leaned a little that way. And of course Digby was an anarchist.

Finding the Cuckoos to Fill the Nest

DICK MARTIN:

Then we had to put the cast together . . . and we just looked around. We found Arte Johnson, and we found Ruth Buzzi from the Billy Barnes Revue . . . Alan Sues was not there at the beginning . . . Henry Gibson . . . Larry Hovis, who was one of our writers, and he also did characters on the show . . . and Judy Carne was in at the beginning. Between the writers and George, you know, we all pitched in.

GEORGE SCHLATTER:

Nobody ever auditioned for the show. We just collected these people who I'd seen. I hadn't worked with any of them except Alan Sues, who'd had an act with Paul Mazursky . . . But the rest of them, Judy Carne had been married to Burt Reynolds . . . and Arte Johnson was very close to a woman by the name of Teme Brenner, who was a dear friend. And she would bring Arte over to the house. I can remember one Easter morning when he was going around the front yard, y'know, like a bunny, in his German helmet. He was the Easter Nazi. And he would do voices for me. So he was hired.

Gary Owens, I was having lunch with once we got started . . . and in the men's room, he said, "My, the acoustics are good in here!"

GARY OWENS, performer:

We went into the men's room to wash up. And George said, "Oh, my God! That's what you've gotta do! You've gotta do that on the show!"

I said, "What, wash my hands?"

"No, you've gotta be the old 1940s announcer guy!"

It was one of those acoustic tile bathrooms, so whatever you would say, it really made your voice almost echo. I put my hand over my ear, doing an impression of the old-time radio announcers who would always announce that way on stage—mainly because they were too vain to put headphones on. It might spoil their hairdo, or their toupee.

GEORGE SCHLATTER:

I said, "Jesus, Gary, that's what I need—I need somebody to say: 'At that very moment, the masked man turned to his Indian companion and said . . . ' " So, Gary was hired in the toilet at the Smokehouse Restaurant in Burbank.

Henry Gibson I'd seen on a talk show. He came into the office, did a poem and a back flip, and I said, "Well, that'll be good. We'll use that." Jo Anne Worley was on the phone—I think I'd seen her in the *Mad Show* or something— anyhow, she was hysterical, just on the phone. Ruth Buzzi sent me a picture of herself as Gladys in the trash bin, a discarded human being. And I said, "That'll be good." So, we collected this group of people.

ARTE JOHNSON, performer:

The next thing I knew, I was doing the show. It was quick, irreverent; it did funny things. I had no idea of what its value would ultimately be . . . and I never thought of it in terms of a series. I thought it was a funny one-shot. And I brought my characters in there . . . I was doing those crazy characters all over the place. I even designed their clothes, I knew *exactly* who they were.

When we finished the show, there were no contracts drawn for any kind of longevity. And I had no aspirations. It was a fun thing, I did it, it was over, it was cute to watch, and it was done. When they went to series, I was stunned! I thought, "Wow . . . how the hell is he going to do it?"

Early Laugh-In *cast: Dan Rowan and Dick Martin, seated. Second row (l-r): Judy Carne, Henry Gibson, Ruth Buzzi, Jo Anne Worley. Third row (l-r): Dave Madden, Chelsea Brown, Goldie Hawn, Arte Johnson, Alan Sues. Perched on top: Dick Whittington. (Missing from the shot is series stalwart Gary Owens, who was busy feeding Morgul the Friendly Drelb.)* © *NBC Television Network*

And he *did* it. George Schlatter pulled together an incredibly talented group of people, all of whom had a track record. Everybody on that show was not a discovery; they were people who had worked before. They had worked on series, they had worked in movies, they worked on the stage . . . so it was not like bringing together a bunch of kids and saying, "Now here's what you have to do." These were all schooled performers who knew techniques. It was an exciting experience in that respect. Everybody on that show was a professional.

DICK MARTIN:

The special did very poorly in the ratings . . . but it only cost $165,000. Imagine puttin' on a show like that today for that? But critically, the reviewers loved it—and [media critic] Marshall McCluhan wrote very fondly of the show. He was pretty hard on television, if you recall. He said that finally people are using the medium for what it's for . . . an electronically driven show.

So, NBC said, "Okay, we'll try thirteen shows" . . . but they put us opposite *Here's Lucy* and *Gunsmoke*. What the hell. We were so happy to just have a job.

GEORGE SCHLATTER:

They had a show that was supposed to go on Monday night at 8:00—and Lucille Ball was killing 'em. The CBS lineup Monday night with Lucille Ball and *Gunsmoke* just killed NBC. They couldn't do anything with anybody. So they said, "Look, we've got this thing. Why don't we throw it in there until we get a show ready, and it would cost no money . . . what're we gonna lose? This isn't gonna work anyhow."

So, they put us in there, and nobody paid any attention until like about the fourth week.

DICK MARTIN:

It was tough to sell, because the network kept saying, "That's very funny, but what in the hell are you going to do *next* week?"

GEORGE SCHLATTER:

The reviews came out, but all of the reviews weren't that positive. Because this was a show they didn't understand. The network didn't like it. The network said, "This isn't a television show . . . it doesn't make sense! What are you doing?"

I said, "You just watched the show and laughed . . . why don't you just leave it alone?"

So, we went on the air with the promise that we would slow it down. Which we didn't do.

DICK MARTIN:

We went along, limping, limping, limping . . . but it kept gaining. And come the eighth show, where the guest stars were Sammy Davis and Joey Bishop, it was the number-one show in the country. It went right through the roof, with like a forty or forty-five share . . . it was wonderful! A lot of our mail was from parents saying, "It's the first show we can watch with our kids." And the *kids* loved it. They loved the psychedelic look—it was exciting, because it was colorful. And we had some goddamn good writers.

GEORGE SCHLATTER:

We had a writer by the name of Allan Manings who made Digby look conservative. And we had an old guy by the name of Hugh Wedlock who had written for Jolson in burlesque. He was great, and he remembered every joke that had ever been done—y'know, "I remember a thing we did once with Ben Blue!"

Digby had worked with Chris Bearde in Australia, and he said, "There's a mad Australian who we've gotta bring in." So, Chris came in. We actually put Chris together with Arte Johnson's brother, Coslough, and they wrote together.

CHRIS BEARDE, writer:

I had come from Australia to Canada. I had a show called *Nightcap*, a late-night satire show. It was kind of like the precursor to *Saturday Night Live*. We were the Peck's Bad Boys of Canada. In those days, there *weren't* any bad boys in Canada. So, I became this cause célèbre of the whole country.

One night I'm looking at the television, and I'm seeing this show come on called *Laugh-In* . . . and a lot of the jokes in it were *my jokes!* What had happened was, this guy called Digby Wolfe—who was a comedy consultant on *Laugh-In*—had taken my material and given it to George Schlatter. Digby Wolfe was the host of the first big Australian variety show co-production with America, called *Review '61*. I wrote all his material with a guy called Alan Kitson. I traveled the country with him . . . gave him lines before he went on stage. Y'know, Bob Hope never wrote a line in his life—well, you can think of Digby Wolfe as being Bob Hope of Australia. He may have had a couple of ideas that he said to George, but I can honestly say I never saw him sit down and write anything on a piece of paper. He was never billed as a writer on *Laugh-In*, he was billed as a "comedy consultant." I'm not saying that Digby isn't talented, because the guy must have had talent to get himself in that position.

The only thing I know is that a lot—I mean, *a lot*—of my material was on the special. And that came directly from my pen, through Digby, to George. Well, as soon as Digby heard the name *Chris Bearde*, he must have gone, "Holy shit! He's alive and he can just put me in the crapper here!"

71

But I didn't. I was very smart to say, "Oh, Digby, I'm glad they used *our* material," so I could get the gig. Because my agent said, "Don't come in on a negative, come in on a positive." And that's how I got to do the show—there wasn't any animosity or any negativity. I just didn't let that happen. And to this day I don't have any negatives, 'cause I'm very thankful to Digby for taking the material and giving it to George. Otherwise, I wouldn't have done *Laugh-In*!

COSLOUGH JOHNSON, writer:
George called me in and said, "Meet Chris Bearde. You'll be writing together." That's how George worked! And because we're both a little off the wall, we got along great. Working with Chris was an exercise. He was marvelous. I mean, he'd have ideas off the wall, and he would scream and shout and holler. He was just a definite character. He's a wild man—but a marvelous talent.

CHRIS BEARDE:
We were the sight gag guys. We came up with all that shit like little people falling over. All the falling over and violence was us. You know, you'd say, "What are we gonna do today?" Okay, a man on a pogo stick. He comes along on a pogo stick; he falls down a manhole. He comes along on a pogo stick; he goes up and doesn't come down. He comes along on a pogo stick and three other people on pogo sticks bump into him and they all fall over. We riffed. It was comedy riffing, that's exactly what it was.

What else did we do . . . oh, Vikings: So three Vikings are in a boat, one of 'em takes one of his horns off, drinks out of it, and puts the horn back. Three Vikings in a boat, they land, and one of 'em falls down a hole.

COSLOUGH JOHNSON:
We did a lot of the visual stuff. And also, the far-off kind of stuff . . . y'know, cheese-throwing contests, that kind of thing. And we did most of Arte's stuff, because I knew all of the characters he had. So a lot of Arte's stuff came out of our office. It's hard to pinpoint, because everybody did a little bit of everything.

CHRIS BEARDE:
David Panich, Marc London, and Allan Manings used to write a lot of the opening monologues for Dan and Dick. Coslough and I weren't even asked to write the monologues. I mean, I could've written 'em with my eyes closed . . . but I found a niche for Coslough and I, sight gags. And it was so easy to do that, and there were so many other writers that were good . . . We never even knew, by the way, what we were gonna see or what

we weren't gonna see. 'Cause we'd just submit the material and go home. We'd have to go home and look at the show to see, "Oh, *that's* my joke!" "*There's* my joke!" "Oh, *that's* my joke!"

DICK MARTIN:

They would write us a monologue . . . but then we would fuck with it, y'know? They used to stand just out of range, Paul Keyes and George Schlatter and Carolyn Raskin, a couple of people, when Dan and I were doing our alleged monologue. And they'd bet how many times they'd hear a word that was in the script, 'cause we kinda just winged it. We had a ball.

Debonair Dan Rowan and goofball sidekick Dick Martin, seen here standing against a "mod," late-1960s-style flat from their smash hit show, Laugh-In. © *NBC Television Network*

CHRIS BEARDE:

We were relegated to a motel. We did not have writers' rooms; we had motel rooms. And it was great—I mean, we didn't want to be in an office. We'd much rather be where we were, in a motel room! It was walking distance from George's office . . . and we went there in the morning. There were thirteen of us in that first year, so it was very easy for us to, say, finish our work by 11:00, take a swim, and just sit around havin' a good time for the rest of the day. 'Cause there were thirteen writers and only an *hour* of television. What the hell is going on, y'know?

People were smoking dope. It was the 1960s, for God's sake. I was the straightest guy there at that time! People made mobiles for their rooms, and went for a sleep in the afternoon . . . I tell you, it was the most fun idea. And then we weren't even allowed to go over to the studio to see the show unless we got a special pass or anything. We were just lackeys, y'know?

COSLOUGH JOHNSON:

Sometimes at night you'd go over there . . . because it was hysterical on the set. But the writers would hide in the back. Because if George saw them, he'd start hollering, "Give me some more lines!" So, a lot of us went, but we made sure we weren't in the forefront.

I'll always remember the first meeting we had with George. George is a big guy, physically. And as I remember, he had a red sweatsuit on, and he looked like a giant whale that just came in. He sat with all the writers, and he starts doing this song and dance of what the show is about.

After that, we all went back to the motel, and went into this one room . . . and there was this long beat of silence. Then, finally, one of the writers said, "What the hell is this show about!?" And another guy said, "I don't know what it's about, but I guess we'd better go write our ten pounds of material."

CHRIS BEARDE:

There were two camps on *Laugh-In*: There was the Paul Keyes camp, which was the sort of Republican camp. And we can't talk about left wing and right wing in comparison to today, where it's Nazis against liberals who are like Communists. Paul Keyes was Nixon's speechwriter—and Paul Keyes got on right great with me, because a satirist should be somebody who can hit all angles and hit on everybody. That's what my philosophy was. Dan Rowan was a Republican but a very *liberal* Republican. In those days, that did exist. And I got on really good with both sides. So, somehow or other, I was this middle-ground guy . . .

One side used to come to me and say, "You know what they're doing? I'll tell you what they're doing, Chris."

And the other side would say, "Well, you know what they're doing?" And blah blah blah.

So, I was kind of valuable to the show in that regard, because I was sort of this Australian/Canadian nebulous political person, and I really kept my politics pretty well clear of everybody. I saw if I took a side, I couldn't have that middle ground—which gave me a lot of my material going on the show.

DICK MARTIN:

Paul Keyes was very insistent that an equal number of left-leaning jokes got in the scripts. We had Allan Manings and a couple of guys on the staff who were really liberal. So, their stuff got in, and Paul supervised it—he saw to it that it *did* get in. Very fair. And nobody would have ever been able to get Nixon to come on the show and say "Sock it to me" other than Paul.

Be Our Guest

GEORGE SCHLATTER:

Richard Nixon was running for president. He was out here for a press conference, and Paul Keyes said, "Why don't you come by and just say 'Sock it to me'?"

He said, "What's that mean?"

Paul said, "Well, it's a show that has a lot of kids watching it, and it would show you in a good light with young America."

So, we went over to CBS, and went into the studio where he was going to tape a commercial. They stood him in front of a flat, and we got him to say, "Sock it to me." It took six takes to get him to say it.

"Sockittome!"

"No, no. Just look into the camera and say, 'Sock it to me.' Be surprised."

"Oh, I've got it. I'm new at this: Sockittome."

"No, no, no . . ."

Anyhow, we did six takes, took the tape, and got outta there like a porch climber. We put it on the air—and the network said, "You can't air that because of the equal-time law."

And we said, "No, it has nothing to do with politics. We will offer any politician three seconds for equal time."

They said, "What do you mean?"

"'Sock it to me' took three seconds. We will offer equal time to every political candidate to say, 'Sock it to me.' Or to take three seconds and say whatever they want."

They said, "Who's gonna do that?"

I said, "Riiiiiight!!"

So, they passed a law: the Richard Nixon Law. It was for equal time, where you could make a non-political statement on a non-political show for under five seconds, and not kick in the equal time. Today it still may be on the books. But now, presidential candidates are all over the place.

DICK MARTIN:

Lena Horne once kicked me in the shin and said, "You son of a bitch, you elected that bastard!" But we also offered the same thing to [Nixon's Democratic opponent] Hubert Humphrey a week later. He was in the building to make thirty-second and sixty-second spots at NBC, and we went down there and cornered him. He had an entourage.

And we said, "You'll come on the show and say whatever you wanna say" . . . but his advisor said no. He said to Humphrey—and I heard him say this: "They'll end up throwing water on you." Like we're gonna throw water on a fuckin' presidential candidate! Absurd. [laughing] That dumb son of a bitch.

GEORGE SCHLATTER:

We chased him! We had four tapings set up for Hubert Humphrey. We wanted him to repeat Richard Nixon's saying "Sock it to me." And Humphrey said not doing it cost him the election. People say that we were responsible for electing Richard Nixon—it was so close—and by showing him in that milieu, with that audience, it may have elected him. I've had to live with that for fuckin' thirty-eight years.

DICK MARTIN:

A lot of the cameos were done just by luck. Douglas Fairbanks Jr. was doing some dramatic thing down in Studio 3 at NBC, and we talked him into coming on and doing cameos. What a coup to get someone like that, because he just didn't fit into that mold. And he had no idea what the show was, 'cause it had never been on the air yet.

He said, "Why the devil would I say *that?*"

And we just kept talking him into it. George was very good at that, y'know, saying, "Oh, c'mon, it'll be a lot of fun." He got him to say all these lines, and then they would just fit 'em in. And then he liked it—so he came back as a regular guest star once. He was adorable.

We got Jack Lemmon just walking down the street. I knew him from the golf course. He came on and did I don't know *how many* cameos. That's how you'd find 'em—it had to be half-social. Then it became very cool. And it was easy. I remember one time I got a call from Greg Garrison, when we were playing Pittsburgh. And Greg said, "I've got a guy who wants to be on your show. He's on our show this week."

I said to him, "Great, who is it?"

"Orson Welles."

I said, "*What?!*"

He said, "Here's a number. He's at the Beverly Hills Hotel, call him. But he won't talk to any producers, and he wants cash."

That's when Orson was having all that trouble with the government. So I said, "Well, sure, absolutely," and called the number . . . and this fucking thunderous voice answers. Oh my God, I was talking to Orson Welles! He came on, did the Halloween show, got his fifteen thousand or whatever it was—in cash—and jumped on the next plane to Europe. Then he'd come back and do a Dean Martin roast, and then he'd fly out that day. He was very fleet of foot.

COSLOUGH JOHNSON:

George would have some of these superstars coming on the stage—and George would just look at Paul—Paul was very facile at coming up with lines at the last instant—and he'd suddenly say, "Okay, say *bippy*." These superstars would look at him like, what the hell's he talking about?! And then if you get four superstars saying *bippy*, you put it together, and suddenly you've got twenty seconds of *bippies*, which is hysterical.

DICK MARTIN:

Bippy came from a drummer named Buddy Rich, and a guy named . . . oh, a photographer, nice guy. And they used to go out looking for broads. Now I did this with Buddy up in Reno and in Vegas, when he was playing with [bandleader] Harry James . . . and he'd say, "Oooh, a bippy bird!"

And I said, "What?"

"Look at the bippy!"

He called girls *bippies*. So, when I started using it, everyone thought *I* had done it. But it's like "Sock it to me." "Sock it to me" is a jazz expression that was around for years. And we just started using it, but we didn't invent it. We popularized it. But we did invent, for this genre, "beautiful downtown Burbank."

GARY OWENS:

That was mine. I had been doing radio for eight years before I went on *Laugh-In*, and each morning I would do an alliterative weather forecast. Y'know, in L.A. the weather is pretty much always the same, anyway, it didn't matter. So, to spice up the weather, I would have *Clinton S. Feemish* come in and tap dance to the weather forecast, and I would have him do: "Here's the weather for magnificent Monrovia . . . romantic Reseda . . . and beautiful downtown Burbank."

It probably is one of the best-known cities in the world now. The day after we started *Laugh-In*, all of the operators at NBC would then answer, "Good morning, NBC, beautiful downtown Burbank!" Every operator was asked to do that.

Hard to Say No to a Five-Hundred-Pound Gorilla

Like a cage full of mischievous monkeys led by the biggest and baddest one of all, George Schlatter, the zany writers, producers, and cast of *Rowan & Martin's Laugh-In* kept the show's three Standards and Practices editors hopping on a steady basis. And with so much material to comb through every week—an average *Laugh-In* script ran hundreds of pages long—it was no easy task. By their own admission, it became a sort of cerebral "hide-and-seek" game they enjoyed playing . . . at times just to see how much they could slip onto the air.

GARY OWENS:

Herminio Traviesas, Bill Clotworthy, and Sandy Cummings were our censors on *Laugh-In*. And they always were very, very careful that something double-entendre was not taking place. See, we purposely would not break up—even though it was easy to do, because it was always funny. It was hard. It was harder than stifling a hiccup, really.

The censors weren't clueless. They were all very bright, well-read men. I don't think you could get that job unless you were well read. Bill Clotworthy and Herminio Traviesas then went on to *Saturday Night Live* after *Laugh-In* ended. Of course, there's a lot of difference between the time periods—they were on after primetime, so they could get away with more things, obviously.

CHRIS BEARDE:

George was the driving force behind it. His persona is huge, his ability to sell in those days was huge. His ability to get things on the air without them being too changed around was an enormous plus to the show, because he did not allow himself to be bullied by people . . . you know, "Put that in your Funk & Wagnall's" was a fuck joke. I mean, we got away with stuff because of George. That was not because of Rowan and Martin, and it was not because of Ed Friendly, and it was not because of anybody else but George and his ability to schmooze people into allowing him to put stuff on that was absolutely out there. And it took years for these people to discover what he was doing, 'cause they were so totally dumb! He was very smart to be able to outwit all the censorship that was trying to go on around it.

GEORGE SCHLATTER:

See, *Laugh-In* happened during the 1960s. There was great political unrest—like it is now. It was a dumb war, a stupid war that we were involved in that we were never going to win—like now. Politicians had been lying to us—mm hmm, like now. And it was a decade of change . . . you had the Beatles, and the pill, and burning brassieres, and miniskirts, and artificial stimulants. Herb had just come into its own.

So, into that environment, with political unrest and the assassinations that had happened, we were a nation that was angry and confused and frightened—and into that, we brought a show that did jokes about *all* of that. Also, the network was innocent at that point.

GARY OWENS:

There's one that we didn't smile at, purposely, 'cause we knew it wouldn't get on: Judy Carne comes on wearing a medieval wig. And she's dressed as a medieval lady. She said, "Hello, hello, hello. You know, I've been out here for thirty seconds, and no one has said, 'Sock it to me' yet today." At that point, a boxing glove hits her in the face, and knocks this huge wig—oh, about two-and-a-half-feet tall—off her head. And she's got a bald wig on. She's completely bald.

And she looks into the camera and says, "Y'know, I've never been balled on camera before!" Which, of course, is quite a bit of innuendo. But nobody laughed, so it passed through the censors.

GEORGE SCHLATTER:

We did three great fuck jokes in a row!

DICK MARTIN:

Up until our show, you had to submit your script to Standards and Practices. And they would go through the script with a blue pencil. If they found anything untoward, they would circle it. Well, they couldn't do that with us . . . 'cause the script was 300 pages long! We had three pot jokes in the first show, and they didn't catch any of 'em. We finally had the first *live-in* censor. They just sent Sandy Cummings down there—and he sat in on every rehearsal and every show.

He would say, "What does this mean? What is this: *At the United Nations today, every nation has agreed on every proposal for the first time in history . . . and they're still trying to find out who put the grass in the air conditioner.*"

And that got on the air! But he said, "What's funny about that?"

George was great at covering this, too. He'd say, "Can't you get the picture of a guy mowing a lawn and throwing grass in the air conditioner?"

I remember one of Jo Anne Worley's lines, at one of the cocktail parties, was, "Boris is so dumb, he thinks a little pot is Tupperware for midgets." Now they say, "Wait a minute. That's offensive to the little people." We had Billy Barty come over and say, "That's not offensive, I think it's funny." So, we didn't argue with 'em. We would just try to teach 'em the errors of their ways. They just didn't know . . . and nobody'd ever tried that before—so we thought we could do it and get away with it.

GEORGE SCHLATTER:

Smothers Brothers were great, cause we could hide behind them. We would say, "You can't say that—but you could if you were on *The Smothers Brothers* show." So, we directed a lot of attention to the Smothers Brothers and hid behind them. And Tommy would keep saying, "Come on, man, be cool."

CHRIS BEARDE:

I don't think it affected us one way or the other. We were a totally different show. As a matter of fact, I think it *helped* us more. Because more people—the public, anyway—came and said, "Well, *Laugh-In* is general, it's funnier, it's lighter, it's people dancing and singing, it's like a vaudeville show. And the *Smothers Brothers* have these two guys, like two avatars from the left, screaming blue murder at us."

George used to take on NBC, but he didn't take 'em on head-on like that. He'd say, "Nah, no, no, no, no. We'll do that differently." He subtly moved that show into the center and kept it there. And it had amazing left-wing stuff in it, but it also had John Wayne on it. It was a balanced show.

GEORGE SCHLATTER:

The difference was, we were just having fun. We were on both sides of all issues, but we did not have a political agenda—there was no *intent* with what we did. And we would do a hard political joke about the war . . . we'd say, "Alright, everybody, let's all get behind President Johnson. And push!" Now if you put that next to a trap door, and somebody gettin' hit with water, you weren't aware that there was a message in there.

That was the technique. Smoke and mirrors, razzle-dazzle, tap dancing.

ARTE JOHNSON:

We would read something in the rehearsal hall. And we'd go, "Oh, come on, George. You know you can't do that!"

And George would say, "I know I can't do that . . . but I want *them* to tell me I can't do that! In the meantime, I'm going to sneak this one through." He played it. He played those censors like a harp! He got away with stuff . . . because there *was* stuff. It was double entendre—but at the same time, it was with single intent. But he played them like a maestro.

GEORGE SCHLATTER:
At that point, to see me thirty-seven years ago with a fifty share, I pretty much was a five-hundred-pound gorilla. I mean, a *two-thousand-pound* gorilla, you know? It was real tough to tell me "No." Not only that, but I was arrogant and cocky anyway. Going *in* I was cocky! And see, we were exhaustive—we put six censors in the home. We would exhaust them, because they would always just stay there, and we would tape till 2:00 in the morning, and at dinner break, they'd just head for the bar. It was too fast a track for them . . . but we were having fun.

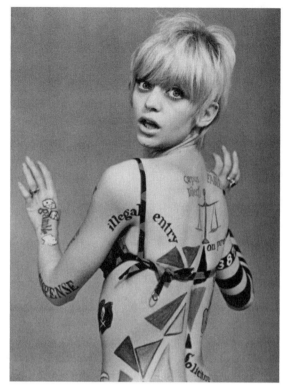

Goldie Hawn, one of the show's first breakout stars, made a lovely human canvas—displaying the handiwork of several lucky decalcomania painters that Laugh-In *employed regularly.* © *NBC Television Network*

Feeding the Monster

Some of the show's recurring comedy bits, like broadcasting the News of the Future, would prove eerily prescient. On just the fourth episode of the series in 1968, resident dizzy blonde Goldie Hawn introduces Dan Rowan's segment, The News Twenty Years from Now: "Item: Washington, D.C., 1988," Rowan intones, deadpan, after a drag on a cigarette. "President Ronald Reagan today denied once again that he is a candidate for office of governor of California!" The absurd line generates huge laughs . . . and, of course, Reagan would actually be president of the United States in 1988.

Laugh-In's producers quickly found that repetition breeds success, revisiting many of the same setups over and over, but with slight variations on a theme: lithe Goldie Hawn undulating in nothing but a bikini, the camera zooming in on clever graffiti bodypainted all over her torso . . . mild-mannered Henry Gibson appearing with an oversized daisy in his hand to recite an absurd poem . . . Arte Johnson's dirty old man Tyrone sidling up to Ruth Buzzi's frumpy spinster Gladys on a park bench, muttering filthy innuendos to provoke an outraged wallop over the head from her handbag or umbrella . . . a grown man in a yellow raincoat pedaling a few feet on a child's tricycle before toppling over . . . and many other recurring bits that came at us fast and furiously. The writers and crew strove to keep up the pace at all costs.

GEORGE SCHLATTER:

They used to say, "Gotta go feed the monster." Feed the Monster. The thing is, it was *dangerous*. It was television without a net. It was what doesn't exist today, because while they were reading the script, we were taping it—there was just no time to fix everything. It was free fall television . . . and it was like a gigantic playpen with acres and acres of prop boxes, and glasses and guns and masks and shit, y'know?

ARTE JOHNSON:

Each show took a long time. It took two days of shooting. And the first day of shooting was really the hardest and the longest day, because of the fact that it had the music at the end of the day . . . and by that time, we were so knocked out. You know, we had to do the music dubbing things, and I hated that; it was one of my most hateful moments, 'cause I just hated lip-synching.

To this day, George always laughs and says one of his favorite things was watching me lip-synch, 'cause I would just go, "Blah blah blah blah blah." I never mouthed a word, I hated it. And I had another propensity, during those production numbers . . . wherever they had me doing dancing things, I would manage to *die* in the middle of them. I would fall to the floor in a faint. Bobby Darin once turned to me and said, "You're the only performer I know that dies in every song he does, and people have to walk over your body."

Comedian Arte Johnson's most enduring character: muttering, dirty old geezer Tyrone, who provoked many handbag whacks to the head by affronted spinster Gladys Ormphby. © NBC Television Network

I got more attention that way. And I didn't have to learn the damn words or the steps. It was a trick. People would say, "There he goes! There it is!" And they'd be walking around my body.

GEORGE SCHLATTER:

Arte never wanted to be in musical numbers. He hated 'em. Any time you'd put him in a musical number he would always fall down, and you'd have to drag him around during the number. Coslough looked like Arte, so when Arte got pissed off and didn't come in, or when Arte didn't wanna do something, we'd put Coslough in his costume.

COSLOUGH JOHNSON:

Which is like saying, "I don't wanna dance. I'll let the one-legged guy do it." If there's an antithesis to a dancer, that's me. Because I'm the same size as Arte and Henry, they could use the same costumes on me—and if you kill a writer, it doesn't mean anything. But you can't kill your stars. The second season, I was the guy in the tricycle who got killed all the time. I performed a lot in the second and third season, doing not words and lines, but just as a body. It was great. I got away from the writing desk!

CHRIS BEARDE:

I did the French Canadian Axe Dancer, which became a college favorite. Nobody knew who I was; nobody ever plugged it or anything. I'd just show up every now and then and do this stupid clog dance, and drop axes on my feet, and walk off swearing in French Canadian. So, I became a cult favorite: "Hey, where's the French Canadian Axe Dancer, man?" And I used to be the Australian Didgeridoo Player . . . I'd play this didgeridoo, and sets would fall down all around me.

COSLOUGH JOHNSON:

The show was a bottomless pit for material. Sometimes it would get heavy, sometimes it would get hard. But somehow, if one team was slow one week, another team would pick up. So, I don't think George ever ran into the problem of not enough material for a show. He was able to cull a lot of the garbage out. And we all handed in some garbage. Some of it's not very good. The funny thing is, sometimes you hand in a piece that you think is really weak, and then they keep it, because they see something funnier than you did in it. And then you'd get it on its feet and get Arte dealing with it—you could give Arte four straight lines, and it would be hysterical.

Or any of those talents. Like Jo Anne Worley. I always say she was the only person in the world who could make "hello" into a two-act opera. Some of the stuff that we gave to Alan Sues, he would do little things to it that'd make it work, and get laughs out of it. Each one of them had their own little things that they added to the material. So, most of the time, you'd get about 120 percent from what you put on the paper—which, for a writer, is quite gratifying.

ARTE JOHNSON:

I came in with an idea one time. I wanted to do my little Russian, Rosmenko, doing a song, singing "Old Man River" or something. And everybody said, "Well, what are you going to do?" I said, "Schedule it, give me rehearsal with the musicians." And I remember that Paul Keyes was totally against it. He said, "What are you gonna do? What's so funny about it?"

And I took this character from behind the Iron Curtain, and I dressed him up in a suit with stripes, and black and white shoes—it was an ugly outfit—and I came out and sang this song in double-talk . . . and I was dancing and singing and screaming and yelling, and the audience—people who just came into the studio, we didn't have tickets—they were *screaming* at the end of this thing.

I came off the stage, and here was Paul standing there with tears running out of his eyes. He said, "I still don't know why it's funny!" And that was one of the great accolades I got from Paul Keyes.

COSLOUGH JOHNSON:

Funny is funny. Forget it—when you start analyzing comedy, you're in a lot of trouble. I remember working for a producer once, and in a sketch we had a guy falling off a chair. Which can be hysterical. And he wanted us to analyze for him *why* it's funny, a man falling off a chair. We knew we were in trouble right there.

I don't think you could do *Laugh-In* today, with all the problems with ethnic humor. Political correctness has killed a lot of humor. God forbid you do a Polish joke now; you get your house bombed. Or if you do an Arab joke—forget it.

Jump Cut To:

GEORGE SCHLATTER:

Laugh-In survived because of what we did *not* put on the air. There was a woman by the name of Carolyn Raskin who did the editing, who remains today one of the most brilliant women ever in television, and a major contributor to the success of *Laugh-In*.

COSLOUGH JOHNSON:

Carolyn, in a very silent way, had a lot to do with everything. She was very talented—not a wild lady at all. She was like the base, the stable part of that team, I think, because the rest of them were a little off-center. There was a lot of strength there, and she got things done.

DICK MARTIN:

Also, we had a marvelous director named Gordon Wiles, who was largely responsible for the look of the show—zoom in, zoom out, quick cuts. It had never been done on TV before . . . he was just feeling his oats. You know, there was a lot of Ernie Kovacs-type photographic stuff. Ernie used it a lot . . . but not much before. And so Gordon, really, in an hour show, was responsible for a great deal of it. And Art Schneider, who was our editor. He won an Emmy the first year—he was *majorly* responsible, too.

GEORGE SCHLATTER:

Art Schneider was a contributing force, and he and Carolyn Raskin were in charge of the editing. Carolyn had a great sense of humor, and Art could make anything work, with all those physical splices. So, all of the editing techniques that you have today grew out of *Laugh-In*. The edge numbers that you see now when you see a tape? Those didn't exist. To edit tape, you had to do it with a microscope, and physical splices.

COSLOUGH JOHNSON:

They used to do these eighteen-hour editing sessions! And those were the days where you had the old reels of tape that weighed about thirty pounds—there would be a stack of these things. And Art Schneider was not himself a very funny guy, a hysterical kind of a guy, but he just put that show together, and got that pacing going that made the show work.

The writers appreciated what he did. A lot of people *didn't* understand what he did, but we knew. If you ever sat in a session with him, he was magnificent. You'd go into the dark editing room, and all you're eating is donuts and eighty-two cups of coffee. So, in eighteen hours you'd gain forty-two pounds and have heartburn for a week. He was kind of pear-shaped, is the polite way to put it. And he didn't mind working the eighteen, twenty hours . . . he would just sit there and do that.

GEORGE SCHLATTER:

Nobody had ever edited like this, because everything had had to make sense. You had transitions. And we *had* no transitions. The network would say, "George, that's a jump cut."

And I'd say, "No, that's the way it oughtta be."

"But you jump cut from the door to the window. How did he get there?"

I'd say, "Beats the shit outta me, Sarge, I don't care." They would always be telling us, "These jump cuts are rattling us."

GARY OWENS:

Laugh-In was a little bit of everything . . . it was a little bit of Olsen & Johnson, a bit of Ernie Kovacs . . . although much faster. And I think the thing that made it work was, we might do fifteen jokes in one minute. Even though Olsen & Johnson, with *Hellzapoppin'*, was fast, it was not *that* fast.

The editing was miraculous. Carolyn and Art worked seven days a week. I mean, they never had a day off until summer would come around, when we'd be in reruns. My gosh, you talk about how difficult it was, trimming by razor blade—whereas today you just go in and press a couple of buttons and there it is. Y'know, there were so many cuts during a show, it was unbelievable.

Because they didn't want to switch directly from one sketch or monologue by Dan and Dick right to another thing where people may be talking, I was always the interim guy between Rowan and Martin and the rest of the cast—in that broadcast area next to that old 1944 RCA microphone. We had a little clock behind me that would grow about a half an inch a week . . . the hands would. They were like cartoon hands. And people wouldn't comment on it or anything, but by the end of the series—after six years—it was almost down to the floor.

Rowan and Martin would end a sketch, and then I would come in: "Meanwhile, in a seemingly abandoned warehouse in another part of town, we hear Tonto say to the Green Hornet . . ." And then Goldie would come in, or Lily Tomlin, or whoever it might be. That was always the quick switch.

Here Come Da Mud! Here Come Da Mud!

Given the steady stream of freewheeling insanity flashing across the TV screen, viewers were unaware of the continuous wrangling going on behind the scenes between *Laugh-In*'s creators and the network censors—as well as within the creative ranks of the show itself. Though most cast and crew members are reluctant to discuss it even today, stars Rowan and Martin did not see eye to eye with executive producers George Schlatter and Ed Friendly.

CHRIS BEARDE:

Here's the bottom line to this story: Rowan and Martin, as far as I'm concerned, think they created *Laugh-In*. And George thinks he created *Laugh-In*. And Ed Friendly thinks he put the deal together. And Dick Martin doesn't like George at all, and Dan Rowan *hated* George.

When I got an opportunity to go work on the *Smothers Brothers* show, I got in a room with George, and George said to me, "I'm not letting you out of your contract."

And I said, "But George, I'm just gonna go sit on my ass and not do anything. You don't want a disgruntled writer."

He said, "You're not going to be a disgruntled writer. Because I'm going to promise you that at the end of this show, I'm going to give you two specials and a blah blah blah. And you've got to listen to me: I'm not going to give anything to any of the other writers—*you're* getting this."

I said, "Okay. So I'll stay."

And I stayed that year. But while I was in the process of leaving, George said, "You can't leave. You're the one that's holding this together, because you're the only one that talks to both sides."

And then I go to Paul Keyes, and he says, "I can't make you the head writer, but I promise you I'll do whatever I can for you this year, Chris." He says, "Please don't leave. Because you're the guy that's between the two sides. If something happens with you, we won't be speaking to each other in the next year."

COSLOUGH JOHNSON:

I know Dick and Dan did have differences with George as far as content was concerned. I don't know if that was ego trips on both sides, or what was going on. It's a shame. They had problems, but you didn't see it on the screen . . . because the format hadn't changed, and the type of content hadn't changed. Whether there was a lot of screaming and hollering in between that, I have no idea. Very seldom did we ever get over the NBC studios.

I'm always oblivious to all that. Y'know, you sit in a room, and write your material, and go home. That was it. And that was another reason not to wanna go to the set . . . you didn't want to get involved in anything. Arte was smart—he stayed out of that stuff, too. Because you couldn't take sides, there was no way to take sides.

ARTE JOHNSON:

I was so out of the loop—I made it conditional that I stay out of the loop. I didn't want to get involved in the politics. I'm finding out *now* that there were certain things . . . I'll have a conversation with George, and then all of a sudden something will come up, and I'll say, "I had *no idea* that was going on." A performer shouldn't be involved. I didn't need that on top of the other stuff.

GARY OWENS:

George and Ed and Dan and Dick would fight over different things. I think part of it was: who created the show? And I don't know . . . I didn't do the special. I joined it as the series began, and did every show. I was not privy—I was *in* the privy, that's when I got signed—but I wasn't privy as to who really created it. I think that Larry Hovis, who was teaching at the University of Texas until he died in 2003, created the word "Laugh-In."

But it was a great success. And the *four* of them owned it. They're still paid to this day, of course.

CHRIS BEARDE:

I quit the next year to go do *The Andy Williams Show*, and for two years they didn't speak to each other. They sent memos across the studio! Other writers would call me up and say, "Chris, my God, these people are not talking to each other."

Armageddon happened in there, because the left went left, and the right went right, and the center disa-fucking-ppeared. Like what's happened in this country right now. And this was in 1970! It was a disaster. I mean it was still getting ratings, because of the power of the people in it, but the show stopped being funny when people were going, "Why you . . ." "Why you . . ." "We created the show!" "No, you didn't!"

DICK MARTIN:

I don't wanna even touch that, if you know what I mean.

GEORGE SCHLATTER:

Interesting . . . It was interesting. [pause] But you've gotta understand the political pressure on *Laugh-In* . . . and the political pressure on *Laugh-In* went up to the White House. When Nixon became president, and Paul Keyes was still on the show, they did not like what we were doing—anything political. We were doing jokes about oil, about nuclear, about the Pentagon, about the President, about the Congress, about corruption, about graft, about greed, about everything. They didn't like any of it. They weren't funny to Nixon.

We said, "There's no truth to the rumor that off-shore drilling will cease when the oil slick reaches San Clemente."

They didn't like that. We got that on the air . . . by saying there's *no truth to the rumor.* We used to do, "No truth to the rumor that [Vice President] Spiro Agnew is against freedom of speech and democracy and equality. He just doesn't want things like that to fall into the wrong hands." Well, they didn't like that . . . so they said, "*Was* there a rumor?" "Yeah!" We're okay, 'cause we're putting down these rumors.

The reason I left the show . . . that was pretty much it. Pressure from the White House that they weren't going to allow us to do any more political humor. They got a fast "Fuck you" and a mighty "Hi Ho, Silver."

When Nixon became president . . . John Mitchell ordered a study from the Rand Institute on: "Due to the amount of political unrest, what would the reaction of the public be if we were to skip one election?" And then, they let it be known that they could question the political balance of any network affiliate for what they aired, even if they hadn't originated it or created it. When you start threatening the affiliates, then you're hitting 'em right in the lap.

So, they wanted to maintain "political balance" . . . and the words that rang loud and clear were: "Or else." It's kind of where we are now. The Fox Network has now replaced Spiro Agnew. Now they're saying, "Fair and Balanced," and all of that stuff. The whole idea has always been to control. Once you control government, then you control information. When you control information, then you control thought. When you control thought, then you control everything . . . and that's where they're headed now: to control thought.

I Am Woman, Hear Me . . . Meow

4

This is a tale so old, by now it's grown a beard. From their very beginnings, most mediums of mass communication have been owned and controlled by men. Even the prehistoric cave wall frescoes were likely painted by men—which would explain why we never see images of cave *women* throwing spears at mastodons.

Fast-forward a couple of years to the dawn of radio and television, and it's the same story: male values, ideas, and viewpoints dominated the airwaves. The biggest stars were men. Producers, directors, network executives, technicians, and most of the writers were men. Women continually saw themselves depicted as faithful secretaries, smiling homemakers, loving wives, purring sex kittens, or helpless damsels in distress throughout TV's first decades of existence. With very few exceptions, a woman had to be extremely attractive to even make it onto the air, while a guy could be fat or skinny, bald, hairy, grizzled, funny-looking, or just plain ugly.

Lucille Ball may have been the reigning queen of comedy in the 1950s, but she was still seen on *I Love Lucy* (even the show's title was from the male viewpoint) as bandleader Ricky Ricardo's wife . . . and a zany, bubble-headed one at that, invariably screwing things up as she schemed to somehow share his bright showbiz spotlight. *Behind* the scenes, however, Lucy was half of Desilu Productions—and quickly became one of television's smartest producers, its first truly powerful female executive and the first woman to head a major television production studio. Today, few may realize that it was Ball who gave the greenlight to and ultimately produced two venerable franchises: *Mission Impossible* and *Star Trek*.

In the 1960s, the women's liberation movement began to stir, and suddenly the testosterone-fueled domination of the industry was challenged. Women started appearing on TV as reporters, schoolteachers, attorneys, nurses, actresses, nuns, police officers, secret agents, witches, genies, and vampires, along with their traditional roles. Slowly, the image of the "new woman" began to emerge, and she was bright, self-reliant, and every bit the equal of her male counterpart . . . even if she wasn't necessarily equally compensated.

Donald Hollinger (Ted Bessell) tries to celebrate an intimate New Year's Eve with . . . That Girl, *Ann Marie (Marlo Thomas) in this late 1968 episode. © ABC Television Network*

That Girl (1966), created by talented *Dick Van Dyke Show* veterans Sam Denoff and Bill Persky, was the first comedy series to embrace this new equality. The popular show starred Marlo Thomas as a bubbly, attractive, hopeful young actress trying to strike out on her own in New York City. Well, not *entirely* on her own: On the very first episode, Ann Marie met the love of her life, magazine reporter Donald Hollinger (played by Ted Bessell), and the two eventually get engaged several seasons later. While *That Girl* set the template for situation comedies featuring independent women, the show often featured larger-than-life situations—which its characters would respond to in similar larger-than-life fashion—and retained the flavor and style of standard sitcoms of the day. Despite the fact that it followed one of ABC's biggest hits, *Bewitched*, on the schedule, *That Girl* never managed to grab huge ratings . . . yet the network kept it on the air for five seasons, and would have kept it on longer. "Sponsors really wanted it to stay on, because they were selling a lot of ladies' hair products and stuff like that," recalls Denoff. "But Marlo wanted her movie career."

Ms. Thomas was, and remains, a staunch and vocal supporter of women's rights. Loyal fans of the series remember it fondly, and *That Girl* opened the door for good to TV shows featuring strong women at their epicenter. "It was a good show for its time," notes Martin Starger, who was

V.P. in Charge of Programs back then. "And it did a hell of a lot better than most ABC shows. We were proud to have it."

As proof positive that times truly were changing, in 1968 Diahann Carroll became the first black woman to star in her own sitcom, *Julia*, portraying a widowed working mom with a young son. The show, though well intentioned, lacked bite and never really caught on with audiences.

And Then Along Came Mary

It took until September of 1970 for viewers to finally embrace—front and center as star of her own series—an independent, successful, single career woman. *The Mary Tyler Moore Show* was something new to the traditional American sitcom. Co-creators James L. Brooks and Allan Burns—a partnership that was forged by famed TV and film executive Grant Tinker (who was then married to Mary) specifically to create *The Mary Tyler Moore Show*—built an ensemble comedy series more rooted in the real world, reflecting what was going on at the time. The show was filled with funny, multidimensional characters who started out painted in broad strokes, but evolved and deepened as we watched them year after year: In Mary Richards's workplace at WJM News, viewers grew to know and love sarcastic head writer Murray Slaughter (Gavin MacLeod), pompous anchorman Ted Baxter (Ted Knight), gruff newsroom boss Lou Grant (Edward Asner), and, a few seasons later, smarmy "Happy Homemaker" hostess Sue Ann Nivens (Betty White) and Ted's sweetly simple girlfriend Georgette Franklin (Georgia Engel). Sharing her apartment house were Mary's self-deprecating neighbor and best friend, Rhoda Morgenstern (Valerie Harper), and Phyllis Lindstrom (Cloris Leachman), their idiosyncratic landlady.

The show developed a performance and writing style all its own—emulated by many other subsequent series—keeping the volume down in contrast to Norman Lear's more theatrical approach, which, it should be noted, would not hit the airwaves for another year. But *The Mary Tyler Moore Show*, which would garner great acclaim and end up one of the best-loved situation comedies in TV history (or *herstory*, if you will), had to overcome some unexpected obstacles before, and even after, it made it onto the air.

GRANT TINKER, producer:
Mary always wanted to go back to work in TV, and she had proved that she was very good at comedy. She had had such a great experience on *The Dick Van Dyke Show* . . . I mean, you can't find a better way to work in television

than a comedy that shoots in front of an audience, because your hours are kind of like banker's hours. You went in around 9:00 or 10:00 every day, and you go home at 5:00 or 6:00. You shoot it in front of an audience on one night, the fifth night of the workweek. And you get what I've always called *psychic income*, as well as getting paid for doing the show.

ALAN WAGNER, former V.P. of Program Development at CBS:

One day I get a call from Artie Price, who was her manager, and he says Mary wants to do a show. I loved Mary from *Dick Van Dyke*. Artie Price says she's really interested, but you know, she's Mary, she doesn't want to get tested again and all that crap. *That* was an easy sell. I said to him on the phone, "You got it. I'll sell this. You can go tell Mary that she's got it."

So I said to Fred Silverman, "You're committed to thirteen of these *Mary* episodes," and he said, "You fuckin' son of a bitch, you idiot!" Oh, man. Then, "What's the show about, tell me the famous idea, and who's writing it?"

ALLAN BURNS, co-creator, writer and producer:

Jim Brooks asked me to come in and look at the pilot of *Room 222*—which was a very *different* kind of show. Talk about shows that you couldn't get on the air today, this was a show that was partly funny, and partly not . . . it was meant to be a sort of slice of life, where comedy came to it naturally. Not being forced in, y'know? A very good show about an inner-city school—basically, a typical inner-city Los Angeles high school.

So, Jim asked me if I'd come and write some episodes for them. We were getting to be pretty good friends. So I did—and I really loved working on the show. I probably wrote five or six episodes that year, and it was done at Twentieth Century Fox. At that particular time, Grant Tinker was a vice president of development . . . I believe that was his title . . . and Grant loved *222*. And he liked both of us, individually and together.

ALAN WAGNER:

I am an absolute firm believer that shows don't normally rise up beyond a concept—that it's all in execution. *Mary Tyler Moore* is shit without execution . . . which is why it was so important to get Brooks and Burns.

ALLAN BURNS:

I remember having lunch with Grant by myself once, and he started asking me if I'd be interested in doing a three-camera show. I had done some three-camera work at Talent Associates . . . I'd worked on a show called *He & She* that Leonard Stern and Arne Sultan had created for CBS, which was a wonderful show that unfortunately died an early death it never should have. And it was the first three-camera show I had ever worked on, with an audience and all that.

But it was tremendously hard work. I learned a tremendous amount from Leonard Stern, but he was a particularly tough taskmaster who was never satisfied with anything. He taught me a lot about not being satisfied with the easy joke. He always was looking for: Where's the *character* in this? Jokes are easy, character is difficult . . . and it was very exhilarating—but it was also *exhausting*.

So, Grant said, "Would you be interested in writing another three-camera show like *He & She?*"

And I said, "Jeez, Grant, I don't know . . . I mean, I'm two years married, I've got a small child, I don't think I wanna work that hard anymore."

Grant said to me, "Well, it seems to me if you're in charge—if you're the producer of the show—you can make it whatever you want it to be. Y'know, you don't have to answer to somebody else." And so I was thinking about it. He was talking sort of vaguely, in general terms. Unbeknownst to me, he was saying the same things to Jim. Having lunch with him, taking walks around the Fox lot together after lunch, and proposing this.

And Jim and I were talking one day . . . we were on the phone. He said, "Is Grant talking to you at all about a three-camera show?"

I said, "Yeah! Is he talking to you?"

"Yeah! He is. What's he up to?" And then Jim said, "Ohhhh, I think I know . . . I bet they've got a deal for Mary to do a show!"

So together—on separate lines—we called Grant in his office, and said, "Grant, is this about Mary?" And he said, "I have to be very careful about this. Because I'm working for Fox, and Mary and I have made a deal to do a show that is *not* going to be for Fox. So I have to be extremely careful about how I broach this with you guys. But indeed, that's the case."

What surprised Jim and me, and probably surprised a lot of other people, too, including the ones that weren't asked, was, why didn't she go back to Carl Reiner? Why didn't Grant go to Carl Reiner to do a show for Mary? It's what *I* would have done.

GRANT TINKER:

I can't answer that question. It just never occurred to me. Maybe because I had just been involved at Fox. Jim was doing *Room 222* there, and Allan did some writing for it . . . and then, when Jim went off to make a movie or something, Allan produced it with Gene Reynolds for a while. So I got to know those guys.

ALLAN BURNS:

Failing going back to Carl, why not Sam Denoff and Bill Persky, who had been the top writers for *Dick Van Dyke* along with Garry Marshall and Jerry Belson? Why didn't he ask them? Every instinct I would have had, were I Grant, taking a big chance as they had, would have been to go to somebody she had worked with before, that she felt comfortable with.

BILL PERSKY, writer, producer and director:

Of course, they came to us. Mary and Grant asked us if we'd be interested in doing it, and we weren't. I worked with Mary subsequently on several specials and things, and we're very close . . . but at that time, it was the last year of *That Girl*—we were moving on to something else, and we just didn't have time. It wasn't like they made an offer and we rejected it. It was a conversation.

ALLAN BURNS:

But Mary had so much faith in Grant, and just went along 'cause he was tapping us to do it. I think it *maybe* had a little bit to do with that *Room 222* was not your typical situation comedy. It had a little bite to it. It felt, I think, extremely contemporary for its time, and maybe that's what he wanted. And he was seeing us doing this, and I think he thought, "Well, I'll go to these new guys. I like 'em, and I trust 'em."

And boy, did he ever back us up!

GRANT TINKER:

Because they were so fucking good. And it was so *obvious* that they were good.

No Jews, Moustaches, New Yorkers, or Divorced Women

ALLAN BURNS:

We came up with a lot of terrible ideas at first.

One was that she'd be working as a sort of leg person for a Hollywood gossip column. That there would be somebody like Liz Smith . . . and you know how Liz Smith has all those people out there, beatin' the bushes for her. That would be what Mary would do.

But what made it even worse, when we took it to CBS, is that we'd decided that Mary should be divorced. I think every comedy writer wanted to do a show about divorce . . . because probably two thirds of the comedy writers in town had *been* divorced, and wanted to write about their own experiences. Divorce had never been done. Not successfully, anyway. There were no divorcées in television. And there were all these women of a certain age, like Doris Day and Lucy—after Desi, when she was back to being Lucy again without the benefit of a husband—but nobody ever felt it was necessary to explain, in those days, why these thirty-year-old women were unmarried.

We wanted to do Mary as somebody who was *real* to us. We didn't want to do Mary as Lucy . . . we didn't want to do her as Doris Day. I mean, here was Doris in those days, who I'm sure was forty-five years old, and still playing this virginal character. That just didn't seem real to us.

And I can remember taking this divorce idea to Mary and Grant. I remember going to their house one night . . . We had never met Mary, by the way. We had been working for probably two or three weeks, maybe a month, and had not met her. And so we told Grant this idea, and he said, "I think you ought to tell it to Mary."

We went to their house on Beverly Drive, and Mary comes down the steps . . .

GRANT TINKER:

There was a little moment when Mary came down the stairs and did a little *drunk* thing, and startled them. Allan said later, "My God, we've committed to make a show with this lady, and we didn't know she's a drunk!" That was just Mary's little introductory joke.

ALLAN BURNS:

And how *nervous* we were, whether this was gonna click with her . . . Well, she loved the idea. Mary had been divorced. Grant had been divorced. They *got* it. And our rationale was, we knew we'd get some flak from the network on this. We knew it fairly early on. But we thought, if we've got good reasons . . . We said, "A tremendous amount of people are divorced. Or their parents are divorced. Or their brother's divorced. And it cannot be this awful thing that the powers that be were claming it was." So we thought if we go in and make that pitch, we'll be all right.

GRANT TINKER:

I didn't give a rat's ass. It didn't make any difference to me. In fact, I thought that was a good idea. But CBS had a big problem with it.

ALLAN BURNS:

We went over to CBS to pitch it, and it was a lunch meeting with Perry Lafferty and Paul King where they already knew the concept, and they tried to dissuade us from this.

Perry said, "But, guys. Everybody's going to think she got divorced from Dick Van Dyke."

And we said, "We've already thought about that. We'll make it clear that she's not, because we'll *see* the ex-husband, he'll be in it—so people will know it's not Dick Van Dyke. And we will know that she's blameless in the failure of the marriage, because two of the characters in the show will be her in-laws, who adore her still, and think their son is a schmuck because he lost this wonderful woman, y'know? We'll *see* this."

Now, *today* she'd be a woman who isn't married, even if she's forty-five. Because it wouldn't feel necessary to explain. We were *just* ahead of the wave that was going to become feminism—*women's lib*, as they called it in those days—where women didn't feel the need to apologize for not having been married. But us two schmucky married guys thought, "God, we have to explain why she's not. She's clearly thirty, and let's explain this."

I remember Perry saying, "Look, if you're determined to do this, you're going to have to run this by Mike Dann and the guys in New York. We'll tell 'em that you really want to do this, and Grant and Mary want to do it, and we'll get behind it, but you're going to have to go to New York and have a meeting about it."

PERRY LAFFERTY, former V.P. of Programs at CBS:

I was under orders from New York. That was not my own preference, 'cause I didn't think it made a damn bit of difference . . . They wanted to have a divorced woman striking out on her own. That was the nub of the whole show. And the network said, "We can't have a divorced woman running a TV show as the star."

And I was uneasy because they hadn't had any big experiences. Jim was on *Room 222*, I don't know where Allan was. They didn't have big credits for, "This is our new half-hour comedy." I did everything I could to *not* have them as the writers. Let's get somebody who's been around the track . . . I wanted Leonard Stern to come in and hire the staff. But Artie Price and Grant Tinker just put their foot down and wore me out. It's again a question of who believes—if you found producers that believed that heavily in something, I think you had to let them run with it.

**LEONARD STERN,
television writer and
producer:**

I felt that *The Mary Tyler Moore Show*—part of that group—was like our graduating class. People who had come from *He & She*, and *The Governor & J.J.*, and were imbued with the spirit of these shows . . . the wit . . . not conceding that people in the Midwest won't understand it. They exist. There are bright people everywhere.

Then the *Mary Tyler Moore* deal was made, with no pilot. And that unnerved the people at CBS, especially the hier-

The Mary Tyler Moore Show's *original core ensemble (front, l-r): Gavin MacLeod, Cloris Leachman, Mary Tyler Moore, Valerie Harper, and Ted Knight. Looming over them all is Ed Asner.* © *CBS Television Network*

archy above and beyond Perry. So they virtually came to me and said, "Would you get involved?"

And I said, "No. These are all people I know and trust. I'm *excited* for them." They said, "Will you read the initial scripts?" I said, "I will. But I'm going to be in support of them, I'm telling you that in advance. I think what has happened is you're all panicking because you don't have a pilot." I was concerned that we were going to have the old classic network problem, interfering with something that was different—yet what they wanted was something that was different!

PERRY LAFFERTY:

I was just doing what I thought was best, what they paid me for. It got so bad that it ended up in New York, in that meeting with the head censors and the head of the broadcast group.

ALAN WAGNER:

That's the famous meeting with Mike Dann, the famous meeting in New York.

So, we fly up from California, Artie and me—Artie was now the executive producer of the show—and Jim and Allan. It took place in CBS's thirty-fourth-floor conference room, which had a semicircle of chairs up on a slight rise, up a step or so, around a table. There was a couch, chairs, love seats. And down in this enclave was a large television monitor, and right behind me in this enclave was a screen.

ALLAN BURNS:

It was the darkest room I'd ever been in in my life. There was not a window. It seemed to be right out of Kafka. There was darkness all around, and this womb-like feeling. The *womb room*, I guess it is. And I remember there were lights shining down from the ceiling, in sort of a circular pattern . . . and there was a circle of people sitting in there. You'd have thought it was a Ku Klux Klan meeting or something like that, because of how mysterious everything seemed. And it was so intimidating!

There we were, under our separate spotlights, and everybody was there: the great Mike Dann, whom we had never met . . . and there's Bob Wood, who had *just* taken over CBS as president. I think Bob was brought in to be sort of an interim guy, that's always what the feeling was. That he was a guy who wasn't gonna rock the boat. Y'know, a corporate guy, a company man all his life. *Nobody* ever knew, at that time, that Bob Wood was going to be the innovator that he was. How could they know that *he* would rock the ship more than anybody ever had over there? But Bob was pretty quiet at this meeting, and he let Mike run it.

ALAN WAGNER:

And I start by introducing the party of Artie and Jim and Allan, and saying okay, this is what the show is going to be about, and "Jim and Allan, why don't you take over?" And Jim explains how the show is roughed out, that Mary Richards is divorced . . .

ALLAN BURNS:

I don't recall anybody saying much except Mike Dann, and the guy from their research department. Very soon after the meeting started, Mike turned the whole thing over to Mark. A rather heavy-set guy. And he started telling us their research: the famous four things that people wouldn't accept on television.

ALAN WAGNER:

We're sitting around at this thing, and there was dead silence. *Dead silence* in the room. We hadn't heard a word, not a snicker, not a word, nobody was breathing. And slowly, everybody turns to look at Mark Golden, who's sitting on that chair, up on that rise. Now, Mark was the "guru of program analysis." And as far as Mike Dann was concerned, nothing could question program analysis.

FRED SILVERMAN, former V.P. of Programs at CBS:
He was Mike's hatchet man. He would write a memo that wasn't even a memo—it was like one line, where he would just say: "The following shows will get below-average ratings." And he would list about half of the programs in development. And on the basis of that, those shows would be dismissed. So, it was very dangerous, 'cause nothing that was new, and nothing that was progressive, could get on the air.

ALAN WAGNER:
And in the silence, Mark says, "There are four things Americans won't stand for: Jews, men with moustaches, New Yorkers, and divorced women." It's fuckin' branded in my head.

ALLAN BURNS:
I was absolutely stunned. I'm not Jewish . . . but almost everybody in the room is, ya gotta remember. And I mean, the whole idea of nobody who wore a moustache—so much for Clark Gable, I guess, and David Niven, and Tom Selleck later, and on and on. And *people from New York*, for God's sake? If you looked at CBS in those days, it was pretty rural, especially in comedy . . . it did not have a big-city feel to it anywhere, and nothing sophisticated about the comedy they were doing. But what do you say when somebody says something like that?

GRANT TINKER:
Well, that may have been their opinion of the audience. I guess it was [former CBS president] Jim Aubrey who coined the phrase, "We program for the people we fly over." Which was kind of true. But they weren't all white-bread guys over at CBS.

ALLAN BURNS:
We stammered, I guess, for a while, and we gave 'em what we thought was our whole card, which was that everybody is touched by divorce in one way or another, almost everybody in America, and people will understand it. And we will make her blameless in the divorce, all that stuff.

And—*flop sweat*. We knew we were getting nowhere, and somebody said, "Well, if you're determined to do this, we urge you to rethink it."

We were invited to leave the room, and we went out and waited by the elevator . . . and Mike said, "Artie, can we see you? We've got some business things we need to talk to you about." We were just dumb enough not to realize that was code for "these guys are toast."

ALAN WAGNER:

Out in the hallway, I heard Mike Dann—whose voice rose about an octave when he was angry—saying, "Fire 'em! Fire 'em all! Get rid of everybody—fire 'em all, those fucking sons of bitches!"

ALLAN BURNS:

So we waited, and said, "That didn't go well, did it?" And we said if they force this on us . . . what are we going to do? 'Cause we don't have another idea at this point. Artie finally joined us and said, "That did not go well, fellas." That was patently clear to us. And we now had the longest flight imaginable back to Los Angeles, the two of us. Artie wasn't on the flight, he had some other business to do, so we got on the plane . . . On the way back, we were discussing if we should quit now or later.

ALAN WAGNER:

We were *horrified* leaving the room, you know. "What the hell does this mean?" That's what was so bad . . . now we're suddenly suspect, we're guys who are shaking the boat, and these are untried people who've never headlined a show before . . .

It was scary. We'd gotten Mary to do a show, and everybody loves Mary, and it seemed harmless enough. And suddenly, Mike Dann was overreacting a lot. He got fired not long afterwards. Program Head was a job I never wanted, because of the short life span. Sooner or later, you're going to fail, someone's gonna get ya—or the pressure gets to be too much, so you quit.

They Were Gonna Make It, After All

ALLAN BURNS:

By the end of the six-hour flight, we had considered the option of just throwing it in . . . but you know what? Grant and Mary had been so terrific, and we could see anything in *Variety*—like "Writers Ankle Moore Pilot"—was going to reflect badly on them. And certainly not well on us, either. We thought, let's give it another week or two and see if we can't come up with something else without selling out what we wanted to do, which was to keep the sense that we have one foot in reality, at least.

So, we just started throwing out all kinds of different ideas. I remember Jim saying, "I used to work at CBS News in New York . . . and nobody's ever done a show in a newsroom. That could give us the reality that we need. You know, that you feel like you're in a contemporary world. And it lends itself to comedy." He started telling me all these stories about people he worked with . . . all very eccentric. And then we started talking about the funny anchormen there were around town, y'know, all these stentorian-voiced guys, most of whom were dumber than stumps but they were delivering the news with such import . . .

We began to get excited about *that* aspect of it. And we said, "Wait a minute—that's much better than her working for this flaky columnist!"

We'd set the show in Minneapolis . . . one of the reasons being, if you're going to do a three-camera show, you're always going to be inside. And wouldn't it be nice to be inside in a place where it feels *good* to be inside, where it's so cold out and you can see snow outside the windows, and all that kind of stuff—and there was something so appealing about Minneapolis, being this sort of sophisticated city in the mid-lands. As we talked about this, we thought, let's explain why Mary is thirty and unmarried. So we invented this idea that she had been involved with an intern at what appeared to be the Mayo Clinic, since we're in Minneapolis.

We thought it was sort of implicit that she and this guy had lived together, and she sort of supported him through medical school, and he's now dragging his feet about getting married, and she's learned not to wait. The handwriting is on the wall that this guy is *never* going to get married—and let's see this guy in the first episode and blow him off, and have Mary out there on her own, in a new city . . . a smaller-town girl in a fairly good-sized city, coming to work for this television station that's sort of the fifth station in a four-station market.

We got real excited about this whole idea. Pitched it to Grant—and he loved it. We said, "We're going to write this up." So we sat down and wrote about a ten or twelve-page treatment—oddly enough, I still have it—and it contains a spooky amount of dialogue that's still in the pilot.

GRANT TINKER:

It was half prose, and half partial scenes. That was the bible—sort of the intro-duction to the show. And years later I went back and found it. Whenever I was leaving some office, I found it—and I looked at it, and where they had dialogue, it was almost word for word what wound up in the show. It was remarkable. Those guys together were incredibly good!

ALLAN BURNS:

The treatment became rather famous for having so well exemplified what a series treatment should be about, 'cause it really zinged along . . . Anyway, we sent it to Grant. Grant loved it. He gave it to Mary. Mary called up and said, "I love this. *I love this!* This is so great."

So, there you go. That's how we eventually ended up with a far better setting for a series than we had originally come up with. And we always were sort of amused at the idea that they were against divorce, but they sort of tacitly agreed to the fact that here was Mary living in sin with a guy for those years . . . and nobody much said *boop* about it. By that point, I think they were so relieved to get rid of divorce, that they were willing to accept anything. And of course, when I say "living in sin," I say it in quotes . . . 'cause in those days, that wouldn't have seemed acceptable to us at all, in terms of what the network would accept. But they did.

When Rhoda and Phyllis spun off into their own series, some memorable new characters were added to the mix. Pictured l-r (front): Sue Ann Nivens (Betty White), Mary, and Georgette Franklin (Georgia Engel). Behind them: Gavin MacLeod, Ed Asner, and Ted Knight, who stayed with the show for its full run.

ALAN WAGNER:
Now, why that was any better than being divorced, I still to this day don't know. She was fucking unmarried, and that was better than being divorced?

GRANT TINKER:
Anyway, we finally made it. CBS couldn't get out, really. It was a pay-or-play thing. And if they hadn't put the pilot on—the prototype—and, ultimately, the other shows, they'd have to pay for 'em. That was a big bill for nothing . . . but CBS had resistance to all kinds of things, and they had big problems with everybody. Mary and Valerie and Cloris, all of them tested badly.

SAM DENOFF, television writer and producer:
We were working on the same lot at that time, and Grant's office was right next door to ours. They tested it after it was shot, and CBS wanted everybody fired except Mary. Ed Asner, Ted Knight, all the guys who became enormous.

VALERIE HARPER, performer:
I never felt in danger of being fired, but I sure could've. In today's world, I would've been. I think so . . . if you don't have producers with backbone.

GRANT TINKER:
This is where, I think, I began to separate myself from some of the things that were sort of part of the business, like research and testing. I began to think more in terms of my own judgment. Your seat-of-the-pants reaction—you know, your visceral reaction to a show, I've always thought—is what you get paid for. And if all you're going to do is look at test scores and TV "Q's" and so on, then you might as well be in another business. There are so many shows that I've been involved with that tested badly, that went on to become really great shows.

VALERIE HARPER:
That was Grant Tinker. Oh boy, did that guy have backbone. And he believed in the creative people. He didn't dictate . . . Jim and Allan would tell us, "Oh, God, Grant saved us again. He gets in there and he doesn't take no for an answer. And he fights for us. It's so wonderful to have that." In subsequent series I've been involved with, you didn't have that.

I said to [writer] Ed. Weinberger one time, "Ed., what *is* it with the network? Giving all these notes . . . saying, 'Wouldn't it be funny if . . . ' and all that? What is with them? These ideas are terrible!"

He said, "Well . . . they're not equipped."

Doesn't that say it all? And Jim Brooks and Allan Burns used to say, "I'll listen to Jerry Belson, I'll listen to Danny Arnold"—y'know, they listed a bunch of comedy writers—"But I am not listening to a manager, I am not listening to people that don't know how to do it. If they can't sit in the writers' room and come up with *funny*, I don't wanna listen to them."

GRANT TINKER:

Well, network stuff never surprised me. It could *anger* me . . . to the point where, you know, you get in your car and you go right over there and do battle with the silly network people. I can say honestly and correctly that as a network guy, I was so in awe of these wonderful writers that I was a helper and not a hindrance. And I *never* thought I could "produce the producers"— as some network people do. It's just amazing, the arrogance and the stupidity of certain people who work for networks, who think they can do it. But they never have, and they never will.

ALLAN BURNS:

We had just two advocates at CBS: Alan Wagner and Ethel Winant. Alan, in those days, was mostly in New York. Ethel was stalwart. She was Horatio at the bridge for us. I felt we owed her such a debt . . . she was the most wonderful woman, and so honest. I know she could be really tough. She was never tough with us. She was nothing but supportive.

She said to me, later, "I loved those scripts. I knew it was going to be a great show, and I *told* everybody, and they would tell me to shut up." She said, "There were times when I felt like if I said one more thing in favor of you guys, that I was going to get fired. Because they were so sick of hearing me defend you."

Daunted, but Not Doomed, by Dr. Death

There was a particular CBS executive assigned to them—their official network liaison, whom they coyly nicknamed "Dr. Death"—who just didn't seem to get the show, or much care for it. All it did was make things more difficult for the series' creators and producers, and *The Mary Tyler Moore Show*'s early going continued to be a rough ride. The week before they were scheduled to film the first episode, they suffered through a disastrous read-through in front of an audience—an almost comically terrible situation fueled by a steaming hot studio whose air conditioning was broken that day, a script that still needed some fine tuning, three enormously bulky experimental film cameras that virtually blocked the view of anyone not on the stage floor, a malfunctioning sound system, and a phoned-in bomb threat. If anyone had scripted this series of circumstances, it would've likely been thrown out as way too exaggerated.

VALERIE HARPER:

That first time, there were no laughs . . . but I hadn't heard laughs all week. Who knew from this? I was completely a virgin. I thought, "Oh well, they're far away, it's television. Maybe all laughs are canned."

ALLAN BURNS:

We knew it was an unmitigated disaster. And I guess CBS was thinking, "We should have fired these guys when the firing was good. When Mike told us to." And that night, the night of the disaster, they were feeling pretty good about that. That they knew we were the wrong guys, and they weren't liking the scripts they were reading. They didn't think they were funny—they thought they were a little twisted in certain ways, and they didn't like anything about the show. It was only when Freddie and Bob saved us that anybody else came aboard other than Ethel.

FRED SILVERMAN:

The first year that I was there, I got there very late in the game, so the schedule had already been set. And y'know, it's that great scheduling, where they'd put *Mary Tyler Moore* on Tuesday night, in between *Green Acres* and *Hee-Haw*. Right in between two of the rube shows.

ALLAN BURNS:

We were just aghast. What in the world were they doing?! We were the sacrificial lamb . . . they had a commitment, and this was their way of canceling us.

JAY SANDRICH, director:

There are a lot of shows—especially in those days, 'cause time slots had so much more to do with it—that just never got seen, even though they may have been good. And if it hadn't been for Fred and Bob Wood moving the show, it probably only would've done twelve or thirteen weeks. Today, people sit in their chair and they press the remote. In those days, most people didn't get up out of the chair. And if they were watching the show that preceded it, they'd stay tuned.

FRED SILVERMAN:

I just said, "This is crazy. I looked at this thing, and I don't care what the testing said, this is a hell of a good show! And we're killing it. Let's take one of those dogs—take *Petticoat Junction*. Take anything. You name it!" We had a bunch of crap on Saturday night, it was kind of a hodgepodge schedule. I said, "Take one of those, put that on Tuesday night with all this other garbage. *Mary Tyler Moore*, give it a shot!"

We had Dick Van Dyke on Saturday nights. *The New Dick Van Dyke Show*. I said, "Put it back to back with *Dick Van Dyke*. Then, at least, you know you've got a couple of new comedies there, and I think this one is really good." And God bless him, that was the *first* time Bob Wood said, "Go ahead and do it," late in the game. The second time was a year later, with *All in the Family*.

ALLAN BURNS:

So we trimmed . . . and we did a little punching up, but not a whole lot . . . and had pretty much the same show—only shorter, and tighter. It was miraculous! And those friggin' cameras that were in the way were *out* of the way . . . so people could see.

And we got big laughs on the first scene—not huge, but big enough that we looked at each other and thought, "Okay. Okay, this is going all right." Then we go into the newsroom, where Mary arrives and has her interview scene with Lou Grant, where he ends up with the famous line, "You've got spunk. I *hate* spunk." It worked like a charm . . . and the laughs started to build for that scene . . . and by the time they got to "I hate spunk," I thought the audience was going to applaud. Y'know, they were just jumpin' out of their chairs.

Jim and I looked at each other, like, "Why didn't this happen Tuesday night?" Ethel came down afterwards and said, "I knew this was gonna work." And it did.

JAY SANDRICH:

If the shows are well written, and you cast them right, they're gonna work. Then the only question is: Is the audience going to like the combinations? We knew how good Mary was. We didn't know how good everybody *else* was, 'cause I don't think Valerie had ever done a television show . . . and Ed Asner was basically not a comic actor . . . and Ted Knight was doing radio and cartoon voices. So, there were a lot of gambles. But having sat there for six or seven days, working scenes and watching this cast work, you could see there was a lot of depth there.

ALLAN BURNS:

We had an opening-night party at my home. It was a sit-down dinner. And we invited everybody, including the CBS liaison, 'cause we just weren't going to offend the network in that way. And I remember that evening, him sitting down at a table with some of the cast and saying something like, "Well, that's gonna get about a twenty-two share."

Well, a twenty-two share in those days was *disastrous*! And we all watched on television sets, watched the thing as casts do, and staffs do . . . and then he very loudly announced that we were going to lose the time slot by a great deal. I think he had had something to drink by that point. And I remember him sitting down and taking my wife's seat—so that when she came back to the table she had nowhere to sit! I had to remind him that he was sitting in her seat.

The next Monday, I called up the CBS liaison to tell him we didn't think his behavior had been very good . . . and I started to get very angry at him. We had a long office, with two desks that faced each other—and I remember looking over at Jim, whose eyes were sort of wide, like, *I was talking like this to the network liaison*?! But I was so angry at him for his behavior that night that I thought, "Well, fuck it, y'know?"

I remember him not putting up a big argument. I think he probably realized that he had not behaved particularly well, and took it for that moment. But that didn't stop him from telling us not to shoot certain shows . . . well, one show in particular.

He called up and said, "This show that you're supposed to be doing next week"—and we thought, "*Supposed* to be doing next week?" He says, "I'm going to forbid you to shoot it. As the network representative, I'm going to tell you you can't shoot the show."

We said, "Why not?"

He says, "One of your main characters, somebody we're supposed to like, refuses to see her mother. How is anybody ever going to like her? And then there's all this twisted, perverted stuff in that first scene."

And we said, "What are you talking about?"

He said, "Oh, the sadism stuff."

"Beg your pardon?"

Beating the furniture, to him, was a kind of sadistic act. I don't wanna be in his bedroom if he thinks that this is sadism. My wife and I had done this with furniture. This silly thing, you know, taking fairly new furniture and whacking it up and then painting it, antiquing it, distressing the wood by hitting it with chains, was something that a lot of people I knew did. But this exec saw it as being sadistic, and twisted, and what was funny about that scene?

GRANT TINKER:

Mary was distressing a table with a chain—and they thought that was just a crazy thing to do, y'know, a *sick* thing to do. That's what I was talking about before, where you just say, "God, what a waste this is, to argue about a silly thing like that."

ALLAN BURNS:

After we got that phone call from the CBS exec, we called Grant. He was still at Fox. And we said, "Grant, we've just been told that we can't shoot next week's show."

He said, "Which one is that?"

And we said, "It's the one about Rhoda's mother."

"That's hilarious! What do you mean you can't shoot it?"

"Well, they told us we can't."

He said, "The deal we've got with them, they can't exactly do that. We have creative control. And if we want to shoot something, we'll go ahead and shoot it. *I'm* telling you guys to go ahead and shoot it."

Quintessential comedic Jewish mom Ida Morgenstern (Nancy Walker) knows that Mary has just been on the phone with Rhoda . . . who's been avoiding her meddling mother at all costs. © CBS Television Network

JAY SANDRICH:

When Grant was running MTM, he would say no to the networks. "No, we're not going to do that. This is what my writers feel." And the notes that would come from the network—the writers would either pay attention to them, or *not* pay attention to them. But they were making the shows, and Grant's was the production company hired by the networks to make the shows. They didn't *tell* him how to make them. And he didn't tell his creative people how to make them. He would make suggestions . . . but the creative people were in charge.

ALLAN BURNS:

What this one had more to do with was, "How can you do this to one of your main characters? How are they ever gonna understand that Rhoda wouldn't want to see her?" And we said, "Because your parents drive you crazy. Everybody's parents drive every child crazy." If you could have been there when that scene was shot, where Mrs. Morgenstern says to Mary, "Just go back to what you were doing."

And Mary says, "No, that's alright."

She says, "No, really, I insist."

And Mary picks up that chain, and barely hits the thing with it—and then gets into it, and starts to laugh 'cause she realizes how ridiculous this has to look to Ida Morgenstern, that there's this pretty lady doing this. And when she starts to laugh, Mrs. Morgenstern says, "Well, it's nice you have a hobby that makes you happy."

The audience went to pieces. It was like when Walter Cronkite walked on in year six or seven, and the audience applauded for five minutes. Well, you have to cut the cameras. And Jay kept cutting the cameras for this in that scene, because the audience was so helpless with laughter. So we had to piece it together that way, so that by the time we got to that scene, the audience laughs but they don't come completely unglued.

Ironic that it was the one Jim and I won the Emmy for that year.

The CBS exec stuck around . . . and then, at a certain point, he just left, to move on to other projects to mess with. But he never liked *The Mary Tyler Moore Show*. He didn't like *M*A*S*H*, either, by the way.

VALERIE HARPER:

The same CBS liaison said I was too abrasive: "Let's have less of her. And no mother. Get that Jewish mother out of there." Which turned out to be a bona fide home run every freaking time she opened her mouth.

ALLAN BURNS:

After the "Jewish" proclamation? I don't know . . . I guess we just decided we were going to do this. We wanted a real contrast to Mary, a real foil. It worked. They never trotted the research out on us, on that one. Never did. And Ida Morgenstern was as much the quintessential Jewish mother as you'll ever find. They hated the show in so many different ways, that maybe that was a little further down their pecking order, y'know, about what they were going to hate about it.

Ladies First, At Last

From the very start, *The Mary Tyler Moore Show* sought to reflect the uniquely female point of view of its central character. Although the writing staff that launched the series was predominantly male—all of them sensitive, brilliant writers like Brooks and Burns, David Davis, Gordon Mitchell, Lorenzo Music, Steve Pritzker, Bob Rodgers, and Lloyd Turner—one of the early guiding forces on staff was Treva Silverman, who wrote the second episode of the series, "Today I Am a Ma'am." This was the show that definitively established Mary Richards and Rhoda Morgenstern (Valerie Harper would win four Emmy Awards in the role) as best friends, and featured the first of many intimate conversations they'd have over the years. Of the 168 episodes that would eventually air, forty of them would be penned by women writers, with Silverman scripting a record sixteen of them.

TREVA SILVERMAN, writer and story editor:

Mary was about behavior. So many sitcoms were about *setup/punchline*. Not that it didn't have its lovely, good share of setup/punchline, but it was about small things that people do . . . nuances. There was *subtext*, the famous word. It's what appeals to me about writing. My favorite kind of writing has always been: What's really going on underneath? What are people feeling but not saying? And *Mary Tyler Moore Show* was about that.

VALERIE HARPER:

I think that Treva Silverman was the only female writer in the beginning. There weren't many women comedy writers in the business at all in 1970. There just were not. There were guys with orange alpaca sweaters, with cigars, watching and saying, "Now that's funny," without laughing, y'know? The quintessential, "that's funny."

TREVA SILVERMAN:

It was a big deal for me, because there *weren't* women. I got a lot of publicity and attention as a woman who actually does this. There were very few . . . I was being written about in columns. And there was a big article in *Mademoiselle* magazine. When I did *The Mary Tyler Moore Show*, there had never been a female executive on a comedy show. I was also the first woman, solo, to win an Emmy for comedy.

And it was very scary for me, because I kept feeling, "God, if I fail, I fail in the name of all womanhood." I really, really did.

VALERIE HARPER:

Our guys were all kinda young, they were in their thirties. And Jim and Allan were writing *great* women. But Jim Brooks said, "I'm in no way chauvinistic, and it's not that men can't write women. But y'know, there's a world of comedy in my wife's purse. And I can't access it . . . I really don't get it when I look in there, and a woman would. That's why having Treva is really important, and we're going to bring along some other writers."

And they did: Mary Kay Place, and Marilyn Miller, and Monica McGowan . . . I mean, there's a ream of young women who started on that show.

ALLAN BURNS:

Mary Tyler Moore was about a woman who was proud of being single. *Unapologetically* single. Because that was something that was really happening at that time. We were a little behind the curve on realizing it, but we quickly caught up with it.

When women began to support the show in such numbers, it was because they saw themselves in it. You know, they were either approaching thirty, or were over thirty, and they were out there in the job market. And they were having a tough time because they weren't being treated as equals . . . which we had some fun with in some of the episodes we wrote, about equal work for equal pay. I think we were able to catch up and finally ride the crest of that . . . that feeling. I guess it's the same women who were watching *Sex and the City* and saying, "That's us."

TREVA SILVERMAN:

My recollection is that, at the time, people who were not married by thirty were like total, untouchable pariahs. Getting married right after college, or at least—God forbid—it shouldn't be past your mid- or late twenties. I remember the first show that I wrote. It was about Mary turning thirty. Somebody called her "Ma'am," and she freaked out. That had actually happened to me. I thought, "That's the line of demarcation. I am called a Ma'am!" Not a Miss, but a Ma'am. At that point, I would say that you had to do a hell of a lot of apologizing if you were past thirty and not married.

JAY SANDRICH:

I don't know that Mary's show ever set out to be the groundbreaking show that it became. That was not the concept. What happened, basically, is that it was the right show at the right time. And Mary was really the perfect spokesperson for young, single women who realized that, number one: they didn't have to have a man in their life full time to be able to have a wonderful life . . . and number two: they could go out and work.

We didn't sit around and talk about this—this was not something that was constantly talked about on the stage. I don't know what was going on in the offices, but I never got the feeling that the show set out to break these grounds.

Dating situations, by that time, yes. I remember doing a show where Mary stays out all night. Her parents are visiting and staying with her. And the mother and father are fit to be tied: "Where have you been? Who've you been with?"

"Well, it's none of your business."

And that was it. But the network had a real problem with it, too—that Mary Richards stays out all night. That she has a healthy sex life, and she isn't married. It was a different era. You have to project yourself back in time . . . to the days when you couldn't show beds. Y'know, on *The Dick Van Dyke Show*, they had to have twin beds. The whole rule was that if a man and woman were in bed, they had to have their feet on the floor. It was a different time.

I remember early on, scenes would come down. Maybe this isn't the exact situation, but . . . Lou would say, "Mary, get me a cup of coffee."

And Mary would say, "Yes, Mr. Grant."

Valerie would say, "You can't do that. You've gotta say, 'Would you mind getting me a cup of coffee?' And, 'If I feel like it, I'll do it.' "

That type of thing. 'Cause that's what feminists were saying at the time: that the secretaries and the assistants were not slaves. And yes, they'll be happy to get coffee for their boss—*if* they feel like it, if he asks them nicely. As *he* would get coffee for *them*. Well, none of us, at the time, were aware of these undercurrents. Mary was certainly not aware of it. Mary was married to Grant, and wasn't really in touch with what was going on in offices. Valerie just is a person who's always been in touch. And so she'd say it to Mary, or to Jim and Allan, and they'd laugh and do a rewrite.

VALERIE HARPER:

I had been doing a lot of reading through the 1960s of Steinem, and Germaine Greer, the Australian feminist—*The Female Eunuch*—but really, the mother of us all, Betty Friedan. That *Feminine Mystique* was so wonderful, and so earth-shaking. And then, in the 1970s, I was already working on the ERA, the Equal Rights Amendment.

JAY SANDRICH:

Valerie just had her finger on the pulse, if I can use that old phrase, of what was going on out there. And she would sort of gradually, in her own way, guide Mary. It was not only called MTM Productions, it was *The Mary Tyler Moore Show*—and Mary was just a wonderful person to work with, because she'd never demand anything. So if it worked, Mary would be happy to perform it, y'know, as long as she was comfortable with it.

But Valerie would sort of say, "Well, why don't you talk to the guys, and see if we can get a different line there."

VALERIE HARPER:

The writers felt it was very important. I think that's why the show has a real resonance about it. You're not writing men or women, you're writing human beings. But there's a sensibility and a detail that comes up . . . I remember one time, Ted says:

"I have a date tonight . . . uh, let's see . . . *BL* . . . *R* . . . *B* . . . "

"What?"

He says, "I have the girls under *blonde*, *redhead*, or *brunette* in my book."

That was the joke. And Treva said to the guys, "You know, you can't have Mary standing there. Get her out of the scene—or she's gotta have a rejoinder. She can't stand there and let that pig remark go."

"Is that a pig remark?"

"Yes. It's a pig remark, that women are in the thing without names. It might as well be a breast measurement. It's a hair color."

It's funny. Ted's a schmuck! The joke was fine. But for Mary to stand there mutely in 1970-something and let it go, that wasn't acceptable to Treva. And then the writers said, "That's right." I mean, so I saw the boys coming along, too.

TREVA SILVERMAN:

It was more when we were in the room together that those things would come up. Because it was the years that it was, I addressed myself more to that no sexism stuff should get into the scripts. We were all just . . . stuff was just happening in the air. It was an interesting group—people who were in marriages, out of marriages, getting divorces.

I remember a line in a script about Mary: Which did she want, a career or a husband?

I said, "If it were a man, would you ask that question?" The conventional feminist stuff. And the wonderful thing was that they *did* listen. I can imagine being on another show, saying the exact same things, and getting some kind of feedback like, "Oh, don't be so sensitive." But no, they absolutely did listen—and Jim and Allan particularly *wanted* that. They were glad to have it pointed out to them.

VALERIE HARPER:

There's an affinity, a knowledge, a ground of being that understands. For instance, one of the female writers did some bridesmaid dresses, where we looked like Little Bo Peep. And Allan said, "We would never have come up with that. We didn't know that was an issue." The idea that the dresses are so God-awful, 'cause somebody is two hundred pounds, and somebody is eighty pounds, and then someone is high-waisted—and we're all shlepped into these ugly dresses that are moderately priced. It was hilarious, but it was out of the truth—and it was exaggerated slightly—although maybe not, I've been in some bad bridesmaid dresses! But that is the truth of the female experience that might not come up. It's not that men can't write women as human beings, and brilliantly . . . but it's that little minutia.

TREVA SILVERMAN:

I always wonder why people say it's a breakthrough show. And then I start thinking about it . . . and what I've come up with is that it's because so many young women, and older women, identified with Mary and Rhoda. Everything that they did was kind of really taken in, and taken as gospel: "Hey, I guess this is okay." Not just because they did it on television, but because of *who* was doing it on television. It was Mary and it was Val.

So anything that happened there, every little thing, was picked up and kind of run with as, "This is okay. I feel better about myself because one of these two women is feeling the same way that I am."

JAY SANDRICH:

Mary was one of these very rare combinations of a really good actress who could do comedy, and somebody you just loved to look at. And somebody you'd like. Valerie was the exact same thing—Rhoda was played, originally, as

Female viewers across the land found they could relate to unapologetically single best pals Mary Richards and Rhoda Morgenstern. © *CBS Television Network*

frumpy and dumpy, and had no self-confidence . . . and yet, she's just an extremely attractive woman. And funny and likeable in her New York sort of way. You know, more aggressive.

VALERIE HARPER:

She was based on a woman named Rhoda who worked in a brassiere factory in the Bronx. Or a lingerie company, something like that. I did a New York accent . . . and I brought an attitude, and a physicalization that wasn't exactly my own. I'd been living in California, and wasn't particularly New York. So I used close friends and family . . . and gestures, things that I'd seen them do.

TREVA SILVERMAN:

Allan Burns has always said he felt that in "Today I Am a Ma'am," I created who Rhoda really became—much more than she was in the pilot. Because what they were trying to do in the pilot was the *opposite* of Mary. Mary Richards was kind of shy, hadn't really found her voice—she'd found a little bit of a voice. So they were very wisely trying to do the exact opposite with Rhoda. Y'know, who's this abrasive *I want what I want* kind of woman? And they did it brilliantly. But I saw Rhoda a different way—I'd seen Valerie perform—and just kind of instinctively softened some of the edges, but kept her spirit.

JAY SANDRICH:

There was a very interesting thing in the show where Mary and Rhoda are bridesmaids at a wedding, and the bride sends them these really horrible-looking dresses. In the run-through, the first time they put 'em in clothes, Valerie walked out and I said, "You are gorgeous!"

And she said, "Don't say that."

She really didn't feel it. Valerie, as a person, probably to this day never thinks she's beautiful . . . but of course, she is. And a really beautiful human, aside from that. A caring, wonderful person. But she was really good-looking, and just didn't think of herself in those terms. That's one of the reasons she could play the character so well . . . because she understood Rhoda. She didn't have a lot of self-confidence in her physical looks.

TREVA SILVERMAN:

Women have always had sidekicks . . . in 1930s comedies and on television. And the main person would always be pretty. That's why she was the main person and, y'know, that's how people wanted it to be. So there always had to be somebody who was *not* the main person—and she would always be kind of funny looking, or real heavy, or she would be man crazy, and the men would never like her.

Well, how lovely that the casting was Valerie.

'Cause Valerie is, and was, an unusually beautiful woman. It was her *attitude* towards herself that made her a sidekick. So many young women in the world identified with Valerie . . . and they weren't identifying with someone who was unpleasant-looking. There was always something undesirable to men about the sidekick. And because it was Rhoda's attitude towards herself, so many women could say, "That's me. That's me! I am secretly Rhoda, because these are the secret feelings I have about myself." Self-deprecating, not really good enough, and sort of a sidekick mentality. I think most of the women who *did* identify, identified with Rhoda and not Mary. And I love that Valerie was such a lovely Rhoda.

VALERIE HARPER:

I think that Rhoda wanted a relationship that would be fun. She had a lot to share. So I never thought of her as man-hungry . . . I thought she was seeking a home, a place to be. And, she had her mother *hocking her tchainik* like you cannot believe to *do* this. She grew up in that—*that* was the measure of success. In the course of the show, Rhoda transformed in a strange way. It got to be that she and Mary would rather sit with each other and have pizza than go out with a crummy date.

TREVA SILVERMAN:

It's the Episcopalian and Jew. The whole dynamic of Mary and Rhoda was: "Oh, I can't do such a thing. Nobody would approve of that." And Rhoda being the "C'mon, c'mon, let's do it. C'mon, you can do it!" That's really the Episcopalian and Jew.

VALERIE HARPER:

One day, fooling around at the end of a scene, Mary said something . . . and that was the end. But I kept talking: "You see, Mary, that's your problem. You trust people. You're too trusting."

And she's going, "Yeah, I know . . . " and she's in the kitchen, chopping, and she's nodding. And Jim and Allan are laughing. They said, "That's great!" So we did several of those. They said, "Valerie, do one of those run-ons."

It wasn't making up lines. It was just staying on something and doing a little improvisation. I felt I wanted to *be* her. I wanted her cute little figure, I wanted to wear white pants without an over blouse, like she could do. A tucked-in shirt, for God's sake. So I loved her, *but*: I was from *New York*, I was from *da Bronx*, I had seen it all and done it all, and this was a Midwestern shiksa. And I was gonna straighten her out. That's when I started—it just came out: one day I called her "Kid."

And I asked them, "Is that okay?" 'Cause you never put lines in, never. You never wrote. You'd ask, "Can I say this or that?"

They said, "Yes, that's fun!"

It was: Mary's got a career, Rhoda's got a job. *She's* got this great apartment, *I* have a garret. But don't forget, I'm from New York, and I've been around the block. She'd say, "Rhoda, why do you go out with these guys? Terrible Ernie, the termite guy, he picks you up with that bug on the truck." She was always my kind of counselor: "Stand up for yourself, Rhoda. Think better of yourself." But it was in such a space of love . . . and I think that's why the friendship was so wonderful. Because we would tell the truth to each other, and we were very different. But we loved each other, and it was very recognizable to women everywhere, of all ages.

TREVA SILVERMAN:

Over the years that *Mary* was on the air, Rhoda changed a lot. She changed from, "God, I'm such a schmuck and who would bother to live with me," and started to get a lot more self-esteem. She blossomed.

We all went away on hiatus . . . and Valerie had been adorably zaftig. When she came back, she'd lost twenty pounds. And Jim and Allan went absolutely crazy, *loving* that she'd lost the twenty pounds, because now we'd get to write about it! So they asked me. I was given this wonderful gift of writing the show where we addressed what it was like for Rhoda. It was called "Rhoda the Beautiful." It was manna from heaven . . . because it was about Rhoda confronting her lack of self-esteem.

Mary brings her up against a mirror and she says, "Look. For God's sake, look!" And Rhoda refuses to acknowledge that she looks good.

She says, "What's wrong with this whole thing is I can never say, 'Gee, if I only lose twenty pounds, I can really look great.' " It was about her coming to terms. That was in season three . . . and she won an Emmy for that.

VALERIE HARPER:

The thing is, they wrote from life. They wrote women they knew . . . and they started writing to people's strengths. We would wanna surprise the guys when they came down, 'cause the material was so good. A lot of times you have to *make* material . . . not even better, but . . . just *presentable*! So that a human person would say these words. But this had such richness that we didn't want to miss all the possibilities that they'd written in. The writing was between the lines, because behavior was going on, and actual human connection, and the foibles, the wants, the desires, the hubris. It was playwriting of the first order.

ALLAN BURNS:

When we were doing *Mary*, we were writing to please ourselves. What made *us* laugh was what was important to us, and as it turned out, people did get it. You're not too smart for the room. As subtle as *Seinfeld* could be, people got it. They never wrote *down*. Who else ever did stories that were about John Cheever being gay? And *Frasier* was so smart . . . it was so sophisticated that twenty years before that, nobody would have dreamt of doing a show as sophisticated as *Frasier*. That incredible dialogue, and the fact that they would throw references in that were fairly esoteric. What some people didn't get, someone *else* got. And there was enough really funny stuff in there to keep everybody watching.

"Chuckles Bites the Dust"—a classic episode of a classic sitcom: at Chuckles the Clown's funeral, grief-stricken Mary is besieged with uncontrollable laughter as Ted and Georgette (Georgia Engel) eye her with consternation. © CBS Television Network

TREVA SILVERMAN:

The night that our show premiered, there was this party. And Jim came up to me and said, "Oh, here's an honest face. Do you think that we're just doing another sitcom?"

And I said, "Absolutely not."

He said, "How can you tell?"

"Because another sitcom would've stopped at 'spunk.' We're the sitcom that says, 'I hate spunk.'"

Another sitcom would've done, "You've got spunk," and it would've gotten applause. But it wouldn't have been funny. It would've been, *let's admire the lead in the show.* Why that particular little sound bite is the most often repeated when they talk about *Mary Tyler Moore,* or when they show it, is because it turned the sitcom on its ear. Lou was saying the unsayable—and *it* was saying: We were not an ordinary sitcom.

A Sitcom Holds Up a Mirror, and We See Ourselves

5

On a crisp winter night in January of 1971, at 9:30 P.M.—a peculiar hour for a new comedy show to debut—American television history was made, and things would never be the same again. That was the night that the dysfunctional Bunker family was first unleashed on the public airwaves, breaking practically every rule and taboo on TV.

That is, if anyone happened to be watching. Not many were, not at the very start.

CBS, the network that dared to put producers Norman Lear and Bud Yorkin's new series *All in the Family* on the air when others would not, was on edge. Fearing a deluge of viewer complaints, they added scores of extra telephone operators to their switchboards that evening . . . but, as Lear later wryly noted, "They thought some state would secede from the Union. Nothing like that happened."

The first few verses of its opening theme song, "Those Were the Days," told us right away where this middle-aged, conservative, blue-collar U.S. citizen and his sweetly scatterbrained but dutiful housewife were coming from. The series' stars, Carroll O'Connor and Jean Stapleton, sat side by side at an upright piano and sang in harmony of a time when their world was a simpler place, back when bandleader Glenn Miller led the hit parade and guys like Archie had it made.

Today, of course, the name "Archie Bunker" is a household word. Residing in a working-class neighborhood in Queens, New York, with a full household to support—including loving wife, Edith (dubbed the "dingbat"); cherished daughter Gloria (his "little goil"); and liberal, atheist, college student son-in-law Mike Stivic (the "meathead")—Archie resented anyone who might invade his turf or usurp any piece of his pie, seeing them only in distinctly stereotyped roles. His long list included African Americans, Asians, Latins, Jews, liberals, Democrats, Communists, gays, lesbians, and anyone from any walk of life or corner of the globe other than his own.

All in the Family was stunningly audacious. In just the first handful of episodes alone, Archie fakes a back injury and purposely seeks out a certain type of lawyer—uniquely qualified, in his mind—to handle his case ("Get me a Jew!"), tries using his own brand of skewed logic to dissuade the black Jefferson family from moving into a nearby house ("There ain't a chicken shack or a rib joint within miles of here!"), vehemently insists that whites and other races don't have the same type of blood ("I bet down in Chinatown, they got a *chinky* Red Cross takin' blood for their own people"), mercilessly mocks one of Mike's artistic friends for being a "pansy," and pontificates about God with a black man ("It's interesting, too, the way you people worked yourselves up from the snakes and the beads and the wooden idols right up to *our* God."). Mike exhaustively engages his narrow-minded father-in-law in heated debate over these and many other twisted notions, while Mike and Gloria's articulate black friend, Lionel Jefferson (Mike Evans), delights in teasing Archie by repeatedly feigning the role of a stereotypically slow-witted black man as seen through the eyes of a bigot.

Throughout, Archie casually tosses off colorfully offensive racial epithets to describe any ethnicity or minority, including *spade, spic, chink, gook, dago, wop, mick, hebe, fruit, kraut,* and *polack,* something the American public may have been used to hearing in their local bar, but certainly not emanating from their friendly TV set in the living room. It shocked and delighted viewers, many of whom reveled in such honesty on television.

It also sparked countless heated debates: Does portraying a prejudiced character like Archie Bunker hold up bigots to ridicule, and reveal them to be the narrow-minded jerks that they are? Or, by showing him as all too human—even lovable at times—does it merely encourage those who think and speak like that, letting them know they're not alone and that it's okay to act this way?

No American TV show before it had ever come close to asking these questions, or tackling so many incendiary social and human issues (including religion, politics, gun control, poverty, racism, sexism, feminism, anti-Semitism, sexual orientation, the generation gap, impotence, menopause, rape, miscarriage, infidelity, divorce, death, and taxes), or simply portraying the average American family so realistically. The reason it all worked so well: brilliant writing that veered from side-splittingly funny to deeply poignant, a sublime cast of actors, a live studio audience reacting honestly—no canned laughs—and superb production and direction.

All in the Family began as just one of many projects that friends and long-time collaborators Norman Lear and Bud Yorkin were trying to get off the ground back in the 1960s. They'd already established successful careers producing, directing, and writing in New York and Hollywood, working with performers like Jerry Lewis and Dean Martin, Carol Channing, Martha Raye, and Don Rickles on television. By the early 1960s they'd largely turned their attention to making feature films, though without ever entirely abandoning their roots in TV. The pair continued to produce comedy specials for Fred Astaire, Jack Benny, and Danny Kaye, "But certainly neither one of us wanted to keep doing live television," as Yorkin recalls. "It's like waiting for your heart attack to come!"

Their comedy films were a mixed bag—some well-received, others box-office duds, but their creativity and talent was never in question.

As fate would have it, way across the pond at around the same time, a BBC comedy series called *Till Death Us Do Part*, created by Johnny Speight in 1965, had begun to cause a sensation. The British viewing public quickly turned a sitcom featuring a middle-aged, misanthropic working stiff named Alf Garnett and his feuding live-in son-in-law, Mike, into a huge hit, and it didn't escape the notice of Americans both in the United States and abroad . . .

In the Beginning, It Was *Alf* in the Family

ALAN WAGNER, former V.P. of Program Development at CBS:
We had a guy working in our research department who loved wine, and he'd gone to London and Paris on a wine-buying trip: Mark Golden. Mark was an ex–Marine who walked around still carrying his service .45. A large, bullet-headed, bald eagle . . . very, very assertive. But his passion was wine. He went to Europe, and while he was in London he saw a TV show called *Till Death Us Do Part*, and called me when he got back and said, "There's this really funny show you should look at."

LARRY GELBART, television writer and producer:
You didn't watch it; you were *riveted* to it! It was blowing my mind. I was living in London with my wife and family . . . and never once having the foresight or the vision or the inclination to say, "This would be great in America." Because it was *unthinkable* that that could ever invade our land, and *Lucy* . . . you know? Interestingly enough, it came from England at a time when almost all television was public broadcasting there. It's a good case to be made for what happens when you don't have to worry about the terrible two A's: affiliates and advertising.

BUD YORKIN, producer and director:

I had also been in England, when I did *Inspector Clouseau*. When Blake Edwards couldn't do it, I ended up doing it. And I did see *Till Death Us Do Part* when I was there. I was amazed at it—what I could understand, the Cockney was so thick—but I was amazed at what I saw, and particularly what it dealt with.

ALAN WAGNER:

We got a tape—I'm not sure how—either Mark brought one back, or we got one . . . and I saw the tape and fell down. It was *really funny*. The one I happened to see was a Christmas show in which Alf pissed all over the Queen of England. I mean, it was hilarious, a screamingly funny show. I said, "This is tricky, nobody's ever gonna put this on the air, but we've got to get the rights somehow, we just *have* to." And we started making bids and inquiries on buying the show.

WILLIAM TANKERSLEY, former Director of Program Practices at CBS:

I was asked by Alan Wagner one day if I would look at this British comedy. So I looked at it—and I said, "That *could* be done here. It's sort of a Jackie Gleason with a little more bite to it . . . but if they take out some of the gross jokes, that could be done!" And then, I didn't hear from anybody about it for a couple of years.

NORMAN LEAR, writer, producer, and developer:

I read a squib in . . . I think it was *TV Guide*, describing this relationship between Alf Garnett and his son-in-law. And I said, "That's my Dad—and how did I never think of this?! That's my *father*." So I started to work on that, to think about that, make a bunch of notes on it. Just on the premise.

I knew that my Archie—he became Archie Justice—I wanted him to have far more humanity. I wanted him to love a daughter, and I wanted the daughter to love her dad. I wanted his wife to love him, whoever he was, *whatever* he was. So he had to have a good deal more. Alf Garnett had none. I was doing something different. I forget how many shows we'd already made before I saw any of theirs . . . I only saw one or two of theirs. It wasn't, basically, what we were doing at all . . . I had all the characters in my family. So I had half a dozen scripts before I ever saw their show.

And then I wanted to *see* it, and I wound up talking to a woman by the name of Beryl Vertue. She represented *Till Death Us Do Part*. Terrific lady. As I remember it, she made it easy. She was selling. She *wanted* to sell.

Till Death Us Do Part, *the pioneering British series that spawned* All in the Family. *Seen here (from l-r): daughter Rita (Una Stubbs), bigoted Alf Garnett (Warren Mitchell), son-in-law Mike (Anthony Booth), and Alf's wife Else (Dandy Nichols).* © *British Broadcasting Corporation*

ALAN WAGNER:

Somebody was bidding against us—we didn't know who. It was Norman Lear, but we didn't know that. Norman got the rights, and sold them to ABC.

BUD YORKIN:

Norman called me. He had read a story in America, and he said, "Jesus, let's do a television show on that." And I thought, "Well, you'll never get it on the air . . . but hey, if you wanna take a crack at it, be my guest! What can I say?" Which he did. Norman did the pilot script . . . and I liked it a great deal. What was there not to like? Again, I still said, "How do we get this on the air?" But we worked together somewhat on the script when I got back.

LEONARD GOLDBERG, former Head of Programming at ABC:

I had always felt that at ABC you had to do something *different* to attract an audience . . . So when the idea was presented, and then I read the script and committed to the pilot, I thought, "This is a very daring show." But if you're ABC, you can't just play it safe. You play it safe, you lose. So, we had to try it—it excited me.

MARTIN STARGER, former V.P. in Charge of Programming at ABC:

ABC was the third network. CBS and NBC were the twin Rocks of Gibraltar—and for Len and I, the challenge was fun. We were able to take chances 'cause we had nothing to lose, much like Fox Broadcasting later. In this era, just to give you the context of time, I had two assistants, one after another: Barry Diller was my executive assistant. He was Len's—and when Len left, he became *my* assistant. Some time later, when I put him in charge of movies for television, Michael Eisner became my assistant. We had some pretty good people in a very small department. It was electric! We were all young; we could try anything.

We needed comedies. *Bewitched* was one. We had a couple, but a weakness at ABC was half-hour comedies.

Norman Lear—who was not the Norman Lear we think of today—had this show that he wanted to do. And it was exciting. It was different. I said to myself, "Great idea. Terrific talent. And an urban half-hour comedy." We would've given anything to have Jackie Gleason in *The Honeymooners*, but CBS had that.

So, we did the first pilot.

Justice for All? Not Quite Yet

With partner Bud Yorkin off directing a feature film in Europe, Norman Lear set about casting their new pilot for ABC, originally called *Justice for All*. (The show's name next morphed into *Those Were the Days* before eventually settling on *All in the Family*.) Finding the right actor to portray his anti-hero, Archie Justice, was crucial. It had to be someone who could utter some of the awful things that Lear knew his character had to say, without completely turning audiences off—a rather tall order. His first choice? A rather short actor.

NORMAN LEAR:

The only actor I had in mind was Mickey Rooney. I called his manager, and I said, "I'm coming to California." I was in New York, editing *The Night They Raided Minsky's* . . . and I was coming out to do some casting, and Mickey Rooney occurred to me. Anyway, so I said, "I've got a pilot I want to talk to him about." And he said, "Well, he's right here! Why don't you talk to him?" So he put him on.

And I said, "I'm coming out. I'd love to talk to you about a show."

He said, "Tell me about it."

And I said, "Given the nature of the show—it's only a few days, Mickey—let me come out and see you, and I'll tell you about it."

He referred to himself in the third person: "No, no, you can tell the Mick anything, come on, come on."

So, I said okay. And I told him, basically, who Archie was.

There was a pause . . . and he said, "They're gonna kill ya in the streets, kid. They are gonna shoot you in the streets. You wanna do a show with Mick? Listen to this: Vietnam vet. Short. Blind. Private eye. Large dog!"

I said, "See ya." [laughing]

So, I came to California, to our office on Sunset Boulevard, Tandem Productions. And I don't remember a single actor reading for Archie but Carroll. 'Cause it must have happened early . . . He came in—his agent had the script—he came in, sat down, read half a page . . . and I knew in a flash. His sound was based on a cab driver he knew in New York. An Irish cab driver.

CARROLL O'CONNOR, performer:

We talked about the character and so forth, and he said some people thought he should be from Texas since he was a bigot. And I said, "No, no, make him a New York Cockney." The guy in the English show was a London Cockney. I was familiar with the British version . . .

So now comes the script and I thought it was terrible. I said, "I'm going to rewrite this script, and if he doesn't like it, then he can just get somebody else."

I rewrote the script all in pencil.

NORMAN LEAR:

He had rewritten the entire first act! That was the first of endless confrontations. This was something that went on for all the years.

JEAN STAPLETON, performer:

My agent called me to come up and see Norman Lear about this part in a series . . . Norman said that he had seen me in *Damn Yankees*, that that's how I came to his attention. And so I read.

And I was just amazed by its quality. Really good script. A comedy based in character and situation and so forth. And I thought to myself, "Wow, this on TV, how wonderful." Even then I thought that. And I read for him, and then I went back to Pennsylvania. Then I think I was called up again . . . Now I don't know their names, but I know that he saw every character actress in town for this part. He read everybody. And that's how I got the part.

NORMAN LEAR:

Marion Dougherty was the casting agent in New York, and she brought her in. She was in a play at the time, and she suggested I see her. She was *glorious*—she read like Edith.

JEAN STAPLETON:

She just had a zinger, about one line a page, that just broke his hot air. Every time it was a laugh. And so I think I said it in quite a wry and wise manner, knowingly, you know, a zinger. [laughs] Burst his bubble. And that's the way I played the

The Bunkers alone together in the kitchen: Edith ruminates while Archie complains. © 1971, 2005 ELP Communications, Inc.

first—the pilots and the first—which became the first show, because I had nothing else to base on. You don't know what comes later. You don't know much about these parts.

BUD YORKIN:

So, I directed the pilot. We quite liked it . . . but ABC tested it, and it tested very poorly. Those are the tests where they press a button if you like it, and another one if you don't like it. And a lot of them *didn't* like it, so the network, going along with those kinds of things, saw their way to not put it on. Two people out of the four—the kids—tested low.

LEONARD GOLDBERG:

In those days, there was a program board made up of the chairman of the company, Mr. Goldenson; his right-hand guy, Si Siegal; the president of the network, Tom Moore; and then the heads of the key departments: affiliates, sales, research, and advertising. We had a screening, and the program board attended. Normally, after a screening was over, I would get up and say, "This is where I think the show can go from here," and invite questions. So before we entered the programming scheduling meetings, they would feel comfortable about what the shows were.

The pilot ended . . . the lights slowly came up . . . I got up. We were sitting, Marty Starger and I, in the front row. We turned around . . . and there was no one in the screening room.

They were all gone. Literally. I looked over at Marty and said, "I don't think that went that well." I had never had that happen in the three years and probably seventy-five, eighty pilots I had made, some of which were pretty bad.

I quickly moved out of the room and down the hallway to the elevator, where I met Tom Moore, the president. I said to Tom, "What's going on? Where *is* everybody?" The elevator doors by now were opening. He stepped in, turned to me, and said, "We in senior management are going to pretend this pilot never happened. And for your own future, I would suggest you do the same." At which point the elevator doors closed. I was like, "I know this was a somewhat abrasive pilot" . . . but clearly, they were not in a mood to take that chance.

I went back to the room, and said, "Lemme say this: I don't think we're going to get a series commitment today."

And that was the end of *All in the Family* that season. I know that Marty managed to resurrect it . . . and he did another pilot.

MARTIN STARGER:

The show was terrific, I thought. It was a fresh breath of air, and it was vastly superior to most comedies. You did not have to be a genius to see that. So, we tried it again. We asked him to tone it down, if he could. Y'know—I'm making this up, but—if you had the word "kike" thirty-one times, can you do it four times? And the word "nigger" . . . could you cut it down? And we did some cast changes, as well. We were very close to the show—not telling Norman how to be funny, no one could—and he had his pulse on everything.

CARROLL O'CONNOR:

Norman said that ABC had said to him, "We want to do it again with two other kids." So when I came back from our trip to Europe—it was January or February—we went over to ABC studios downtown and we taped another pilot with another boy and girl. ABC rejected that, too. I forgot about it. I went over to Europe.

BUD YORKIN:

Again, ABC passed. Didn't think it was gonna work. I think there were several reasons . . . I don't think Leonard Goldenson was in love with hearing about *hebes* and *jungle bunnies* and everything—which was in the first one. We wanted to show where we were heading. Maybe they tested it again and it tested poorly, too.

MARTIN STARGER:

I couldn't get it on the air. Couldn't get it past our management. They were good people, and they took a lot of shots on a lot of things, believe me. But when faced with management who was getting input from the sales department . . .

"The advertisers are not gonna buy this," was what they said. "We have to sell commercials, we're a third network. Why would you give us a burden like this? It's hard enough." CBS was sold out; NBC was sold out. The ABC salesmen were going up and down Madison Avenue, trying to sell shows. What advertiser is going to go into a show that is going to offend people? Who's going to buy that in the South?

At any rate, it was probably better received than the first one, because it was toned down a bit . . . but we could not pick it up, and that was the end of it.

FRED SILVERMAN, former V.P. of Programs at CBS:

What happened was, ABC had acquired a show called *Turn-On*, from Bristol Myers. It was from George Schlatter—he was then very hot, doing *Laugh-In*. And it was in such bad taste that it literally never made the West Coast! They cancelled the West Coast feed of it. They only showed it wherever the live feed was.

GARY OWENS, performer:

Turn-On, the world's shortest show. I was the announcer on that. There was a sketch about two nuns talking, and as I recall, they're chatting about using contraceptives and the pill . . . and as the camera rolls back, you see that they're both pregnant. That was kind of shocking even then, in the 1960s. I was busy that night that it came on, and so I've never seen the show!

LEONARD GOLDBERG:

It was going to be ABC's irreverent answer to *Laugh-In* and *Smothers Brothers* . . . but because we were third, we had to push the envelope even further.

I'll never forget this. It went on the air on a Wednesday night. I got a call from ABC that the switchboard was lighting up, and most of the calls were very negative. In fact, one call got through to my apartment—and the man was not complimentary. Somehow he got my number, I don't know how. He said, "Where do you find your ideas, on the walls of bathrooms?"

What happened was—talk about perfect timing—there was a groundswell building in the country against all the drugs, perceived sexuality, the whole liberal, hippie movement. And I caught the tip of the wave. If I was surfing, it would've been perfect. But I happened to be the final straw . . . and so all the pent-up fury that had been building in society amongst the more conservative groups—the "silent majority"—I gave them an opportunity to vent their spleens, and they did. Was it any more than *Laugh-In* or *Smothers Brothers*? No. But it was the straw that broke the camel's back. Maybe I got the perfect wave, but I wiped out!

So, that was the end of *Turn-On*.

FRED SILVERMAN:

They got so criticized for running this thing that it scared them off. It scared them off from doing *anything* like *All in the Family*. And as a result of that *Turn-On*, they walked away . . . They said, "We just can't do this." They were fearful, and they dropped the show. Or else I'm pretty sure it would have gone on the air then.

ABC's Nay Becomes CBS's Aye

BUD YORKIN:

From that point, Norman and I went to David Picker at United Artists—and got a deal to make a low budget film based on *All in the Family*. That was the next move. We had talked about it somewhat, and I think Norman was about ready to sit down and open up the story. We knew where we were going . . . it was going to be a small-budget picture and a fairly intimate one, which you can still do with that family . . .

MICHAEL DANN, former V.P. of Programming at CBS:

One day I got a call from [agent] Sam Cohn. We had worked together—I was the chairman of the Democratic National Committee for Television when McGovern ran, and Sam was active. And Sam called me and said, "Mike, can I show you a pilot? I want to know, we respect your opinion. Can I come down with it?" I said, "Yeah, come on."

And when I looked at it, it was the goddamnest thing I ever saw! And then I called up Fred Silverman, Irwin Segelstein, and Alan Wagner, my three top programmers, and *they* loved it. I figured we'd learn something from it, if nothing else—I certainly didn't think we were going to *buy* it—and they went absolutely bananas over it. They thought it was the best thing they ever saw . . . and they knew all the problems.

WILLIAM TANKERSLEY:

I was getting ready to go to Washington—we were going to a hearing . . . and I had grabbed my briefcase, when Mike Dann came down the hall and asked, "Can you come down and look at a pilot film?"

I said, "I can't do it. I'm headed for a plane."

"You've gotta see *some* of this, at least!"

So I said all right, and I went down—they'd just started the film before I got there. The lights were dim. And all of a sudden here came this show, with more bad taste, and toilet flushings, and everything in the world. To whoever was in there in the darkness, I said, "My God! We're in trouble in Washington, we're going down there, and now you throw *this* at me, for God's sake?!" And I left.

FRED SILVERMAN:

Then we called Bob Wood in to look at it. He didn't know what to make of it, but he just laughed to death, he thought it was the funniest thing he'd ever seen. Y'know, he was a USC guy, so I'm not sure whether he was laughing *with* or *at* Archie Bunker!

MICHAEL DANN:

And then we showed it to Bill Paley.

FRED SILVERMAN:

Paley hated the show. *Hated it.* He thought it was vulgar, it was coarse, and really, really disliked it . . . but he ultimately couldn't overrule the whole network. Or he'd have had an awful lot of unhappy people. I think if anybody was responsible for *All in the Family* coming to CBS, it was Bob Wood. He totally embraced the show, and he was just very, very courageous, and had a mind like a laser beam. He knew exactly what he wanted that network to be.

NORMAN LEAR:

Bob Wood said, "Come on in. I want to talk about this." I just had finished editing *Cold Turkey*, and the powers that be at UA offered me a three-picture deal on the spot, to write, produce, and direct. I remember their saying, "There's just Blake Edwards, and Woody Allen . . . " and somebody else maybe . . . "and you. You've *gotta* do this, there's nobody else that writes, produces, and directs." So it was a thrilling offer.

And the week I'm considering *that*, there's Bob Wood and an offer to do the show! So it didn't take a lot of courage to say, "We're going to do it my way." All my family and friends said, "You've got to do the films, you've got to take the three-picture deal. They'll never pick up the show . . . they'll air it once, they'll take it off . . . it's too different, they won't stay with it . . . " You know, all of the advice you'd expect. But I guess I felt the three-picture thing isn't going to go away after a month, or six, or whatever—they'll be there—so we took the CBS deal. It was pretty secure. I mean, I don't think I'd get points for that . . . but that was the situation.

And then he said, "Why don't we do it first as a pilot?" 'Cause he hadn't seen the two young people I was going to do it with, two new young people. I said, "No."

CARROLL O'CONNOR:

I was over in Europe for more than a year when I got the call that Norman had sold the show. He'd got it back from ABC and he'd sold it to CBS, and CBS wanted to do it. No pilot. They just wanted, well, a pilot in the sense that our pilot would be the first show on the air . . . That was it. And we were bought for a firm thirteen shows.

BUD YORKIN:

We did the same show, the third time. I knew that show by heart at that stage. They gave us thirteen, but they had an out after three. They could pay off the cast, which they would do and so forth—they had a way to get out. So we went on the air with only three . . . I think only three episodes done.

ALAN WAGNER:

The *next* big problem was finding a name for this thing. We couldn't call it whatever the hell ABC called it, and we weren't going to call it *Till Death Us Do Part*. So I ran a contest in Television City. Everybody wrote down four or five names, and *All in the Family* won—not because it was so good, but because it was the least offensive of all the things we had!

MICHAEL DANN:

There was practically an opening line in it, where they all got uptight about it. It's Sunday morning . . . and his son-in-law was coming down the stairs, buttoning his pants . . . and then his daughter is coming down. Archie says,

"On Sunday morning?!" You've gotta know—that set the stage that this is going to be a different kind of show from anything else you've put on. That was the major breakthrough for situation comedies.

NORMAN LEAR:

The story was that Archie and Edith were in church. It was the very first episode. And Mike and Gloria ran upstairs to make love. When they came down, I had Mike adjusting his shirt . . . I don't remember whether it was adjusting his shirt, period, or adjusting it a certain way with his trousers . . . but it was a big deal for a couple of days, 'cause they were watching *very closely* at dress rehearsal, and so forth. There was a line that went with it—Archie had a line, "Eleven-ten of a Sunday mornin'!"

PERRY LAFFERTY, former V.P. of Programs at CBS:

I think a few stations didn't take it, as I recall . . . not too many, but there's always a few. It was too far out—the sex had gone on when they went to church. Well, they didn't want to do that.

ALAN WAGNER:

I thought the show was going to be a long shot. When it finally got scheduled, they scheduled it in the least dangerous spot in the world . . . so if it flopped, it was going to kill a news program, it wouldn't kill anything else. And everyone was certain it was going to. I tested *All in the Family*, and it was the worst testing show in history, at that point: "A guaranteed failure, guaranteed less than a twenty share," which in those days was heinous.

FRED SILVERMAN:

We all recognized that it was a funny comedy. God knows, we didn't know if it's gonna *work* or not, and they may burn the building down, but it was the kind of thing where you said, "We'll put it on in the middle of the season."

And we put it on in the worst time period in the schedule: on Tuesday night, 9:30. The lead-in was *Hee-Haw*, and the lead-out was the *CBS News Hour.* So I mean, it was the *worst* time period—opposite the *Movie of the Week* on ABC, which was then the number-one show. We had to go easy . . . You know, we weren't going to put it on following *Beverly Hillbillies*. You just couldn't do that. So we kind of snuck it on the air.

NORMAN LEAR:

And then I got word that they were going to air the *second* show first, and I said, "No, I don't want to do the second show, I want to do the *first* show first." I thought the first show showed 360 degrees of Archie. And I used to say that to them, and then I used to say, "Look. With the first script, we jump in the water and we get all wet. You can't get wetter than all wet—and this is the one that does it. We need to get *all wet* together, so that we know what we have." But they were going to do the second show first.

WILLIAM TANKERSLEY:

I said, "Lord, we can't open with that pilot! We can't edit it—I've looked at it. You can't edit that." I'm a good editor, but that one we couldn't work with.

I came back from meetings in Florida one day . . . deep snow in New York, and warm in Florida . . . and I caught a cold, and was hoarse. And had to go to the office before I went home to Manhasset. So I was in there, maybe 8:00 at night . . . and Norman had left a call. I called him back, envisioning him sitting beside the pool, in warmth, while I'm in New York in the snow. And he wanted to open with the pilot.

I said, "No, you can't do it. That's gonna blow the roof off."

He argued, and argued, and argued—he *wanted* to blow the roof off! And he turned out to be right, I think. He just lucked out. Because if you read all the reviews, everybody in the country thought it was horrendous.

I finally said, "Alright. You're going to blow the whole series, Norman, but go ahead."

He wore me out! With the hoarseness and everything else, I just decided, "Fine. Why should I protect you if you want to do it?" That's why I gave in. God.

NORMAN LEAR:

It wasn't until the night before we were going on the air—I was still working on the fifth script, or the sixth script, it was at night—I remember calling my wife and saying, "I just got a call. They're going to do the first show." That was twenty-four hours before—three hours later in New York. Because I had convinced them I wouldn't be there—and I *wouldn't* have been there—if they hadn't done it.

FRED SILVERMAN:

Norman would just not budge an inch. He said, "You bought this show, and this is the show I'm going to deliver. You don't like it? Then we're not gonna do the show."

Great, But Is Anybody Watching?

That week's issue of TV Guide had, in fact, run a "Close Up" sidebar entitled, "A Lighthearted Look at Prejudice," which alerted the public to the network's insecurity: "Due to the series' controversial nature, the subject matter for tonight's episode was undecided at press time," the blurb concluded. "CBS executives might even change the program's title." On January 12, 1971, anyone who tuned in to CBS at 9:30 P.M. saw an unusual disclaimer appear across their TV screens:

> *WARNING: The program you are about to see is* **All in the Family.** *It seeks to throw a humorous spotlight on our frailties, prejudices, and concerns. By making them a source of laughter, we hope to show—in a mature fashion—just how absurd they are.*

WILLIAM TANKERSLEY:

I don't know who drafted that statement at the beginning, the disclaimer— I didn't. Maybe the law department. I never believed in those things, anyway. Anything I approved didn't need a disclaimer! But that one—I don't remember, I might have said fine, but I didn't give the language.

ALAN WAGNER:

One of the agents for the show—for Norman, I guess—was Herman Rush. He had this huge house over in the flats of Beverly Hills, not far from where I lived, but he had a *real* mansion. And he and I sat, almost literally holding hands that night of the premiere, certain that our careers were over, certain that we had taken this fatal step into the abyss. CBS had hired extra phone operators to handle the flood of phone calls from the first episode—and we sat there in Herman's den, mourning the end of the universe in effect, and hoping that we'd be able to recover from this. Because we had done this very brave thing.

And nobody called. The show got no numbers . . . Nobody paid any attention to it . . . and it kind of just sat there.

NORMAN LEAR:

I remember it very well because of all the anticipation. They had, y'know, eighty-some phones—a lot of people on phones. They put on extra lines and extra operators. So I remember it from that standpoint—that nothing much happened. I don't remember being nervous, because we were working that night on the fifth or sixth episode—*writing.* I mean, writing was a nineteen, twenty-hour day. So I was working too hard on the next script. But my *interest* was, will there be so many phone calls?

I knew by then it worked. The cast was just too good, too funny. I'd seen it too many times not to know. And I'd seen it with a live audience when we made it, so I knew it was going to do well with an audience. I didn't know what the response would be to Bunker . . . but, as the network realized later, it just didn't happen. The people are way ahead of the people who think *for* them!

BUD YORKIN:

I think it was basically Fred Silverman who kept pushing for it, to give it a chance. And we picked up nothing, 'cause we were following *Hee-Haw* on Tuesday nights. [dryly] That was a great lead-in for this show. So y'know, it had nothing going for it, to be honest with you, as far as helping it. But then some reviews started coming out. There was a big story in the *New York Times* . . . that caught everybody's attention.

NORMAN LEAR:

It had gotten this terrible notice from Laura Z. Hobson, who wrote *Gentleman's Agreement*. She wrote a big article condemning the show . . . a major piece for the *New York Times* Sunday section, *killing* the show because it was insincere that I never used the word "niggers." And then they allowed me to answer it the next week, or two weeks later. It was an interesting exchange.

BUD YORKIN:

She was pissed, but on the other side of it there was a very big "pro." There were *two* stories in the same paper. One was very positive, and then there was Laura . . . the *New York Times* dedicated that whole page to *All in the Family*. We thought that was great. It certainly helped.

So, we were kind of struggling along . . . but the shows got better. I was proud. And certainly Norman was spending more time with it than me, 'cause at the same time I was trying to edit *Start the Revolution Without Me*, and a few other things. Norman was really running it far more than I was. I'd read scripts, and make my notes, and then talk, and go to tapings . . . I didn't have time to direct it. That's how John Rich got in. We couldn't keep a company going if we both were doing the same thing.

NORMAN LEAR:

We were going to be dropped. I think the reason the show *made* it was, it was *on* long enough. And the only reason it was on long enough was that it went

The classic sitcom's main cast, as constituted when All in the Family *finally made it onto the air: (rear) Rob Reiner and Sally Struthers; (foreground) Jean Stapleton and Carroll O'Connor.* © 1971, 2005 ELP Communications, Inc.

on in January . . . so that there were shows left to be seen when the other two networks went into reruns. That's when two things happened: The other networks went into reruns, and the show that they'd heard discussion about, they started to turn to.

The Emmy Awards asked me to do a cold open with the Bunkers sitting down to watch the Emmys that year. So, before the credits, before anything, boom! It was the family. We did a three, four-minute scene about them anticipating the start of the Emmys—that's how they got into the show that year. And *that* was a big boost. After that, the ratings really started to go up.

MARTIN STARGER:

Bob Wood stuck by it. But they didn't have the station relation problems that ABC did, they didn't have the sales problems that ABC did. You didn't want to go through schadenfreude, but I think I was guilty of hoping it didn't work . . . but then I'd say, "That's wrong. Because Norman Lear deserves it to work, and it's going to be a hit."

Everyone said, "See? See?" the first few weeks.

I said, "Wait. Just wait."

And that's what happened. As a result of that, look at all the spinoffs that came out of that show. They would've all been on ABC, and it would've changed the history of television.

On May 9, 1971, just a few short months after it had debuted, *All in the Family* took home its first set of Emmy Awards. The show was lauded as Outstanding Comedy Series as well as Outstanding New Series, and Jean Stapleton won her first Emmy for her portrayal of Edith Bunker, beating castmate Carroll O'Connor to the honor by one year. Over the series' nine-year run, its cast, crew, and creators would go on to numerous Emmy wins.

JEAN STAPLETON:

[Edith's] character evolved in the first thirteen weeks, as it did for all of us. And she evolved into this woman. I didn't even use the nasal quality in my voice in that first reading. We saw one episode of the English series called *Till Death Us Do Part*, and that wonderful actress who played the wife was as abrasive as Archie, as whatever his name was in the series. That was a hint about how to go with this.

But, of course, when we got into rehearsal, and the fact that we were in New York where I knew everybody hurried, and the abusive demands on Bunker's part, pushed Edith into a run. She was hurrying to get things on the table, etcetera. That's how the little run rose and became a part of the charac-ter . . . And I added the nasality because I had used it in *Damn Yankees* for the woman, for comic purposes. I thought, "Well, I'll give her that nasality. I'll steal it from myself." And that's how that developed.

BOB SCHILLER, writer:

The sweetest thing that ever lived . . . and funny. She developed that little walk that was so characteristic—that little half-run—to be subservient. Wonderful character.

NORMAN LEAR:

Edith was *open*. If she thought it, it fell from her mouth. The question we asked ourselves was, "In the toughest situations, how would Jesus react?" That's the way we wrote her. That's why she didn't see a transvestite as anything unusual . . . she saw the humanity of the person.

JEAN STAPLETON:

A very compassionate individual . . . a peculiar way of arriving at things and thoughts . . . not very bright, not well-educated, but a great sense of wisdom and heart. I guess I would describe it that way. And also fun—a sense of joy about her, and just great love for everyone, and a perception about people that was instinctive, intuitive. But certainly not intellectual.

NORMAN LEAR:

Y'know, this is the kind of miracle in casting . . . it's in the stars. I don't mean the stars of stage and screen. You *can't* take credit for this. You can take credit for the good fortune . . . but the chemistry that existed between the four of them, in every direction—whether it's Gloria to Archie, or Archie to Gloria, or Archie and Mike. In every direction. Edith and Gloria, Edith and Mike— that's a gift of the gods. I never think I cast it. It *happened*.

One of my favorite pieces of philosophy was by Goethe, who said, "At the moment of commitment, the entire universe conspires to assure your success." And this was that kind of conspiracy.

JEAN STAPLETON:

It was very honest and very funny . . . and it was true and it was contemporary and it brought up issues, too. I loved that. But I remember Norman telling us never to count on a success, either. And there wasn't much attention paid in the first thirteen on the air. It's when we started the reruns that summer that the audience began to grow and grow and grow, and we went zooming ahead.

ALAN WAGNER:

Clearly, it was a quality show . . . so it started getting numbers against repeat competition, that's where Freddie had moved it.

FRED SILVERMAN:

I remember traveling out to the coast that summer, and I looked at some of our new shows. We had a show called *Funny Face*, with Sandy Duncan. That was scheduled at 8:00 on Saturday night, and it just was awful. Just the worst! She was cute, but the show stunk. This was my first year on the job. And I said to myself, "Jesus Christ, if I don't do something—I don't know what to do, 'cause we're gonna have a disaster on Saturday!" And then Saturday night was a lot more important than it is now. There was very high viewing on Saturday.

And so I called Bob up and I explained how terrible this *Funny Face* was. And that, y'know, we have a show that just won all these Emmy Awards, and the damn thing looks like it's growing. I said, "Let's take a deep breath, and let's change the schedule. Let's move it to the beginning of Saturday. We'll take *My Three Sons* and move that in place of *All in the Family* on late Monday."

See, this is how courageous he was. He said, "Go ahead and do it."

And we changed the schedule in August, recognizing that all the promotional stuff had gone out already. There were ads, and all that. He said, "The hell with the ads. Let's just get the schedule right." So we put it on at 8:00. In those days, you got overnights from New York, Chicago, and Los Angeles . . . and I thought that the research guy was *drunk* when I called him.

I said, "So?"

And he said, "Well, New York: seventy-five."

"I beg your pardon? What was that?"

"Chicago: eighty."

I said, "Jay, have you been drinking!?"

From the very moment it went in there, it ignited all of Saturday night. *Funny Face*, bad as it was—we'd slid *Funny Face* in at 8:30—ended up the number-two show. *All in the Family* had a sixty-five, and *Funny Face* dropped into the high forties. It had such a halo effect. *All in the Family* just singularly made the CBS television network. It gave us that one hit, that one defining show. Not only was it an enormous audience hit, but it just was kind of a model for what Bob Wood and I wanted that network to look like: being very, very progressive . . . being very, very urban . . . being very cutting edge.

Nobody Fucks with Success

BUD YORKIN:

We were breaking a lot of ground. So much so, that I don't believe you could get that show on the air today. I think it would be much more difficult today, living in a much more conservative time. They don't want to deal with the subjects that we dealt with . . . they were too honest.

FRED SILVERMAN:

When the scripts start coming in . . . You know, week in and week out, the Broadcast Standards department, they were used to policing the *Beverly Hillbillies* and *Green Acres*—and then, all of a sudden *this* thing! And they had just gotten over the *Smothers Brothers* experience. They didn't want another *Smothers Brothers*.

NORMAN LEAR:

There's an expression: "Getting away with." And I hated that. We never tried to *get away with*. We never put three "shits" or "fucks" or whatever the equivalent would be in there in order to get away with one. We just didn't play *any* games at all . . . we were dead serious about what we wanted to do. And I think they caught on to that—that we were not playing games.

The things they would often carp about—this was not Tankersley, this was people in his department . . . these were just average executives. I mean, they were not professionals in this arena—and their ideas of what you *could do* and *couldn't do* were silly. Sometimes there'd be something and you'd say, "How could they not pick on this? And they're dealing with *this*?!"

But executive life is full of people making stupid decisions. That's why the boss works.

PERRY LAFFERTY:

They didn't talk Norman Lear out of doing much, I'll tell you that. He was older, he had more experience, and he was very tough. And he just held the line. It was like, "You don't wanna do it this way? Let's not do it at all." The battles came down, in the early days, mostly to lines: "You can't say this." It wasn't about whole shows, it was more about lines, and fights about maybe a scene or something . . . but the minute it got numbers, that was over!

FRED SILVERMAN:

I really, very wisely, tried to stay out of the Standards arena. I pushed Norman to go as far as he wanted to. Y'know, then it was up to Tankersley to pull his hair out—that wasn't *my* problem. I understand that there were really great battles . . . but you couldn't have a battle with Norman, because he had all the ammunition. And the network was not about to lose *All in the Family*.

NORMAN LEAR:

One of the great truths of show business is the old saw that nobody fucks with success. It doesn't work 100 percent, but it works 80 percent.

MICHAEL ROSS, writer and story editor:

In effect, compared to other shows, we had carte blanche. From the writers I spoke to, friends of mine, they would get so much flak from the network—every week, every week, they wouldn't let up. I'm sure some of them were jealous . . . But fortunately, they didn't know the leeway that we had. And we wouldn't lay that into them. We wouldn't want them to feel bad.

SUSAN HARRIS, writer:

They were writing *people*. It was not set-ups and jokes. Before that, comedy was really about nothing . . . "Honey, I burned the pot roast." Or "crashed the car." It was really very simpleminded stuff. This was really *about* something. And the people were characters. You didn't laugh because of a joke—people don't talk in jokes. You laughed because of who they were, and how you could expect them to react. And that was a dream. That was writing!

I wrote some episodes. I was freelancing, and Norman had me in to see the pilot that had not been aired yet—and I thought it was remarkable. It was like nothing I'd ever seen before. And I wrote an episode . . . and then I wrote more. I wasn't on staff. He had asked me to be on staff, but I had an infant, and I would not take a job that took me away from the house.

BARRY HARMAN, writer:

Another show that I had tried to write for was *The Mary Tyler Moore Show*—we did a sample script for it—about Mary finding out that a guy she was dating was gay. And the comment that came back was, "Understands the characters, but we'd never put this story on." This was not the kind of humor she was doing.

BOB SCHILLER:

We were always very jealous of *The Mary Tyler Moore Show*, because they were doing fluff. And, y'know, we were sailing, we were doing things that nobody had ever done before. So [my writing partner] Bob Weiskopf came in one day and said, "*The Mary Tyler Moore Show* got wind of the fact that we're doing a two-parter on abortion. They're retaliating: they're doing a *three*-parter on mayonnaise."

MICHAEL ROSS:

I really don't remember *any* subjects that were off limits to us. I mean, we weren't stupid . . . When we spoke to each other, or to Norman, about what we wanted to write next, we knew there were limits to everything . . . and we would not get *too* extreme. Although, we got extreme sometimes. Oh, boy. But we were not suffering from the networks, 'cause we were doing so well.

WILLIAM TANKERSLEY:

Norman was reasonable, and the fellas on the coast dealt with him. Once I had to write him a letter, saying, "Norman, I wish you would listen to [Broadcast Standards editor] Tom Donner. We respect his judgment. I ask you, please listen to Tom. He knows what's acceptable." So, things like that took place. And he would call me on occasion.

NORMAN LEAR:

Sometimes they were *right* . . . and sometimes questioning something resulted in a better way to do it. I think it would be unreasonable for anybody that has gone through this to say they never learned that something they were doing was a little more over the top, that it could have been *another* way, or would sit better another way. You know, you learn from questions. And you learn from your decisions being questioned.

Producer Norman Lear on the set with his talented stars, Jean Stapleton and Carroll O'Connor. © 1971, 2005 ELP Communications, Inc.

ALAN WAGNER:

Norman Lear had balls of steel. He would hide scripts under his bed so you couldn't see them until it was too late. He *earned* that success with *All in the Family*. Those were brilliant shows. Brilliantly cast, and brilliantly directed, and the scripts were really high quality. There were very few things, on all the shows that I'd loved, that didn't pass through the hands of the creator. Norman had his hand in almost every word. Even shows that his name didn't appear on.

BOB SCHILLER:

Oh, yeah. We used to argue with him constantly, 'cause he was constantly rewriting. And we always were complaining . . . because we felt what *we* wrote was fine, and it should go in just as we wrote it. And Norman would say, "Well, we made it better." I'd say, "No, we didn't make it better, we made it *differenter*."

He'd put in stuff, or make *you* put in stuff. Very hands on. He had his own sense of humor, and it didn't always jive with ours . . . but he owned the store, so there was not much we could say. So, that was that. But he was certainly an innovator, and had guts, and changed the face of television.

LARRY GELBART:

Look what *All in the Family* did. With that first flush, you know, all of television's inhibitions and ridiculous rules went down the drain, literally.

NORMAN LEAR:

The toilet flush caused a tumult because it had never been heard before. I knew it would be a giant laugh. If you remember the circumstance of the flush, it wasn't just a throwaway: we flashed back to Gloria and Mike getting married, and everybody's standing around . . . the preacher just arrived, and they're ready to go and everything, and Archie isn't there.

[imitating Edith] "Archie? Archie?"

"I'll be right down!"

And while everybody's standing there waiting for him, on a wide shot of the whole stage, you heard the *flush*.

The most spiritual experience in the world is watching from in back of— we had about two hundred and fifty seats—in back of an audience, when there is a real belly laugh. You watch an audience rise, as one, as if they rehearsed . . . they rise a couple of inches out of their chairs . . . they go forward . . . and then they come back. And it's the purest moment. *Deeply* spiritual, I always felt.

Understanding the Bunker Mentality

ALAN WAGNER:

Norman *always* pushed things. Let me tell you about Norman Lear: Norman is the tiger's tail-tweaker, par excellence. He *loved* to do that. He's the guy who, legend has it, negotiated with Carroll O'Connor—who was a terribly difficult man to negotiate with, or to deal with—and would always end up pulling a script out of a drawer titled "The Death of Archie Bunker." And Carroll would acquiesce. Carroll was a great actor, but simply was not in the creative class of Norman Lear.

NORMAN LEAR:

Well, we didn't do *that* . . . but we did work on a story that killed him. Because we thought we might get to that. But I never used it as a threat, ever. You wouldn't do that out of good common sense, let alone decency.

BARRY HARMAN:

We wrote one which was dictated by the fact that Carroll O'Connor was holding out for more money—the very first one of a four-episode saga. And at the end of the fourth, Norman Lear had declared that either Carroll O'Connor came back, or he was writing him out of the show. So basically, the storyline was that Archie disappears.

It's a funny episode, but it does absolutely nothing, because Archie's not in it. Basically, it just leads up to the end of the episode where they find out Archie's gone away on a convention, and he's missing. And then for the next two episodes, he's still away, and other things happen and they go looking for him, and in the fourth episode he either comes to the door, or you find out that he died.

And of course, they settled everything. Carroll basically felt he deserved more money, that he was a major star and he deserved it—and he did. The network came up with the money, y'know, it wasn't really Norman who had to come up with it. But, as a ploy, they threatened to write him out of the show.

NORMAN LEAR:

What's really interesting about it was that the Irish intellect in him disagreed with much. *Always*. And the Irish intellect and I—and really the writers and directors—collided. Sometimes these collisions went on for a couple of days in rehearsal, and wound up in meetings with his agents and manager . . . and major scenes. But then sometimes it would never get to that when he was right. 'Cause when he was right, it was easy to see, and adjustments were made. But I'm talking about when the Irish intellect, mischievous intellect, just made trouble.

But then this *miracle* would occur when we passed through the difficult part, and he knew he had to do it. He would morph into Archie—suddenly, Carroll O'Connor wasn't playing the scene—it was Archie! And then, *none* of us could write as well for the character, in terms of dialogue, as he could . . . marvelous things would happen. It was an acting miracle. It just poured out of him.

So, a good deal of what was written for him, to be fair to all the writers, came out of him. And we locked it in. I mean, he wasn't ad-libbing on the show, it was dead set. But he found a way to say whatever percentage—y'know, 40 or 50 percent of it—better than we had said it. But he didn't construct anything . . . he didn't decide who he was.

BOB SCHILLER:

He couldn't write. He *thought* he could. He wrote a play once, but it never got produced. But he would take his hand at rewriting things sometimes. And usually it was better . . . he knew the character better than anybody.

CARROLL O'CONNOR:

Archie, like his counterpart in England, was a dumbbell. He didn't know why he was conservative. Had no idea. I think I knew why Archie tended to move towards conservative. He thought that they would keep the country racially pure. Or close to racially pure. And that was stupid. Because the country is not racially pure. But he thought, you know, he had his inbred dislike and distrust of blacks. He didn't dislike Jews, but he didn't trust them. Except, as he said to Edith, if you get a cold or something, you can go to anybody. But if you get something serious, you got to get a Jew doctor every time. And also a Jew lawyer. His lawyers were Rabinowitz, Rabinowitz, and Rabinowitz.

Now, one time somebody said to him, another character said, "I'm going to sue you, Bunker."

"Get out of here," he says. "You sue me, ha ha, wait till you see my lawyers . . . Seven savage Jews will strip the back right off you!"

That ended an act, and the house came down over at the studio. This was live, you know. So that was Archie. All his preconceptions keeping him from enjoying life. That was my message. Because Archie never enjoyed anything . . . He came in the house, he never smiled, never had anything

149

Archie won't touch newly affluent neighbor George Jefferson (Sherman Hemsley)'s money, as wives Louise (Isabel Sanford) and Edith look on. The Jeffersons spun off into their own hit sitcom, which also ran for years. © 1971, 2005 ELP Communications, Inc.

nice to say about the day. Was always something poisoning life for him. He didn't realize the person who he was from inside of himself, and that his father had passed it onto him. It was Archie's heritage.

JEAN STAPLETON:

On the surface, he was that incredible, ignorant bigot, but of course, she saw more than that. Edith saw. They were in love, she was in love with this man and, of course, I guess we had some tender moments that were dramatized, perhaps more off camera. I mean, the whole substance of their marriage is something that was probably very sweet. And that came out sometimes in some shows, like the anniversary show, twenty-fifth anniversary . . . of course, a person like that has tender moments. There is a mixture of qualities, so I presume that is part of their relationship, which wasn't seen on the screen a lot, but it was in some way.

NORMAN LEAR:

Archie is somebody who is simply afraid of the changing culture around him. Afraid of the new. And we see a great deal of that today. It's been said very well a number of times over the centuries, but the human of the species always needs somebody to look down on.

One of the most memorable moments in all of film, for me, is a two-reeler with the Little Tramp—Charlie Chaplin—who has been picked on, and picked on, and picked on . . . and then suddenly this *old, decrepit man* is trying to get up a dozen steps. And Charlie is carrying a package—this blanket with a bunch of shit in there, or something—and he puts it on the old man's shoulders and beats his ass with the cane to get him up the steps. Y'know, he finally found somebody *he* could look down on!

BOB SCHILLER:

Great character. From a comedy writer's standpoint, he was gold. Almost everything he said was funny. He was a total bigot—and nobody had ever done it on television before. Archie Bunker was new to television . . . a realistic character. Everybody knows somebody like that, who's a bigot.

NORMAN LEAR:

I have a great nose for narrowness, for intolerance. I used to listen to Father Coughlin as a kid. He was a radio *hater*—a major figure. And an anti-Semite. He spewed a lot of vitriol on the radio. Anyway, I didn't know any other kids who knew about these guys, but I listened to them. I found them, I don't know how.

Then I served in World War II, and I ran into it. I don't remember anybody coming up to me and saying, "You dirty Jew" . . . but standing on a line, waiting to get into a meal, two guys were talking and one guy made an anti-Semitic remark. As a matter of fact, I decked him.

It was terrible . . . being filled with fear after the fact. Not fear of being *hurt*—but fear of my own violence. My own violence scared me. I wasn't afraid that he was gonna get up and hit me back. It was, "What did I do? What did I do?" We did an episode of *All in the Family* based on this: doing something violent, and then fearing.

FRED SILVERMAN:

Norman was very smart. When he did *All in the Family*, he reached for all the guys that he worked with on the *Martin & Lewis Show* . . . most of his writers go back to *radio*. These were all old-fashioned guys . . . guys with a lot of gray hair. But they knew what was funny. With Norman's sensibilities, and their experience just writing funny stuff for strong characters. Y'know, a lot of his writers came from *The Jack Benny Show*. Aside from writing jokes, there were very vivid characters on that show.

NORMAN LEAR:

I think I see life through the end of the telescope that finds the comedy in *anything*. But I'm a serious man. So, the things I wanted to deal with—or found that I wanted to deal with—were the things out of my own life . . . having a marriage, to then two, and then three marriages, and six kids . . . and an inveterate reader of newspapers . . . It was so *easy* to find serious subjects in which you could find the comedy.

So, the people attracted to doing that—men and women with their *own* families and their *own* lives, who loved coming in and telling what happened last night, what they read or what's going on out there—that's where we cobbled our stories out of. What was happening to us. And in the greater culture.

BARRY HARMAN:

What was funny was that they sometimes censored *themselves* . . . You would pitch ideas to them, and most of the writers and story editors were guys that Norman and Bud Yorkin knew from their early days in television. Essentially vaudeville writers who'd moved into television. And, y'know, their idea of what was funny and *wasn't* funny was a very certain type of humor that they'd been writing all their lives. The only time you'd ever have a "gay" joke was to make fun, or say that a guy was effeminate, that kind of thing. And a story which we won an Emmy for—"Cousin Liz"—that *also* was: "Lesbians are not funny."

It was so weird, because they dealt with so many difficult issues on *All in the Family*, stuff that had never been on television before. And the boundaries kept on being pushed further back and further back, but the writers—a lot of them from a different era—didn't know how to deal with that, and couldn't imagine those things being funny. 'Cause they had never been asked to think that way.

To their credit, they ended up doing it, and in most cases doing a terrific job, but they were really affronted, as I recall, by some of the ideas you would bring in . . . and you felt like you *had* to come up with some really outlandish ideas to get an episode.

Originally they threw out the lesbian idea, and said absolutely not, even then, that far into the series, in 1978. And then, about three months later, they sort of sheepishly called and said, "Well, this is weird, but we were going through all the ideas we were pitched, and we pitched this one to Norman and he goes, 'Why aren't we doing that idea?' "

Mike comforting his wife Gloria . . . on a comedy series that was not afraid to address many issues which had never before been depicted on television. © 1971, 2005 ELP Communications, Inc.

And at that point, Norman had an agenda there because it was about schoolteachers. The two lesbians in the story, one of whom had passed away, were schoolteachers—and there was a proposition being floated in California to bar homosexuals from teaching. So Norman wanted to say something about it.

Archie needed to go to a funeral of their cousin, and then Edith finds out that her roommate was her lover and doesn't want them to take something that meant something to the two of them. That's how Archie finds out about [her being gay]. Norman had really liked that idea. Also, it aired for the *second* time the night before the election in which the proposition was going to be voted on. And it was defeated. So we always felt really good about that.

NORMAN LEAR:

Oh, God. There's one of my favorites. I recommend that to people all the time, 'cause that issue has never been treated better.

Must See TV—Every Saturday Night

ALAN WAGNER:

That night—that Saturday night that we built at CBS—was the last time that Saturday night was ever important. Anywhere. Nobody watches TV on Saturday nights anymore. Now it's the lowest audience numbers of any night of the week, but in *those* days, it was appointment viewing. People stayed home to watch *All in the Family, M*A*S*H, Mary Tyler Moore, Carol Burnett,* all over America. But the linchpin had been *All in the Family* moving to that time period.

FRED SILVERMAN:

It was great. It won the network Peabodies. And all of a sudden, we were prepared to take the next step—and the next step was putting shows like *M*A*S*H* on the air, and *Maude*, and some of Norman's other shows. And then you're like a squirrel, kind of acquiring nuts. You're building up this terrific collection of shows, mostly comedies.

BUD YORKIN:

When people ask about *All in the Family*, I say to them that the first thing we used to think about was not only to make a social comment, but, is it *funny*? Can we make it funny? Where does the story take it *funny*? We looked at it as a comedy, not a social comment. Sometimes that's why it took so long, some shows. Everybody worked on them for months before they could get the final draft done on one of them.

People, in my opinion, if you lecture to them about what abortion is, or what gay is, nobody's gonna watch that. When they're *laughing* . . . when it's all over, they'll say, "Gee, I guess the change of life is not a bad thing. I can go home and make love to my wife." Men were living under the belief that once their wife went into menopause, the sex was over. Women all over America wrote us letters, thanking us for dealing with this subject and laughing at the same time! That's why we were able to make a comment . . . but in the end, you'd better be funny.

NORMAN LEAR:

We loved playing on that line . . . the old saying was, and people still say, "I laughed till I cried." And conversely, "I cried until I got hysterical." So, I mean, laughter and tears walk a line together. I used to say, "Not tee-hee's and ha ha's." We were looking to bring the fuckin' audience to its knees. That's the way I always felt: bring 'em to their knees!

Also, it never escaped my notice—I don't know if we knew this before, or learned it quickly as we were making the shows—that the more concerned and involved you can get the audience, when it was *funny*, the bigger the laugh. And the more they cared, the more they laughed. Yes, we were doing a show on a serious subject, we were going to be respectful . . . but what we were going to do is wring laughter out of it—and, in some cases, tears. Sally losing her baby, and Archie in the bedroom with her . . . I loved the *feeling*, as well as the laugh.

MICHAEL ROSS:

It dealt with what was happening in the world at the time. It dealt with what I talked about with my friends and everybody else all the time.

NORMAN LEAR:

It's America looking in the mirror. It isn't *every* aspect of America looking in the mirror . . . but it's a clear picture of who we are.

Birth of a Genre: The Dramedy

6

Air-raid sirens wailing, bullets flying, and bombs exploding . . . young soldiers gasping for life, rushed into primitive military tents for emergency medical attention . . . gruesome injuries, amputated limbs . . . blood-spattered sheets, surgical gowns, and operating gloves . . . doctors downing martinis minutes before performing delicate surgery . . . a transvestite soldier reporting for duty each day in a lovely dress . . . married men and women casually cavorting with many partners . . .

Not the typical ingredients of your average American sitcom.

In his bestselling 1968 novel, *M.A.S.H.*, Dr. Richard Hornberger (writing under the pen name Richard Hooker) turned his experiences as a surgeon at the 8055th Mobile Army Surgical Hospital during the Korean War into the fictional adventures of a trio of medics . . . which was followed soon after by a savagely witty 1970 feature film scripted by Ring Lardner Jr. and directed by Robert Altman.

Like the book and movie that preceded it, the 1972 TV series *M*A*S*H* was dark and funny and serious all at once. Eschewing the standard production techniques of most half-hour comedies, the show was lit, filmed, and edited cinematically. Shooting with a single camera on the feature film's studio and exterior sets—which were still standing—ensured that *M*A*S*H* would look and feel like nothing else on television. Comedic and dramatic storylines were deftly interwoven, creating the template for a new form of TV eventually dubbed the *dramedy*. As writer/producer Larry Gelbart notes, "*M*A*S*H* became famous for its ability to deliver a laugh and a cry in the same show."

Producer/director Gene Reynolds had first toyed with the form a few years earlier on *Room 222*, a highly regarded, Emmy Award–winning schoolroom comedy/drama hybrid he developed with James L. Brooks that went largely unappreciated by its network, ABC. "When *Welcome Back, Kotter* came on the air," Reynolds recalls, "Michael Eisner said, 'This is what *Room 222* should have been!' I got fired off of *Room 222* after the second year, because of what we were doing."

A few years later, he and collaborator Gelbart perfected the format with *M*A*S*H*, and created a modern classic.

The show's setting was South Korea during the conflict of the early 1950s, but with the United States still polarized by the war in Vietnam, its stories and themes resonated deeply with audiences—thirty million each week, on average, at the height of its popularity.

M*A*S*H focused on a group of doctors and nurses charged with treating wounded GIs being rushed in from the front lines by chopper, jeep, or ambulance to the makeshift facility. The men and women of the fictional 4077th M.A.S.H. unit lived and worked in a state of nearly relentless stress, in a compound of drab tents virtually cut off from the rest of the world by stark

mountains on all sides. Needing to do whatever they could to alleviate the tension, they'd hop from one army cot to another, consistently flaunt rules and regulations, pilfer, steal, and lie if it served the greater good, flippantly crack wise while performing some of the most delicate (and bloody) surgical procedures, and generally display a total lack of regard for bureaucracy.

The unofficial leader of the quirky ensemble was sharp-witted, intellectual Captain Benjamin Franklin "Hawkeye" Pierce

As in the film that preceded the TV series, Hawkeye (Alan Alda) enjoys a homemade martini in the Swamp . . . possibly mere minutes before heading into the O.R. The show did less of this as seasons went on. © CBS Television Network

(Alan Alda, in his breakout role), through whose eyes and ears we witnessed the senselessness and futility of war during *M*A*S*H*'s entire run on television. Hawkeye held court in his living quarters—a tent nicknamed "the Swamp"—where he illicitly distilled homemade gin and jawed with his bunkmate, fellow surgeon and sly co-conspirator Captain John McIntyre, also known as Trapper John (Wayne Rogers). Just two other characters went the distance with Hawkeye for the full eleven seasons: prim head nurse Major Margaret "Hot Lips" Houlihan (Loretta Swit) and Father Francis Mulcahy (William Christopher).

Many other faces came and went over the years, including Trapper John, who was eventually replaced by clean cut Captain B.J. Hunnicut (Mike Farrell); impish company clerk Corporal Walter "Radar" O'Reilly (Gary Burghoff, the only actor to reprise his role from the movie); the supremely arrogant Major Frank Burns (Larry Linville); the unit's affable but bumbling commanding officer, Colonel Henry Blake (McLean Stevenson, whose character was written off by perishing in a downed plane over the Sea of Japan); his wry successor, Colonel Sherman Potter (Harry Morgan); Corporal Maxwell Klinger (Jamie Farr), who cross-dressed daily in the hopes of being discharged as mentally incompetent; stuffy Bostonian Major Charles Winchester (David Ogden Stiers); and literally scores of nurses. The many changes even worked conceptually, in large part thanks to the show's military setting, where characters transferring in and out was a very natural occurrence.

From the beginning, the developers of *M*A*S*H*, the TV series, knew they were crafting a project that was different from anything else that had been on before. And everyone, including the network execs at CBS, were just pleased as punch in the early going . . .

CBS Declares War—On Primetime

ALAN WAGNER, former V.P. of Program Development at CBS:
I was out in California, and I got a phone call from Bill Self. Bill was head of Twentieth Century Fox Television, and a really good guy. One of the class acts in television, I thought. And I got a call one day in my office, asking if I had seen the movie. I said yeah, that I thought it was very good.

He said, "Would you want it as a television show?"

And I was absolutely taken aback. It never occurred to me. You'd had *Gomer Pyle*, *Hogan's Heroes*, things that really were farcical. Not a show that took the problems of people who were facing death.

So, I said, "Yes, I'd be interested. What kind of option are you talking about?"

"No option. It's gotta be firm."

I said, "In that case, okay."

In those days I had that kind of power. I couldn't put it on the air . . . but I could make a pilot. Pilots I could okay.

PERRY LAFFERTY, former V.P. of Programs at CBS:

That was almost unheard of in those days, to give a pilot commitment. You would give 'em a *script* commitment. It was a big deal to get a pilot commitment.

GENE REYNOLDS, producer and director:

ABC wanted it very badly; they wanted it desperately. Had it gone to ABC, and they had had their way, it would've been a much different show. Look at their taste from *Room 222*—they didn't appreciate shows with that kind of a premise. There's a bunch of guys with enormous responsibility and very little talent at the networks. So, Bill Self had the good judgment to say CBS was the better home for it than ABC.

And then he asked me to do the pilot.

He said, "Here you go," and so I read the novel. Of course, I had seen the movie a couple of times . . . I loved it. I thought that Ring Lardner Jr. did a great job, and that Altman did a splendid job. So, I called Ring in New York, and said, "I'm going to do the pilot of *M*A*S*H*. Can you write it?"

He said, "Well, I'm on a job . . . but I suggest Ian Hunter, a writer friend of mine. Wonderful writer."

I said, "Thanks, but I don't know . . ."

And so I put down the phone, and the first guy I thought of was the best comedy writer I knew. It was completely reasonable for me to go to Ring first, because he had done such a fine job on the film. However, I realized the guy that I really wanted to get was a friend of mine named Larry Gelbart who was living in England.

LARRY GELBART, writer, producer, and developer:

In summer of 1970, I was living in London with my wife and family. And, as was always the case, you're entertaining visiting firemen. American firemen, anyway. And one of them was Gene Reynolds. Gene and I knew each other in Hollywood—we'd never worked together, we just knew each other socially. He always struck me as what he *still* strikes me as: a pleasant, decent, nice man. Good man. A cut above, really, people who aren't . . . or anything above or below.

I'd been living in England almost nine years by then, and he said, "Are you ever coming back?" I said, "I don't really know. I know I'm not here forever . . . but if I get sick from this meal, this might have been forever, you know?"

He said, "Well, if I find something that I think you'll find appealing, would you entertain the notion?"

I said, "Yes, of course."

Not too many days later, my wife and I went to see the motion picture *M*A*S*H*, which was playing in Leicester Square, and liked it very much. Another couple of days later, Gene called and said, "Listen, Bill Self has talked to CBS, and they've agreed to pay for a pilot script. Would you do it?"

I said, "I'll do it . . . we can't be as bold as the picture, but if we can be as bold as we can be, if we don't trivialize the war"—because we were still active in Vietnam at that time—"and if we can capture that anarchic flavor, and just the spirit of it, yes. But if they want another *Hogan's Heroes*—which was one *Hogan's Heroes* too many for me—or *McHale's Navy*, then no." So they did agree to that.

I was drawn to it for a couple of reasons. I always envied Abe Burrows—Jimmy Burrows' father. Because he got his really huge break when he doctored *Guys & Dolls*. *Guys & Dolls* was ideal for Abe, because Abe was so sort of a prototypical New Yorker . . . and I always thought, "Wouldn't it be wonderful if something came my way that I *knew* from the inside out a little bit?"

So, when I was offered the opportunity to work on *M*A*S*H*, two things came to mind: One, I'd been there. And not a lot of comedy writers could say that. I'd been there because I'd worked with Bob Hope, and we toured Korea during the war . . . and also, prior to that and after that, I'd visited every kind of military installation with Hope as he did his show. So, I kind of knew the life. It wasn't *Guys & Dolls*, but it was close to what I thought would be an ideal place to go to work.

GENE REYNOLDS:

I didn't think the *M*A*S*H* film was all that condemning of war . . . I thought it was somewhat fun and games, and doctors are all getting laid, they're walking up to nurses and opening up their gowns and so forth. It didn't look like a big condemnation—it looked like a lot of fun! The feature ridicules war, but it doesn't really say *this is detestable* . . . it didn't go as far as we eventually went. But, of course, we had many more opportunities.

LARRY GELBART:

I wasn't worried about the comparison. I knew the take that I had on it was going to be different than Altman's, and I should say Ring Lardner Jr.'s, because he gets so little mention when people talk about the motion picture. A brilliant writer, who had also served in Korea.

I saw the film just one more time. What I did do, though, was read the book. Several times. Just to stop and reflect on the characters. Also, you know, searching for story possibilities. And there were many that we took from the book. If nothing else—and it was *everything* else—it encouraged us to do a lot of research, to talk to a lot of doctors who had been there, a lot of nurses who had been there, pilots who had been there, *patients* who had been there, so that we really kept that background very much in the foreground. We didn't want it to just be another half-hour comedy.

I was working on a television show called *The Marty Feldman Comedy Machine*. Gene flew over, and I was working in a northern suburb called Elstree—we were shooting the shows there—and Gene and I, during off periods over a week, worked out the first storylines. What became the pilot.

GENE REYNOLDS:
Larry was producing the *Marty Feldman* show, so we met at night. He was tired, so sometimes we'd work for an hour, an hour and a half, and he'd say, "I think I'm run down." And I'd say, "See you tomorrow." Larry, of course, is a very bright guy. He sees the possibilities or the lack of possibilities in situations. And so we finally laid it out.

LARRY GELBART:
And then I remember we called Alan Wagner and pitched it to him on the phone.

ALAN WAGNER:
I got a phone call from Larry, saying, "Would a story like this work: A Korean kid is hurt or wounded, or loses his parents, or something like that happens on the battlefield, and Hawkeye and Trapper decide that they've gotta help the kid, and they want to send him to the United States on some kind of scholarship, so they need to raise money. How're they gonna raise money in Korea? Auction off a nurse—a weekend with a nurse. Would you buy that story?"

I thought it was a funny story. He said, "By the way, I'm going to name her Nurse Dish."

LARRY GELBART:
He said, "Sounds great! Go ahead."

So, Gene went back to America . . . and I was *so* involved with *Feldman* 'cause I was producing it and writing it. Finally, about two months had passed—and I hadn't done a thing. And he called me. I was in the control booth, shooting one of the *Feldman* shows.

Gene said, "How's it going?"

GENE REYNOLDS:

I was out there building sets, and doing a number of the things you've gotta do to produce a show. It's a lot of junk. So I called Larry in London and said, "I've gotta see a script." And Larry says, "I just put it in the mail!"

LARRY GELBART:

So, having said that, I was bound to write it and mail it! And because we had been so thorough, and because it had been marinating for so long—this sounds boastful, but I'd been thinking about it—it only took a day and a half. I had it in my head, and I had the craft, and I had the experience so that I could get it down on paper. And you know, it really helped that there had been a motion picture, as opposed to doing speculative writing . . . I mean, I saw the *sets*, I saw the *costumes*, I smelled the camp because I had been in Korea . . . kimchee was in the air.

Then I *did* mail it.

GENE REYNOLDS:

Shooting the pilot, I worked my ass off. I had it pretty well worked out in my mind . . . and it went well. The network got so excited they couldn't stand it!

FRED SILVERMAN, former V.P. of Programs at CBS:

M*A*S*H was an unusual show in that it came from a successful movie. And they got very lucky with the cast. Because of Larry Gelbart and the people who were involved, they were able to attract Alan Alda, who at that point was hot as a pistol. He had just come off of *The Owl and the Pussycat* on Broadway, and everybody in the world wanted him. And we got him and made a perfect pilot, I thought. Probably the best pilot I've ever seen. You didn't have to change a frame of film.

LARRY GELBART:

Alan is only one of two actors I ever knew for whom I never wrote a parenthetical, for whom I never wrote a direction: *sadly, brightly, melancholy*, whatever. It just jumped into his head off the page the way it jumped off mine *onto* the page. It was very exciting to work with someone like that, who just *got it*. I had seen Alan only on Broadway in *The Owl and the Pussycat*. But it was fabulous working with him, just fabulous.

GENE REYNOLDS:

Alan Alda had said, "Can we meet the night before we're supposed to start rehearsing this thing?"

So, we met in the Beverly Wilshire Hotel coffee shop, Gelbart and I and Alda. What Alda was saying was, "I don't want to do *McHale's Navy*. I don't want it to be one of these jerkoff things. The pilot is very good, but are you gonna stick with it? What's it going to be?"

And I said, "Well, the premise of the show, I think, is the wastefulness of war. We have a lot of humor with it, but I think we've got to recognize that boys are dying and that war is a goddamn folly." At any rate, whatever I said, it was the right thing, and he agreed—that was exactly what he wanted.

We had a great time with Alan the whole time. He was a wonderful actor, and a very decent professional guy who's very considerate of other people. He's very unusual.

Most of the original M*A*S*H *ensemble (l-r): Larry Linville, Loretta Swit, Wayne Rogers, Alan Alda, Gary Burghoff, and McLean Stevenson.* © *CBS Television Network*

LARRY GELBART:

First of all, I think Gene cast $M^*A^*S^*H$ brilliantly. I mean, starting with *me*! I'm talking about people behind the camera, as well as the ones out in front. Gene, and to be fair, Burt Metcalfe. Burt, like Gene, was a former actor. They just had a green thumb. I mean, they just picked wonderful, wonderful people. I was living in London, so I couldn't physically be there . . . and anyway, between the two of them, they knew every page of the Player's Directory, and they'd worked with a lot of people; they had good instincts. Both as former actors, and, in Gene's case, as a director, as well. They made great choices. We only changed one person from the pilot cast to the permanent cast: the character of Father Mulcahy.

BURT METCALFE, executive producer:

Gene asked me to come help him cast the pilot. When I was in casting, he'd directed episodes that I worked on and he felt very comfortable with me. So, I started as casting director and associate producer of $M^*A^*S^*H$, and then after four years Larry left, and after five, Gene left . . . so I gradually worked to the point of *taking over*, and wrote and directed, as well. It was a nice growth cycle for me.

I would also cast each episode, although there weren't that many additional characters because we had a large running cast. But as associate producer, I got into some very specific areas, as well: that is, all the post-production. I was very much involved in editing and dubbing. And then I'd sit in on story meetings and try to contribute some there . . . although I was with Larry and Gene, who were just brilliant at it. But it was enormously helpful to me for later on, so it was really a training ground for me.

Give Us Blood and Guts (But Not Too Much)

Like most of the TV series profiled in this book, all of which broke the mold in their own way, $M^*A^*S^*H$ was subjected to much scrutiny by its network— in this case CBS, which seemed to be quite literally the eye of many hurricanes throughout the early 1970s. Despite their excitement, the executives weren't always comfortable with what their creators were up to, and in $M^*A^*S^*H$'s case, some of the early problems were quite basic to the show's premise. *All in the Family* and *The Mary Tyler Moore Show* had begun to pave the way for more adult-oriented comedy on TV—but still, the network worried: Would viewers tune in to a weekly "sitcom" that depicted the horrors of war, gritty medical procedures, and so much casual adultery?

LARRY GELBART:

They generally did have problems with anything that deviated. To CBS, if it's a half an hour duck, then it's a duck, you know? But they were used to having a lot of non-conformity in those days. Perry was a good daddy. He was helpful. Perry was creative, and he didn't have a three-piece-suit mindset—but there were other shleppers that worked for him that weren't that endowed or inclined.

PERRY LAFFERTY:

The problem we had in the early days was that, if you recall the movie, there's blood all over. You can't even look at it if you just had dinner, but that was the whole point. They had to keep laughing during this horrible part of the war. And they would perform operations, and the whole operating tent would be full of blood, and their uniforms . . . and that became a big deal. How far do you want to go on television now, to adapt that movie with what you saw in terms of blood? That was the main thing, the trouble with the blood.

LARRY GELBART:

Well, there were *two* things: Everybody was fucking everybody in the original script. And they were all married. They said, "Could some of the people *not* be married?" So, Hawkeye got a divorce on paper . . . but very few others.

I gave a letter to the Smithsonian Institute—I should've kept a copy of it—from Program Practices at CBS, asking that certain things be toned down. Primarily: Did there have to be so much in the O.R.—in the operating room? And I thought inasmuch as this was a show about doctors that we should be in there from time to time.

GENE REYNOLDS:

Paul King, who was their point man, said, "I was in the theater watching *M*A*S*H*, and when they got into that O.R., two women got up in front of me and walked out."

I said, "Fourteen million of them stayed!"

And Bill Self was with me—we were at lunch at CBS, and Bill nodded his head. We *had* to go into the O.R.! That was the dumbest damn thing in the world. Because you have to justify these guys—they're heroes. In the "Swamp," they're frat guys . . . I mean, they're crazy, they're insane, they're loud, they're funny, they're out of their minds. But when the goddamn bell rings, they go in there and they perform valiantly. You've gotta justify their zaniness with their seriousness.

That was their position. They really felt that, oh, Jesus, you can't go in there. Cause they pictured wall-to-wall blood. We were much more discreet with blood than the feature. We would never show an open cavity—we'd drop the camera down, so you'd see blood on the apron of the surgeons and nurses, and on the hands and so on, but we soft-pedaled the trauma.

LARRY GELBART:

"Not so much blood please," and "not so much O.R." . . . I wish I had that letter.

What they did *not* have a problem with—which was the most welcome thing, of course—they did not have any quarrel with the politics. We could say anything we wanted about the futility of war, the wastefulness of war, alternatives to war . . . the fact that these guys were working on basically healthy people who just happened to have a bullet intrude upon their lives. And they supported us completely.

My contention was that if this network could have Walter Cronkite on the *Six o'Clock News* being so anti-Vietnam, we could certainly be anti-Korean War at 8:30. And by that time, if you remember in the 1970s, the dramas of the early days of the 1950s were gone. There was no drama on television. It had given way to melodrama. It had given way to whirling blue lights on police cars, to cowboys. And we—a small group of us—probably encouraged by one another, not unconsciously, we formed some kind of a group who dealt with social issues.

This was all really because of the success of *All in the Family*. Norman Lear was busting barriers every week! So we could always say, "How come they can do *that*, and we can't do *this*?"

BURT METCALFE:

You have these liaison guys from the network . . . first of all, there's the Head of Programming, but then you'll have guys who are his disciples—who go out to the individual shows. The ones who specifically watch that you don't stray too far from the network party line . . . in this case, the Fred Silverman line.

LARRY GELBART:

That first year was rough. We had a very queasy Program Practices person assigned to us . . . but it got better in the second year, I believe, or the third and the fourth, when we were assigned a young woman. She was so much more contemporary and understanding, that I could hardly get angry at all. The best example of that is, in the first year, they didn't want us to use the word "circumcision." And in the third season, we *performed* one.

Then there was the "Family Hour" thing. It happened during the fourth year of my stay.

Wholesome Fun for Everyone!

In 1974, members of the U.S. Congress decided they'd heard enough outcry about all the violence and sexual content on primetime television, and urged the Federal Communications Commission to *do* something about it. The FCC in turn leaned on the TV networks, whose corporate heads (particularly the CBS brass) decided to create a nightly "Family Hour"—an early-evening time slot featuring only programming deemed suitable for children and sensitive viewers. Some popular shows found themselves moved to later hours . . . while others stayed put, attracting a whole new barrage of meddling by their network. Outraged TV producers eventually filed suit against the FCC.

ALLAN BURNS, co-creator and producer, *Rhoda:*

The "Family Hour" . . . that hit us hard. *Rhoda* was a show about an adult, married couple. And we wanted to be . . . not *explicit*, exactly, but implicit, certainly, that they were having a real sex life. We were on at 8:00, which fell into what became the "Family Hour." And the rules changed. They kept coming down on us for stuff that we had done the year before.

And we said, "But we were doing this stuff last year!"

They said, "Well, you can't do it *this* year, 'cause now you're in the 'Family Hour.'"

So, we said, "We never changed the time—the time is still 8:00. Give us some guidelines."

And I remember their famous quote: "We'll only know what doesn't work for us when we see it."

LARRY GELBART:

The case I always cite was one show where Radar was stopped at the compound late at night by a very, very green GI who was on guard duty. The kid was very nervous, and he had a rifle in his hands . . . he was screwing up and Radar was nervous that he was going to get shot.

The kid said, "Forgive me, sir, I'm a virgin."

And they wouldn't let me say the word "virgin." Because of the "Family Hour" rule.

I said, "You mean, it would be difficult for a family to explain to a youngster what a virgin was?"

And they didn't want to get into it. You just didn't talk about it—if they said no, it was no. They were that intransigent. Then, an episode or two after that, I had a busload of wounded soldiers come in . . . and Radar was on the bus, making notes for the purposes of triage, talking to each one to find out what the problem was. And in doing so, of course, asking their names. He asked this one kid his name, and said, "Where are you from?"

And the kid said, "The Virgin Islands."

They make you play these silly games.

FRED SILVERMAN:

I was never consulted. That ultimately was done by Arthur Taylor and the people upstairs. I'm not even sure that Bob Wood had anything to do with it. *He* didn't want to get involved—why would we wanna move *All in the Family*? It was the stupidest. I think that ultimately it hurt the network. But, y'know, my voice was not that strong a voice—it's ultimately why I left to go to ABC. 'Cause I said, "Fuck this! Who the hell is this guy to come in here? It's taken a long time, and the work of a lot of people, collectively, to finally put a schedule together that was a work of art. And then he's coming along, and to gain favor in Washington, he's totally screwing it up!"

Which is basically what he did. 'Cause we had to fill all those 8:00 time periods, and for the most part, filled 'em with a lot of *junk*.

PERRY LAFFERTY:

It was a pretty tough cross to bear. Because Arthur Taylor was the CBS president, and he was determined that we would have a "Family Hour." And *family hours* were different at different times in the country . . . it was kind of a mess.

LARRY GELBART:

I was one of the people that sued the networks. Norman Lear was another plaintiff, and I think MTM . . . and Danny Arnold. I stuck out like a sore thumb because I was the only individual—I was not the owner of anything.

NORMAN LEAR, producer, *All in the Family*:

We *were* the lawsuit. It all started around *All in the Family* . . . and it was just plain silly. Just thinking that we were going to protect all those kids in the east and the west . . . but screw them in the middle of the country, 'cause there it's going to run an hour earlier. Y'know, if the "Family Hour" meant anything at all, they were left totally unprotected. So, it was silly on the surface. We had to destroy the "Family Hour." It was a ruse.

Following quite a bit of extensive legal haggling, a U.S. district court judge ruled that the FCC had acted improperly by privately persuading network representatives to impose the new policy without holding public hearings, and the "Family Hour" viewing policy was finally scuttled. But the damage had already been done to some shows, as well as the schedule.

LARRY GELBART:

I did not enjoy dealing with the censors, who always bristled when you used that word about them. That was probably the least pleasant part of the job. I did it more than Gene. There was much that Gene did that I *didn't* do—I mean, Gene was really responsible for all of the nuts and bolts of production, scheduling, budget, and so forth. Because he had the experience, and God knows, I was busy enough. But that was the least attractive part of the job.

Gene and I were called to lunch one day by some executive . . . and this was the period before television executives looked like fetuses in three-piece suits, you know? They were mature—anywhere from idiots to terrific guys. He said, "Someday I'm going to tell you two guys how you screwed up *M*A*S*H*."

The lascivious nature of Major Frank Burns and Hot Lips Houlihan's affair irked the show's conservative network liaison. © *CBS Television Network*

GENE REYNOLDS:

We had kind of this grab-ass relationship between Hot Lips and Frank Burns, and the guy thought it went too far. He thought it was in poor taste, and wasn't all that funny. I mean, it didn't always work with those two, but a lot of the stuff I thought was funny as hell. But I never took him seriously anyway . . . he was not a heavyweight. Very few people at the network, in my experience, were the kind of people you listen to and say, "This guy really knows what he's talking about. I'm going to be very careful." There were a few, but very few.

LARRY GELBART:

We did it "wrong"! We didn't do it the way *he* would've done it. It could only be that we were too . . . I was going to use the word "serious." But, you know, the truth to me about what the network thought about the show is reflected in their insistence that we use a laugh track.

Permission to Laugh, Sir

PERRY LAFFERTY:

We had another *long*, drawn-out argument with them: They didn't want a laugh track. We wanted a laugh track. And we had all kinds of proof to show you that it was better . . . I must say, the evidence of using a laugh track was sort of convincing in those days. And they still do it, y'know. Everything that they said on *Friends* wasn't as funny as the laugh track said it was. But they had a laugh track on, full blast.

    M*A*S*H without a laugh track—we were afraid maybe the audience wouldn't tune in to what they were doing. "They didn't have a laugh track in the movie," was one of the big arguments. "But if you go into the theater, everybody's roaring."

ALAN WAGNER:

With *M**A*S*H, it was a very noisy fight, from day one. Would we have a laugh track on the show or not? And early on, network brass—research, sales, my bosses—insisted on a laugh track. There was no way out. Gotta have a laugh track. Because they always *had* had laugh tracks. This was so people would distinguish it from a drama. That was what they kept saying: They're not going to know it's a comedy unless they're *permitted* to laugh. The laugh track is the permission to laugh.

    And there's something to be said psychologically about that . . . because you're watching comedy on TV in an isolated environment. You're not watching with a crowd, where there's an audience responding jointly, like a communal experience or theatrical occasion. You're seeing it alone. It's not as funny that way. I've looked at some of the funniest movies ever made—alone—and they're not as funny as when seeing them with friends, or seeing 'em in a theater. Laughter is absolutely infectious. So, it was not an irrational argument they were making; it was very rational.

PERRY LAFFERTY:

We had evidence. We did an experiment on *Hogan's Heroes*, where they played it without a laugh track—and it was a horrible failure. Nobody liked it much, and it was kind of weird. We put a laugh track on it, and it just went through the roof! So, there was some evidence that laugh tracks made a difference.

FRED SILVERMAN:

I just believed—and I still believe—when people look at a comedy show, that by and large they want it to *feel* like it's a comedy show. And, with very few exceptions—I know *Wonder Years* was an exception—but I can't think of another show, other than *Wonder Years*, correct me if I'm wrong, where it was written for comedy but there were no laughs on it.

But I didn't ask for a laugh track . . . I said, "Just put a couple of chuckles in there."

GENE REYNOLDS:

What we had was a very discreet track. At the end of the second year, some guy wrote me a letter that said, "Well, you finally folded. I'm looking at *M*A*S*H* the other day, and you put in a laugh track. My God, you really sold out."

So, I wrote back to him and said we'd had a laugh track since the first day. But it was discreet. We made the damn joke *earn* the laugh. Some sitcoms, you see 'em and Jesus, that laugh comes in there *whappo*, whether it earns it or not. We had a very good guy. He was the best guy with the old laugh machine. We said to him, "We want a discreet track. For God's sake, don't lean on it."

Y'know, I worked for George Burns one year. For a whole year, I directed a show that he was in and produced. And he'd say, "I'll show you how funny that joke is—lay in a big laugh on that!" *That* we didn't do.

LARRY GELBART:

I fought it till the day I left. There were some exceptions. There were shows where they let us not use a laugh track . . . and portions of shows. Whenever they were in the O.R. or serious surgery, there was no laugh track.

ALAN WAGNER:

The laugh track is *overused*—and I'm guilty of that as much as anybody. I've overused it badly, with some pretty core pilots, trying to goose the audience's response. And the guy who invented that machine, I don't think he did a very good job. There are some pretty raucous sounds in there—it's very hard to make it subtle. Hard to get a *chuckle track* out of that.

LEONARD STERN, television writer and producer:

I think it's the thing that's done the greatest disservice. It eliminated standards. In fact, I'm concerned about it. I think it's worth investigating—I think people's understanding of what's funny has changed radically because of that machine.

Say you're a discriminating listener, and you have a sense of humor. But now you're undergoing a Pavlovian experience: You're hearing laughter . . . to something that you don't consider funny. How long does it take before you're brainwashed? And say, "It *must* be funny, and I don't understand it." Then suddenly, you want to be part of those who respond. You don't want to be iconoclastic—you're back to elementary school. You want to be accepted. So you say, "That's funny."

ALAN WAGNER:

With $M*A*S*H$, we tried to utilize, in effect, the aesthetics that were implicit in the program . . . utilize the same kind of psychology that Hawkeye would use: It's okay to drink gin and laugh in the tent, or the "Swamp," as they called it, but not in the operating room. And that was the demarcation early on: There was no laughter in the woods, there was no laughter anywhere outside the swamp or the mess hall.

LARRY GELBART:

It's all bullshit. In fact, in the last year of my stay, I said at one point, "Why don't we use a preview house? Show audiences a show with a laugh track, and a show without a laugh track, and ask them which they enjoyed more."

And we did. Half the people said they missed it, and half the people said they thought it was better without.

So, I said, "Well, there you go."

And they said, "No, there *you* go! We'll go with the 50 percent. Why fool with it?"

So, that's the way that went.

And we were the people who were forced to cheapen our own show . . . Gene and Burt and I. We would be present at those sessions, and we would say, "That's a five. That's a four. That's a three. That's a chuckle . . . Can you get that hyena lady outta there?"

It was sort of like being forced to disfigure your own child. It was terrible.

ALAN WAGNER:

On *M*A*S*H* you had guys who died, or a man who'd just lost his right hand. You can't deal with matters like that, you can't deal with bombs exploding, you can't deal with Radar saying, "Who'd we kill?", you can't deal with that in the opening credits, which were, from the outset, the arrival of the helicopter, and that wonderful minor music, and the worried faces taking you into that helicopter—you can't deal with that with a laugh track.

LARRY GELBART:

Twentieth Century Fox has released the show season by season, in DVD form. And the owner of the DVD has the option of watching the show without the laugh track. If you watch the show *without* the laugh track, you see the show as it was intended. The laugh track trivializes it . . . the laugh track makes them seem like a bunch of wisecrackers.

I think I won, thirty years later.

A Matter of Gravitas

"Sometimes You Can Hear the Bullet," the seventeenth episode of the series, was the first instance when *M*A*S*H* skillfully integrated its comedy with starkly dramatic situations. The story follows three threads: (1) Hawkeye discovers that a gung-ho teenager (played by Ron Howard) has lied about his age in order to enlist and fight in Korea, and assures the kid that he won't betray his secret . . . (2) a brief reunion between Hawkeye and an old friend whom he hasn't seen in a while, Tommy Gillis (guest star James Callahan), a journalist who's penning a book about the war while traveling through the front lines . . . and (3) obnoxious Major Frank Burns suffers a non-war-related back injury while canoodling with his lover, Hot Lips, but quickly applies to be awarded a Purple Heart, having been technically injured at a frontline unit.

Later in the show, the journalist friend reappears—now mortally wounded, on the operating table—where Hawkeye, for all his skill as a surgeon, is helpless to save his pal's life. Tommy's death hits Hawkeye hard, leaving him in tears—revealing a side of his character we hadn't experienced until this point. The traumatic event leads him to go back on his word to the young soldier, and he has the resentful boy sent home—with Frank's ill-gotten Purple Heart—so that he can hopefully live a long life.

GENE REYNOLDS:

The turning point for $M*A*S*H$ was somewhere in that first year, with "Sometimes You Can Hear the Bullet." From then on, we recognized that the show had these possibilities.

LARRY GELBART:

It pointed out that we could really go much, much further in the dramatic area. Because after a while, you know, however many compliments you get, there was always the fear of trivializing what was going on. So, this was a chance to make sure that didn't happen . . . without giving up the ability to laugh in the same episode where, in fact, someone cries, as Hawkeye does.

BURT METCALFE:

We see how Hawkeye is affected by a personal death . . . it's a famous scene where he and McLean are standing in a doorway, and Hawkeye's in tears. And

Radar O'Reilly and Hawkeye Pierce share a serious moment on a series that set the bar for blending comedy and drama. © *CBS Television Network*

he's saying that so and so is dead, "And I'm a wreck. I'm falling apart. I never cried for all these other kids who died." I'm just paraphrasing, but McLean Stevenson says, "Well, you didn't *know* them. I learned two things in medical school: Young men die and doctors can't do anything about it."

LARRY GELBART:

A writer named Carl Kleinschmitt came to us with the idea of a civilian friend of Hawkeye's coming through the camp as a writer—exactly as it is in that script—and then coming back as a casualty. And we liked the idea very much, but we wanted the guy's death to amount to something . . . we didn't want it to just be the story as presented, where a guy goes into a war to find out what war's about, and gets killed. We wanted to make his death *count*.

So, we invented the character of the fifteen-year-old Marine, played by Ronny Howard, and tied that into the Tommy Gillis story. What we're forgetting is, we did something that I'm pretty sure had never been done on television before: That guy was real uninhibited . . . and in putting the script together, we had him kiss Henry Blake right on the lips! Which was, I think, a first.

GENE REYNOLDS:

What we always wanted to do was have plenty of humor in the show . . . and if it had two curves, if one curve was very serious, to have something that added levity by bringing in another story.

LARRY GELBART:

Well, *M*A*S*H* let you be sad. You know, we were doing *M*A*S*H*. We didn't think of it as television, we didn't think of it as a sitcom. It was certainly not "Hello, honey, I'm not home." It just was what it was. A show about these people, in that place, and others like them from day one in western civilization. Perry Lafferty coined the word "dramedy."

BURT METCALFE:

The thing that made it so memorable and theatrical was that you could rail against the war—the insanity of war, the futility of it, and the insanity of *romanticizing* war. The credo was that these doctors went insane in order *not* to go insane. Their behavior, and the practical jokes, and the fooling around, all the bizarre things that they did—that was in order to not have to deal with the reality of where they were and what they were doing . . . trying to patch up kids so that they can go out again and get killed! That, really, in essence, is what it was about.

LARRY GELBART:

For me it was, you know, a four-year Letter to the Editor. And a freedom. It was about *something*. We were a generation away from the time when we'd celebrate a show because it was about "nothing." This was about something . . . and something very key to people's lives. That's what we were doing every week: We were shooting *relevance*.

Writing from Experiences

BURT METCALFE:

Over the years we interviewed a great many doctors, and men who'd been in the military. We'd tape these long telephone conversations—'cause they'd be all over the country—and we would have that put into manuscript form. Then we'd go over them. They were like *gold*, they were like textbooks that had all the answers . . . I don't care how creative writers are, they can sit and stare at a ceiling all day and they're never gonna come up with some of the stuff that these guys did. Because it happened. Because it was true.

And it became cathartic for the doctors, because it had been years since they thought or talked about any of this.

LARRY GELBART:

I think we realized that, after we picked the bones of the Hooker novel fairly clean, we just wanted to go to some authoritative sources. People who'd been there. And it just seemed pretty obvious that that was the way to go. One of the things I gave UCLA, along with my papers, were some very, very thick volumes of transcriptions of conversations with doctors. They were invaluable, because they just kept us in touch with the truth—and once you know the truth, your inventions are likely based on those. You don't stray too far, if you're lucky. Which is not to say we didn't, from time to time . . . but it just kept reality in the foreground of the series, and in our work process. It's largely a matter of cooking to taste, you know, after a while.

BURT METCALFE:

You would have three or four threads running though, and you would get countless numbers of these from the research, as well as major arcs. It varied, but it was so rich. As a producer, it's one of the reasons I felt that I never got involved in anything thereafter that could remotely compare in quality or durability to this show. It was because of that singular fact: None of the other projects I was involved in could deal with life, where there is a source that is so rich . . . in half-hour comedies, there aren't that many opportunities to do that.

LARRY GELBART:

Reality has a way of trumping fiction every time. I recall that when Gene and I came back from our visit to a M.A.S.H. unit in Korea after the second season, it was very hard to manufacture events. Because we had seen the real thing, we'd been in an O.R. We'd seen real blood—not something from the prop department. Not that we were there in a wartime atmosphere, but blood's blood. What doctors do, and how they do it, and then how they live their lives *because* of what they do, was just driven home.

I remember one of the first things we saw in visiting a ward. This hospital was in fact the site of the original 8055th, which was the real-life basis for the fictional 4077th . . . and it was not mobile now, of course, because there was no war. It was in a village called Uijongbu.

And the first thing we saw was a young person who was a multiple amputee. Even that many years after the action in Korea, kids were still going out and retrieving shells—and unexploded shells, as it turned out—to get the brass, to convert into some kind of product that can be sold. And this kid touched a hot one. So, when you're standing next to someone who's not an extra, swathed in bandages and going through this really traumatic experience, you're not so glib when you get back.

We cherished those notes. They were just inspirational, literally. And sometimes they gave us whole episodes, sometimes just a scene. Sometimes, it gave us—probably, for me—the most memorable line in the whole series.

BURT METCALFE:

We had seen an episode of that wonderful CBS series that Ed Murrow did called *See It Now*. It was brilliant. And Ed Murrow did a one-hour show in which he literally went into the foxholes in Korea . . . he went up to the front, took a primitive camera, and interviewed guys in foxholes, or in their bunks and mess tents.

So, Gene and Larry had this idea: Why don't we do *our* version[5] of *See It Now*?

I got a wonderful newscaster here in town named Clete Roberts, and in essence he was Murrow. There was no script. What we did was, in just a matter of hours, Larry wrote down some provocative questions, and

---

[5] *"The Interview" [February 24, 1976], the fourth season finale. Written and directed by Larry Gelbart, it was his very last episode of* M*A*S*H.

The men (and woman) of the 4077th, as the war dragged on: Alan Alda, seated. Second row (l-r): Mike Farrell, Harry Morgan, Loretta Swit, David Ogden Stiers. Third Row (l-r): William Christopher and Jamie Farr. © *CBS Television Network*

some funny questions, and a kind of comedic response for them as in the mouth of an individual actor, be it Hawkeye or whoever . . . and he gave all those questions to the actors—just five or six basic questions: "How do you like the army?" "What were you doing when you got the letter?" Whatever.

LARRY GELBART:

And then I did one other thing: I got Clete Roberts aside, and said, "Look, why don't you make up some of your own questions and ask them? And I'll get the actors' responses on camera. They'll be hearing the questions for the first time, so it will not be so much acting as *reacting*. That should make for some fresh pieces of film here and there."

BURT METCALFE:

The actors loved it. First of all, they went home and thought about the questions that were posed in advance. By then they all knew their characters so well, and they were all so wonderfully glib and creative and funny themselves, that they could come up with some really good stuff.

LARRY GELBART:

And the power of one speech that we assigned to Father Mulcahy . . . In a very early script, in an O.R. scene in the winter, somebody made a reference to warming themselves over the wound, over the body—this was a written line, this was not research. But the amazing thing was, down the line, one doctor *did* say that it was so cold that sometimes the doctors would hold their hands over the open wound to warm themselves. So, we adapted it to Mulcahy.

BURT METCALFE:

We always point to it as the quintessential $M*A*S*H$ concept. It became the end of the first act of that show, and was a question that was posed to each actor:

"Has being here changed you? How have you changed?"

We went down all the different people . . . Larry Linville says, "Oh, I haven't changed at all!" Everybody, in their own way, has a very meaningful response.

But Bill Christopher, from this research, has the one that just knocks everybody for a loop. He says, "When it's cold here, like it is today,"—and you see the wind blowing on the tent where he is—"and the doctors are operating, they will make an incision and steam rises from the open wound. And the surgeon will warm his hands over the steam of the open wound. How could anyone look upon that and not be changed?"

LARRY GELBART:

To this day, I think it's just so beautifully poetic. I don't think the guy tossed it off when he told it to us over the phone—but he certainly bowled us over. And that line was in those binders for two or three or four years, I don't know how long. It's something I'd look at or go past constantly, never saying, "Boy, some day, some day" . . . but when the moment came, you just knew *this* was the spot for it.

We delivered the final cut to CBS for airing . . . and included was—for the very first time—a script for it. They had no idea what was on that footage, because there was no script. That was a first, probably *last*, and never-to-be-repeated experience for network television, to have such faith in a group of people putting on a show for you, that you would air it without ever having seen a script!

The totally experimental nature of it . . . the total freedom to not be hemmed in by plot . . . the total participation by everybody. It was remarkable—to this day, I'm probably inordinately proud of it.

BURT METCALFE:

The research kept things fresh. That, and the cast changes. The cast changes forced you to shake up the chemistry, it changed all the relationships. And it didn't mean that, y'know, Mike Farrell was better than Wayne Rogers, or Harry Morgan better than McLean. No. It meant they were *different*. You made the character different, and the actors were different. The last thing in the world you would wanna do—certainly this was apparent very early on—would be to replace a guy with someone who was similar. The whole point was to try and go in another direction.

So, when Larry Linville left as this straw man, this wimpy ignoramus, we thought, "Let's get a guy who'd be a real formidable adversary. He won't be as much of a pushover for them. He'll be a good doctor, and he'll be a brilliant guy. Winchester." And then the whole thing about him being very rich and condescending, and the last place in the world he should be in is this cesspool. That became *enormously* rewarding creatively, because it helped to keep it fresh.

Victory and Controversy

LARRY GELBART:

The first year, our ratings were so poor that it looked like we weren't coming back at all. We were on at 8:00 at night on Sunday, the one day of the week we probably shouldn't have been on. And legend has it that Babe Paley—Mrs. William S. Paley—loved the show, and that we were saved by some pillow talk! It's a great story . . . and if we say it often enough, it will be the truth.

GENE REYNOLDS:

We didn't have a good lead-in: It was a show that I'd produced for the first thirteen weeks called *Anna and the King* with Yul Brynner. And we failed with that.

But you see, *M*A*S*H* began to grow . . . even from the very beginning, it grew. But gradually. You could see, "Well, it's doing better this week, now it's doing even better *this* week . . ." And it got strong enough so that in the second year, they gave us a very good position. That really did it for us . . . but also, it was a matter of people seeing the show, sampling the show . . . and showing what happens if you give it a chance.

FRED SILVERMAN:

If something is good, you just have to stay with it. If you honestly believe in your heart that it's gonna work, then you've got to support it. And that was the case with *M*A*S*H*. At 8:00 on Sunday night, it didn't work. And *that* was a half-assed schedule, I remember that. Its lead-in was *Anna and the King*. Ultimately we moved it to 8:30 Saturday, in back of *All in the Family*.

BURT METCALFE:

We used to get a lot of letters. There were people who felt we had battered and bruised the sacred institution of the U.S. Army, and more specifically the U.S. government, in a very unpatriotic way. It's that old story of, if you're not for the policies of this country, I'm questioning your patriotism.

Richard Hornberger, who wrote the original novel, was a violent foe of the show! We didn't get that many letters from him, but we got a few early on . . . and he'd write to the networks. We were made aware of his views. Or he'd be quoted in interviews. He was very much against us 'cause we were so totally left wing, that we were so totally anti-government, anti-military, and he was not that left wing at all.

LARRY GELBART:

You know, there's so much talk these days about people being *right* and being *left*, I'm so sick of it. But he clearly thought we were far more liberal than he was. And we were. His book was completely devoid of any influence or comparison to the Vietnam experience that was going on, and our series very much included feelings that spilled over, or spilled over backwards into the 1950s . . . and I think he resented it. I'm not faulting him. He just felt these were not his doctors.

He was also mad as hell that we killed Henry Blake. He had a M*A*S*H book industry going . . . with a collaborator, he was doing *M*A*S*H Goes to Paris*, *M*A*S*H Goes to Las Vegas*, M*A*S*H goes here, M*A*S*H goes there. So, he was making a tidy living with Henry Blake very much alive and kicking—and we had him dead and buried! Or drowned. So I think he was a little pissed off about that.

BURT METCALFE:

M*A*S*H changed the landscape of TV. But only for a brief shining moment . . . because we have the tangible example of how it *didn't* do any good in terms of where this country is now with war. The success and the durability of that show was in no small way contributed to by the fact that the country was involved in Vietnam at the time. We were doing Korea . . . but the resonance was Vietnam, and the meaning of it to many, many people was Vietnam. The *context* was Vietnam.

We would like to think that perhaps, in some miniscule way, a show like that and what it was talking about could have some meaning and some significance in terms of the way our country then approaches going to war again.

And Then There Was *Maude*

7

All in the Family shattered so many television taboos in 1971, one might think there were none left to conquer. But then *Maude*—the popular show's first spinoff—came along just a year later and went even further than its progenitor, harpooning subjects that even *All in the Family* had shied away from. *Maude* quickly became one of the most talked-about TV shows of the 1970s, and a lightning rod for controversy.

A storyline on the second season of *All of the Family* found most of the Bunker household sick with the flu, leaving poor Edith running herself ragged trying to care for everyone at once. Swooping in to the rescue: Edith's indomitable cousin, Maude (Beatrice Arthur), a tall, tough, brazenly outspoken liberal Democrat and the quintessential anti-Archie Bunker—who naturally couldn't stand the sight of her. Maude Findlay was the first character to appear on *All in the Family* who was every bit Archie's equal, destroying him with withering putdown after putdown. Watching the two verbally spar on "Cousin Maude's Visit"[6] was a riot:

Maude: Are you waiting for a special invitation? I said, breakfast is on the table!
Archie: I heard ya. So did every moose up in Canada.
Maude: You can either come to the table and eat, or you can lie there and feed off your own fat.

The potential of this new character wasn't lost on CBS executives, who were looking to build on the success of Lear's first hit. The episode and subsequent series also unleashed a powerful life force upon the television-watching public

[6] *Written by Philip Mishkin, Michael Ross, and Bernie West.*

185

in the person of Ms. Arthur, well-known at the time mostly for her work on the New York stage. When Maude made her second appearance on that same season of *All of the Family*, the episode was designed to spin her character off into its own comedy series, and set up her basic situation:

Maude lived in upper-middle-class Tuckahoe, New York, with her fourth husband, Walter (Bill Macy); her divorced daughter, Carol (Marcia Rodd, replaced by Adrienne Barbeau for the *Maude* series); and Carol's young son, Phillip (Brian Morrison, and later Kraig Metzinger for the show's final season). Maude's best friend, Vivian (played by Rue McClanahan, who would reunite with Bea Arthur several years later on Susan Harris' show, *The Golden Girls*), would eventually marry her arch-conservative next-door neighbor, Dr. Arthur Harmon (Conrad Bain).

Maude, though a died-in-the-wool liberal, nevertheless always had domestic servants working for her. The first, an African-American lady named Florida Evans (played by Esther Rolle), was spun into *her* own series just two years later, *Good Times*, yet another smash hit for Norman Lear and Bud Yorkin's Tandem Productions.

Stories on *Maude* generally tackled the joys and frustrations of middle-aged sex, unwanted pregnancy, abortion, vasectomies, politics, and many other issues, all filtered through Lear's by-then-well-known sensibilities.

Cousin Maudie Visits . . . and Stays for Six Years

NORMAN LEAR, creator and producer:

The way Maude came about was that the whole idea came from my own family. The greatest arguments in my family lived at the top of their lungs and the end of their nerves. *Always.* And the greatest ones came from arguing about the oldest relationships. When my Aunt Fanny came—who hated my father for twenty years, as opposed to somebody else who only hated him for four—she could kill him.

I wanted a character like that in an episode of *All in the Family* . . . so we wrote Maude as a cousin of Edith who didn't want her to marry this guy in the first place. It's an old, old [enmity], and so she would be lifting the club from the fuckin' ground.

ROD PARKER, writer and executive producer:

I had been doing the musical *Honeymooners* with Jackie Gleason and Art Carney and Sheila MacRae. So, my agent called Norman, and since I'd done *The Honeymooners*, he said, "Yeah, I'd love to talk to you." I went and pitched a story [for *All in the Family*], and he bought it. He liked the way I did the one script, and he liked working with me.

Then Norman called me and said, "Do you know Bea Arthur?"

I said I didn't know her, but I knew who she was. So, he said, "Do you want to do a spinoff?"

I said, "Yes, of course!" Spinoffs are very hard to write, because you're introducing all these characters nobody knows, but you're doing it in the context of a show that everybody likes . . . where the regular characters are known and beloved by everybody else. So, it's a little strange, you know.

BUD YORKIN, producer and director:

We had Bea Arthur on in that guest spot on *All in the Family*, and everybody loved the show and liked *her*. Norman and I had always loved Bea, going way back to New York, when she was in a play [called *The Shoestring Revue*]—she wore a raincoat and sang.

But anyway, the mail was incredible on that show, and particularly about her. Even though she was very liberal coming in, and we were certainly pushing the other way with her, getting ready for the election. I think because of that, and because of Norman saying—to *himself*—I don't know how many times he told *other* people that she was like Frances, God bless her . . . [but] *Maude* was really based on Norman's wife at that time, Frances. Frances *was* Maude. Frances had a very strong mind, like Maude did . . . she also was very opinionated, like Maude was. I must admit, I don't think Norman was quite like her husband. He may have taken a few beatings himself, I'm not sure. [laughing]

NORMAN LEAR:

There were similarities. She was, y'know, a tough lady.

FRED SILVERMAN, former V.P. of Programs at CBS:

I had never seen her before. And Norman thought that was very funny, that I didn't know who Bea Arthur was . . . but what do I know? I was television, and she was a stage actress. And I just thought she was terrific. I said, "That lady is great! Let's do a show with her."

NORMAN LEAR:

Before it aired, I knew that I was going to get a call very quickly to build a show around her. It was so clear. There was nothing like her around. And indeed, before I went to bed that night I got a call from Fred Silverman. Immediately: "You've gotta do a show with that woman, right away."

FRED SILVERMAN:

And he didn't want to do it. He just—I don't know, he had to be talked into everything.

I said, "Just bring her back, once! Bring her back, and we'll do a book-ended show." And he did. And it was just an enormous hit—it tested through the roof. And *nothing* tested well. Even *All in the Family* died on their testing. But this really tested well, 'cause she was a great character. Unlike Archie, she was a screaming hard liberal.

NORMAN LEAR:

Well, she was the same as Archie. As little responsible for *her* point of view and *her* passion as Archie was for his. That's how I used to think of her . . . she was a horseshit liberal.

SUSAN HARRIS, writer:

Exactly. She was liberal, but it was *radical chic* kind of liberal. She was great. She was strong, she had opinions. I mean, no woman spoke the way Maude did. Again, Norman broke ground . . . it wasn't about the pot roast anymore—it was about a facelift or an abortion, it was about real stuff.

ELLIOT SHOENMAN, writer:

I would describe her character as highly opinionated, intelligent, and against the grain. Ahead of her time to a large extent, as far as standing up for her principles. A liberally oriented show that ran during the Nixon presidency, counteracting some of the conservatism. God only knows— I wish we had the same show now! And I'm sure you couldn't. Certainly not with the religious right. I mean, we were doing things about abortions, and jokes you couldn't get near in a million years now.

The indomitable, "compromising, enterprising, anything but tranquilizing" Maude Findlay herself, Bea Arthur. © 1972, 2005 ELP Communications, Inc.

BOB SCHILLER, writer:

Maude was a great character. A woman with her allegiance in two generations. She was right in the middle of the women's movement, but still couldn't accept the whole thing. She was troubled—because she wanted to be a modern woman, and yet she held on to the old-fashioned clichés . . . the old-fashioned woman who took a backseat to her husband.

ROD PARKER:

First we had to figure out what the story was. Walter Findlay—that name I got from Findlay Galleries. I was passing by, and I said, "That's a strange name for a gallery . . . Walter Findlay . . . gee, that's a nice name. I'll use that." So then I started to produce it. And back in those days, there was *a* producer. And an executive producer. The second year, I became the executive producer, along with Norman.

Norman really ran the show. I ran the show, but he liked to come in and change things, and do things. In some cases he'd dictate into a tape recorder—which I learned to do later—in the middle of the night, to redo a scene or something. It was Norman's baby, and I was the hired help. We started *Maude* with three writers. And one of them was the producer: me.

Then we finally got help when we got Schiller and Weiskopf. But after that, I convinced Norman that we needed more of a staff. Because there's just too much going on. And with Norman, he'd get an idea—he'd call up and say, "Let's do this." And all of a sudden, you're looking at a whole new act! This was in the first year.

ALAN WAGNER, former V.P. of Program Development at CBS:

Norman said, "What's different about *Maude*, and what have we not done before?" He'd already talked about having babies, losing babies, cancer, and defecation on *All in the Family*, but not really sexuality in the usual sense. He'd talked about erectile dysfunction . . . but when *Maude* started, that pushed into an area in view of things he couldn't deal with earlier.

And that was a whole new window on the world. Just like *The Jeffersons* opened another window on another world. Norman wasn't afraid of anything. And he wanted the show to be a hit. I mean, he was building an empire; that was part of it, too.

BOB SCHILLER:

First of all, it was honest. It dealt with things—with humor—that ordinarily were very somber subjects. I always say *Maude* went off the air because we ran out of problems! And we did everything . . . rape, alcoholism, middle-aged pregnancy . . . instead of fluff. We handled human problems—and, certainly, human problems are funnier than fluff. It struck a chord. That's Norman's doing. Writing that stuff, you're plowing fields. It was very satisfying.

ROD PARKER:

We also spent time having middle-aged sex, so that they were not your average couple on television at that age. In fact, when the English actress who played the maid, Hermione Baddeley, and Pat O'Malley were going to live together, we had a line, "Why do people think that old people don't get horny?" Well, that was *my* personal battle with Program Practices.

"You can't say that!"

I said, "What do you mean, you can't say *horny*? It's funny. If Carol says it, then you've got a point. But coming from this woman, in her eighties, it's funny. And it's not dirty. Look at it!" And so I finally convinced them. That was my big thing: *look at it.* Which they did, and they said it was okay.

BOB SCHILLER:

I mean, they wouldn't let us stick our wanger out and wave it in front of the camera, but they allowed us a lot that they wouldn't allow other people. Other shows got annoyed at us.

Maude's Right to Choose, and Other Uproars

FRED SILVERMAN:

They did a two-part show on abortion . . . I thought Norman was going to quit. That really became a cause célèbre. It's a hot potato *now*, so you can imagine what it was like in the 1970s, to do a two-parter on it. Where she decides to have the abortion! You're taking sides on a very volatile issue.

ROD PARKER:

We just fell into the abortion show. I called Susan Harris to do it, 'cause she'd done one show for us, and I loved Susan Harris. Now, in that episode, originally, Maude was not going to get an abortion. It was a friend of Maude's who we called Vivian. 'Cause what we really wanted to do was Walter getting a vasectomy. That was the whole argument.

Husband Walter (Bill Macy), best friend Vivian (Rue McClanahan), and daughter Carol (Adrienne Barbeau) are there to bolster Maude during a moment of crisis. © 1972, 2005 ELP Communications, Inc.

SUSAN HARRIS:

The story that was assigned was: How about if we get her neighbor Vivian pregnant, and do an abortion episode? I said, "Great," and I wrote it.

ROD PARKER:

So, the first draft came in—for a single episode—and Norman asked how Susan's script came out. I said, "The wrong person is funny."

He said, "What do you mean?"

"Vivian is very funny. Maude has nothing to do. It has to be the other way around."

And he got excited about it. He said, "Yes!"

So, now we said we can make it a two-parter. I called Susan and said, "Don't worry about a rewrite, cause you're going to be doing a two-parter. You're going to be rewriting your first one, but then you're going to do a second one." She was delighted.

But the point is, we couldn't have it phony—a false pregnancy. That would be terrible. We couldn't have a miscarriage, because Sally Struthers had just had one on *All in the Family*. So, it had to be Maude getting an abortion. We couldn't have her having the baby because, well, the show was not about an older couple with a baby. That would completely tilt the show in the wrong direction. So, Norman made the decision.

BUD YORKIN:

Everyone said, "You can't do it"—including the network—but we went ahead and did it! With money out of our pocket. 'Cause we knew: What are they gonna do? Are we gonna come out in the press and say, "We did this show, here we are, very successful, the first two top shows at their time"—what are they gonna say to us? We say we want to treat this issue, and here's this big strong network that won't let us do it?

So, we put our own money where our mouth was and did it. They didn't want to go through that in public when we told 'em, "We're gonna do it, and if you don't want to put it on, then we'll have to break the news and have a big press conference."

ROD PARKER:

We were getting mail, y'know, unborn fetuses and everything else, as soon as it got out that we were doing the show on this. We had made part one, which nobody could yell about, 'cause she had not said she was getting an abortion then. But before we even finished shooting part one, we were getting hate mail.

CBS got scared. And, I mean, the hate mail came like crazy. We were getting terrible letters. We were "New York liberal Jews"—that was a big one. Some came right out with "New York Commie Jews." It wouldn't have stopped us. We were going to do the show.

And then Norman put the master in the trunk of his car and said, "Okay, you guys don't want to do it? I'll sell it to somebody. We'll show it. And CBS will not have had the guts to do the show." Norman said, "Don't pay me for the show." Norman was rich enough, he could do that. So they said okay.

FRED SILVERMAN:

There was an outcry. And internally, with the affiliates. You have to remember that a television network has a lot of affiliates in those red states. And there are a lot of people in the *blue states* who are anti-abortion.

ROD PARKER:

It was a big fight. But it didn't take long—I mean, Norman was powerful. He and Bud had six or seven shows in the top ten in one week. It was amazing. No one had ever done that before in television. Or since.

And the reruns went on—without any sponsor. It was all promotional stuff. There was one sponsor, and they dropped out at the last minute. Norman said to CBS, "If you don't show the reruns, that means you were wrong to show them in the first place. You've gotta do the reruns."

My favorite thing was that in Peoria, the guy who owned two stations there would not show *Maude*. Y'know, some of the stations showed it at 12:00 at night, even though it was out of its regular spot. The guy in Peoria said, "This show is not fit for the American public to see." So he substituted reruns of *Let's Make a Deal*!

On a personal level, my wife was born in Shenandoah, Pennsylvania. Her parents were Catholic, and her mother was thrilled that her daughter was married to a "Hollywood producer." She put all this stuff in the paper, and told all her friends every time we came to visit. One day she went to church on a Sunday, and the sermon was all about how "those terrible people on *Maude* were murderers." We're for *murder*. And all her friends were kind of looking at her.

CHARLIE HAUCK, writer and producer:
I did one script in which Maude's nephew, whom she loved—he was like a young hippie—comes into town on his motorcycle, and he's got his girl-friend and she's pregnant. And the kid says, "Well, I have to be free!" Maude's trying to get them married. And in all of that, there was never a mention of abortion. The club had been beaten down on us so badly—I wasn't there when it happened—but there was such, like, "Don't even get into that! 'Cause we're just trying to do the show." I don't think we even did a joke about it.

ROD PARKER:
The thing that I learned on *Maude* was: Tell the network as little as possible. And since we always read a week in advance, I'd never clear a story with any-body. I'd just say, "You can hear the show a week in advance. So, you've got a whole week to worry about it. And so will we." Because I always found out that if we could keep up that schedule, and be that one script ahead each week, that it made the shows a lot easier. We had a lot less work to do on a show that we were gonna do that week, because we had spent time the week *before* rewriting after we heard it.

The battles are kind of silly, most of the time, with Program Practices. And I got along with them. Network people just come and go, and you don't know when, how, who . . . They gave me a cartoon: a picture from an old movie of some Mexican police grabbing a Mexican bandit, and they said it's "Program Practices having a meeting with Rod Parker." So, they had a sense of humor, too.

CHARLIE HAUCK:

There was a controversy on a three-parter we did, when Walter was a manic-depressive. It was based on Norman's experience with his wife, Frances, who was a manic-depressive and found lithium . . . and we ended up advocating lithium, in effect, through the context of Walter. 'Cause that's what worked for him. And there was a hue and cry about that from some quarters in the press, like *Time* magazine.

ROD PARKER:

We were the first comedy where a character said "son of a bitch." I was on the phone with Program Practices, saying, "It's the only thing she can call him. And it's so sweet, the way she says it. You've got to see it." So, they saw it—and still said, "You can't do it."

ELLIOT SHOENMAN:

It was a *Maude* episode where Walter had a heart attack. He went over to Jill Clayburgh's house—she played somebody who was working for him. And he had a heart attack while he was there, and it *appeared* that he'd been having sex with her even though he hadn't. Maude was just steaming. But because he couldn't be dealt with, she was overly nice to him.

And then finally he gets a prognosis at the end saying he's okay. And she said, "I'm so glad you're okay, but I have just one thing to say."

"What?"

"You son of a bitch!"

That was the end of the episode. I remember that being a very big controversy.

NORMAN LEAR:

So, that's the way Bill Tankersley saw the script. And he called and he said, "You can't shoot that." He thought I was kidding.

I said, "Bill, this is Maude. This moment, everything builds to this moment, and I can't think of another thing she'd say to him." And we went back and forth.

WILLIAM TANKERSLEY, former Director of Program Practices at CBS:

I said, "You can always find a word to replace a bad word. You can say it in another way." In any event, it *was* absolutely a perfect thing for her to say—"Walter, you son of a bitch"—there was nothing better than that. And I said so. But for gosh sakes, we can't *do* that!

NORMAN LEAR:

Finally, because I respected him, I said, "Tell you what. If you can come up with something, and you can look me in the eye over the long-distance phone and say, 'Norman, I think this is every bit as good,' and tell me what she should say . . . I'll do it. But you have to be able to say you really mean it."

And he called me back and said, "Okay." He took me up on it. Then he called me back a few days later, and he couldn't really think of anything. I said, "I have to hold you to it, Bill." And he did. He let it go through.

WILLIAM TANKERSLEY:

I didn't have time to think about it. [laughing] But if I had, I probably couldn't think of anything better than "You son of a bitch" . . . In any event, Norman still laughs about it. He says I still owe him fifty dollars. I told my wife, "One day I'm going to send Norman Lear a fifty-dollar bill, and he can hang it on the wall."

I won't tell him I don't remember the bet . . . I remembered it as a hypothetical thing, but it wasn't. I asked one of the editors, "That didn't really happen?" He said, "Yeah, it did!"

NORMAN LEAR:

But that's who *he* was. I mean, he really believed *of course* there was something else she could say. I didn't have to *agree* with him. That's the stunning thing, actually, as I've repeated this for I don't know how long, and thought about it. But our deal was that I didn't have to agree—he just has to tell me he believes it. That's how much trust we had in one another. And he couldn't do that. Y'know, he was one of us. But he had a job, and other people that he answered to.

WILLIAM TANKERSLEY:

Well, that's either generous or ignorant, because I had nobody to please but myself. My job was very independent. If I had anybody, it would be the affiliates as a whole. And the public as a whole. I don't want to argue with Norman if he wants to be generous . . .

He called me one day, two or three years ago, and said, "I'm just calling you to tell you about the great respect I've had for you over the years. That's all I want to say."

The last time I called him, I returned the favor and told him what I thought of him as a patriot who would spend eight million dollars on one of the copies of the Declaration of Independence. And I said, "I hope that you're still a good Democrat." He assured me that he was. So am I.

They Worked Hard for the Funny

ELLIOT SHOENMAN:

I learned real quickly that *Maude* was a very hard show. In certain ways, harder than *All in the Family*. I would notice, occasionally, that the *All in the Family* guys would leave earlier than we would . . . and what was explained to me was that, because *Maude* was a highly intelligent show, there were only a couple of shortcuts that you could go to—which, fundamentally, was Maude saying, "God'll get ya for that, Walter"—and there was an amount you could use that for in a season without overextending it. So, when you were sitting there at 2:00 or 3:00 in the morning, the scenes tended to go toward her saying something really clever. That was the nature of Bea Arthur, and that's what worked about the show. Meanwhile, at 2:00 or 3:00 in the morning, it's murder coming up with that stuff!

Whereas with *All in the Family*, I discovered quickly, they had some shortcuts built in. They had Archie doing a malaprop, Edith doing a dumb joke, him

A smiling publicity shot of the Findlay family: Adrienne Barbeau, Bea Arthur, and Bill Macy. © 1972, 2005 ELP Communications, Inc.

calling her a *dingbat* . . . y'know, they could go to the lower brow—so to speak—thing. And then I started to notice that a lot of shows had a dumb character or shortcut. A Latka or Reverend Jim. Where, when you're sittin' there at 2:00 in the morning, you can go to the old standby and, you know, do variations on it—which were very clever and smart—but they're a thousand times easier than Maude doing some wonderful, liberal, intellectual joke.

ROD PARKER:

We had an awful lot of rewriting on that show for the first couple of years, but after about the third year, we became human beings. The writers got a break, 'cause they knew what they were doing. And they knew the characters—so that helped a lot.

BOB SCHILLER:

The writers' meetings were very interesting. You'd think of a problem: "Let's see . . . we did abortion . . . how about rape?" Alcoholism . . . all kinds of wonderful things. Probably, there were some stories we never really licked—but not many. Because we'd say, "Here's a theme for a show" about so and so . . . and Norman would say, "Do it." He'd never say no. We had to clear all the stories with Norman . . . and he was very, very good with story.

ELLIOT SHOENMAN:

Rod ran them. They were very small groups. Schiller and Weiskopf as a team, and then Bud Grossman and I as individuals. That was the whole staff—people can't believe it nowadays. And sometimes Norman . . . but mostly it would be short meetings with Norman where you talk subject matter.

CHARLIE HAUCK:

Norman was very involved, very wisely, through story. All the stories we worked out, we either pitched to him, or *he'd* often come in with story ideas. But we'd always go to his office and talk out the story quite a bit. On every episode. And then, especially as the company got bigger and there were more shows, he might read the script and maybe have some notes, but he'd come to the Friday runs. We taped on Tuesday, so Friday was the big run-through. And he'd have input there. Then, he may or may not come to the show—often he did, but not always. He had enormous energy, and his story fearlessness was really impressive.

ROD PARKER:

I had a line quoted in *TV Guide* when they did an article. I said, "One thing about Norman: He's never afraid to admit that he's wrong. He's also never afraid to admit he's right!"

He got mad at the way they handled the story. He said, "There's only one line in here I know was true: That's yours!"

NORMAN LEAR:

All the writers used to surround the table in my office . . . on all of our shows. All of the conversations for the first four years or whatever, with the scripts—I don't know how we did it. If they shoved a broom up my ass I would have swept the floors—that was always the repeated joke. But somehow, you know, whoever said, "If you want something done, ask a busy man," had it right. You get in that groove, and there's time.

Anyway, stories were conceived. We had a wonderful conference table, and a microphone in the center of it. Five minutes into it, somebody was typing down the hall . . . and by the time the writers left on that show, there were five or ten pages waiting for them. And the next group would come in. Those were the days.

ELLIOT SHOENMAN:

I know there were times when certainly I was frustrated, saying, "Why didn't Rod stand up to him more?" But I was in awe of the whole situation. I remember Norman very fondly, but I suspect that he was a lot tougher than I remember him. What stands out in my mind is the amazing likeability of the guy, and that we were always in crisis on one show or the other with the network, and there were always rumors that the show was going to shut down . . . because CBS didn't want to do the abortion episode, they didn't want Maude to say "son of a bitch," and there was always some unbelievable standoff whether the show was actually gonna be done that week!

ROD PARKER:

I've worked on good shows, I've worked on bad shows, and I've worked on so-so shows. You work just as hard on a bad show as you do on a good show. And when something comes out that you're proud of, that you're happy with . . . when you enjoy writers' sessions, when you sit around and talk about it, and rewrite, and create stories . . . it's worthwhile. I never felt,

"Oh, God, I wanna quit this show. I can't take this." No matter how hard the work was. It didn't do much for my marriage, but . . .

I think it's the best experience I've ever had. And that says a lot. Working with Gleason or Carney, I felt the same way working with Bea Arthur. I was dealing with the same kind of talent. She was going out there, and she was gonna *dare* that audience to laugh. I mean, you better laugh. I'm going to *make* you laugh! Regardless. And the material might be very good, and everything else, but she wasn't happy unless she got the biggest laughs in the world. And we *got* some of the biggest laughs in the world.

BEA ARTHUR, performer:

It was just such fun, working with Norman. I mean, he was there every minute, and we had [director] Hal Cooper, and we had the writers, we had Schiller and Weiskopf ... we tackled everything except hemorrhoids. But we had a chance to do over-the-top comedy. I mean, really, really extraordinary comedy, not just funny lines coming out of people's mouths.

I see it now; I go to bed early so I can wake early and see it at four-thirty in the morning now, on TV Land. And I look at this, and damn it, we were good. We were good. Bill Macy and Connie Bain and Rue McClanahan. I mean we did great shows. The writing was wonderful, and the acting ... And everyone contributed. There were never any egos involved—it was just pure unadulterated fun.

But it was hard work. It was hard work ... I remember being up nights thinking, "Oh God, how are we going to get through this?" But, anyway, it was a hell of an experience.

Soap Bubbles Up . . . and Pops in ABC's Face

8

No show in the history of television has generated more controversy—before it ever even aired a single episode—than *Soap*. With this broad comedy series about two Connecticut families, their passions, infidelities, indiscretions, and secrets, creator Susan Harris knew she was going further than any show had gone before . . . but she and her producing partners, Paul Junger Witt and Tony Thomas, never expected to incur the full wrath of the religious right.

Before *Soap* hit the airwaves in the fall of 1977—a year dubbed the "season of sex" by some wags no doubt also referring to the double entendre-laden *Three's Company*, as well as that ripe serving of cheesecake called *Charlie's Angels*—ABC was barraged by an organized campaign that dumped over 32,000 letters of complaint on their desks. The initial uproar was fueled by a piece of reporting in *Time* magazine's July 11, 1977 issue about the upcoming show. "Until the ABC censors got wind of it," the article read, "the show's writers had plotted Father Flotsky's seduction in church by Corinne, then an exorcism for their baby." From the day the network first announced the show for their upcoming schedule, *Soap*'s racy content had already begun generating controversy—but the *Time* article kicked it into high gear, result-ing in picketing, protests, threats, and considerable fear on the part of spon-sors and their ad agencies. ABC hoped to quell some of the opposition by running "Parental discretion is advised" warnings at the top of each episode, but the damage was already done.

The show at the center of the firestorm? A stylized, cleverly plotted and scripted half-hour weekly comedy featuring a diverse, quirky ensemble cast of veteran stage and screen character actors . . . engaged in some highly farcical and sexual situations.

Soap's intentionally tangled storylines revolved around the eccentric families of two sisters: wealthy, kooky Jessica Tate (played by Katherine Helmond) and her more sensible middle-class sister, Mary Campbell (Cathryn Damon). Jessica's pompous husband, Chester (Robert Mandan), has been cheating on her for years, and she in turn has taken to cheating on him—with the same tennis pro, Peter Campbell (Robert Urich), that their daughter, Corrine (Diana Canova), has been secretly schtupping. The Tates' insolent butler, Benson (Robert Guillaume, in a role he would spin off into his own hit series, *Benson*), does as he pleases in their home, while Jessica's demented father, the Major (Arthur Peterson), still crawls around the house in his battle fatigues as if WWII has never ended.

Across town, Mary's jittery second husband, Burt Campbell (Richard Mulligan), is impotent, mainly because he killed Mary's *first* husband and can't bring himself to tell her. Mary's offspring from the first marriage include Danny Dallas (Ted Wass), an aspiring mafia soldier in the service of "The Godfather" (Richard Libertini), and her younger son, Jodie Dallas (Billy Crystal), who's quite gay, and—at least early in the series—seeks a sex-change operation. *Soap* grew wackier as the years went on, with stories like Benson rescuing Billy Tate (Jimmy Baio) from a religious cult; Jessica's unjust

In the Campbell kitchen, three dummies—Danny (Ted Wass), Bob (the one with the wooden head), and Chuck (Jay Johnson)—sit and watch Burt (Richard Mulligan) grow ever more apoplectic.
© *CBS Television Network*

conviction for murdering Peter (who had turned out to be Burt's son), followed by Chester confessing, being convicted and sent to prison, escaping, and developing amnesia; Corrine marrying her ex-priest lover and giving birth to a baby possessed by the devil; Chuck Campbell's (Jay Johnson) ventriloquist dummy Bob talking—on its own; Burt kidnapped and cloned by aliens, which led to Mary having sex with his clone; and much more.

Soap managed to balance its nuttier elements with some rather dramatic ones, making statements along the way about the human condition with honesty and compassion. To this day, there's not been another TV show quite like it, before or after it ended its four-year run. The series was enormously popular in the United States and abroad—one of the top-rated programs on television almost as long as ABC kept it on the air. Condemned by the Roman Catholic and Southern Baptist churches, as well as the National Council of Churches and the so-called Moral Majority, that *Soap* lasted for four years was a testament to the willpower and creativity of its creators, as well as the faith of its beleaguered network.

Interestingly, *Soap* is often labeled a *satire* on soap operas—a misconception that Susan Harris and her partner/husband, Paul Junger Witt (who both went on to even greater success with the beloved, long-running *The Golden Girls*), would like to clear up . . .

No Soap, Comedy

SUSAN HARRIS, creator, writer, and producer:
Actually, there wasn't an "idea" at first. I wanted to do a continuing story. Probably truly for selfish reasons, because I found it impossible to do stories every week with beginnings, middles, and ends. So, I figured if it was a continuous story, I would never have to wind it up and it could just dribble on and on.

So, I went to Paul and Tony just with that idea. A continuing story about a family—and that's how we started. We didn't consider ourselves a parody of soap opera.

PAUL JUNGER WITT, executive producer:
It's called *Soap* 'cause we didn't know what else to call it!

SUSAN HARRIS:
That was a working title that stuck. None of us watched soaps . . . all we knew about soaps was that basically they had no story end, and that they were pretty silly. It just gave us license to do what we wanted to do.

PAUL JUNGER WITT:

It's really the story of two families . . . of class, of marriage, of parenting, of sex. All of the elements that go into a family life, and contemporary life in America.

Y'know, there certainly were elements of satire. But I think we were satirizing the *status quo* more than soap operas. The storytelling form was not dissimilar in that it was a continuing storyline. What *we* were anxious to do was not only free ourselves of the shackles of a really difficult storytelling form—which is, a brand-new story told every episode in twenty-three minutes and thirty seconds—but also to have characters that were more representative of what we saw going on in society, instead of this generic family that we tended to see in show after show after show.

FRED SILVERMAN, former president of ABC Entertainment:

They took it to Marcy Carsey and Tom Werner, who were running comedy for ABC. They reported to me. I thought it was *great*—I said, "Take the shot!" It represented something new, and at that point in time the Norman Lear comedies were starting to wane a bit. I just thought it would be an attention-getting show, both for its form and content. It was a little more *way out* than the Lear shows, which were more reality based. This was several degrees beyond that.

PAUL JUNGER WITT:

They were enthusiastic from the get-go. They had concerns . . . about Standards and Practices. But we had a very solid relationship with Al Schneider, who was running Standards and Practices for ABC at that time, and we were determined to work together. And I'm sure we turned his hair prematurely gray! But on the other hand, he understood the creative process, and he knew that he could be more than a roadblock—he could be someone that we could work with, rather than around. And he was that for us.

SUSAN HARRIS:

Oh, yeah. You do have to work with them on a weekly basis.

PAUL JUNGER WITT:

That's not to say that we didn't have words. That's not to say that there weren't times we were incredibly upset because we really wanted to do something that they really didn't want us to do.

**ALFRED SCHNEIDER, former V.P. of Policy
and Standards at ABC:**

The toughest part was finding the balance between saying that we were exercising restraint, and at the same time accepting some of the very good arguments that Susan and Paul would make about, "Why can't we include this?"

Like women at a table, talking about sex—which we'd originally said no to. And then they came around and said, "But you let *men* talk about sex!"

They were quite right. So we permitted women to talk about orgasm for the first time on television.

PAUL JUNGER WITT:

They knew that we were anxious to do something that was very different. The form was different. We presented them with a bible, so they could "see" the first season—which you rarely get in initial pitch meetings. And we wanted to have *fun*. We had all worked on a number of series . . . sometimes we were creatively stimulated, other times we were shackled by the kind of storytelling that had gone on for thirty-some odd years, and was relatively unchanged. We were determined to stimulate ourselves as much as possible.

And as the three of us look back at this thing—at our careers, in general— it may have been the hardest work any of us ever did, 'cause we were a very small company. Susan *was* the staff until later on when one other writer joined us—but it was also the most fun we've ever had!

SUSAN HARRIS:

It was the worst experience, and the best experience.

Stop, in the Name of the Lord!

JAY SANDRICH, director:

You can't even begin to know how *Soap* was being challenged . . . we weren't even sure we'd get on the air until a week before! There was a lie—or let's say it was a terrible mistake—printed in *Time*, that we were going to seduce a priest in church. Which was *never* part of it.

PAUL JUNGER WITT:

Time raised a red flag that was really unfair, that had any number of bits of misinformation . . . such as the priest being seduced in the confessional. None of which was ever even conceived of, much less done.

FRED SILVERMAN:

They got a copy of a storyline that had been rejected—and *printed it* like that's what the show was going to be about. I mean, in a million years it would never have been approved. Once *Time* printed that story, then it became the summer of *Soap*, and it was just totally occupying all of my time . . . defending it, trying to keep the affiliates in line. A lot of the affiliates didn't want to clear the show. A lot of them cleared it an hour later—we had to give two feeds of the show. One at 9:30 and one at 10:30, believe it or not.

And for those stations that scheduled it at 10:30, it ended up being a hodgepodge schedule, 'cause we had *Family*[7] on the air . . . and that meant that *Family* would play at 9:30 and *Soap* would play at 10:30, and it made absolutely no sense from an audience-flow point of view.

But it was always going to air. After all the time I personally spent on the stump for this thing, I would've thrown myself off a building if it didn't air. I had a lot of other things to do, y'know, and this was just one show! At that point, the entertainment head was in charge of all entertainment programming, day and night. So, it really did a take up a lot of my time.

ALFRED SCHNEIDER:

We went around the country and spoke to various special-interest groups, and tried to explain to them what our procedures were. And that we would be reviewing the scripts, that we would certainly not consider things that were irresponsible, that we would certainly try to balance the portrayal of the homosexuality, and that there was a review process in terms of the script stage through the final rough cut before it got on the air. And that was our intention.

But what happens is that in special-interest groups, they have their advocates. And they're going to *use* the programs for whatever their own purposes are . . . whether it be to instill responsibility, or to advocate a position.

JAY SANDRICH:

What happened was, Susan and Tony sat down and wrote a bible for the first year. And in it, the priest—who had a high-school crush on Diana Canova's character—quit the priesthood, 'cause he loved her. But never were they going to seduce him in church. *Never.*

PAUL JUNGER WITT:

There was a scene in a confessional . . .

[7] *An hour-long dramatic series that ran on ABC from 1976–1980.*

SUSAN HARRIS:

But there was no *seduction* in the church. They took some license.

PAUL JUNGER WITT:

It was damaging to us in the following way: Before we went on the air, we were condemned by half the churches in America. I remember speaking at churches, and at synagogues . . . and of course, no one had *seen* this thing. But we were condemned by some huge organizations. We also became a target of the Moral Majority—Jerry Falwell's group, at the time—which really had a fad constituency. They claimed to represent several hundred thousand people. Their membership was really several thousand.

But they managed to frighten Madison Avenue. They managed to frighten the agencies to the degree that, despite our numbers, which were huge, we never got the kind of pricing that the show should've. Because a lot of sponsors were afraid of it. National sponsors, rather than paying the full freight for a show that was, in fact, a huge hit, were being discounted . . . or we had companies advertising that didn't pay full freight. Because of the pressure of the Moral Majority.

FRED SILVERMAN:

We ended up getting the sponsors. Y'know, there were only three or four minutes of commercials in the show, so there was certainly a big enough pool of advertisers that we could fill that time with. But I don't think we got the blue chips, like P&G and General Foods. I think they were afraid.

JAY SANDRICH:

So, before the show had even been seen by anybody, we were being attacked. And gays were attacking the show, too. Some Southern stations wouldn't carry it. We originally shot two half hours. It was going to be an hour show, and they decided they were going to break it up—but out here in L.A., they ran the first half hour, followed by a half-hour discussion on ABC between a priest and a rabbi and a minister about the show!

PAUL JUNGER WITT:

It sounds like a joke, doesn't it? "A priest, a rabbi, a minister, and a network executive walk into a bar . . . "

I remember debating Jerry Falwell on *The Phil Donahue Show*, and it really wasn't a reasonable debate. We *were* dealing with infidelity. We *were* dealing with subjects that were part of the fact and fabric of American society, but had been verboten on television. And we didn't set out to be pioneers or sexual liberationists—just honest storytellers, wanting to have as much fun as possible . . . and to stretch the envelope as much as we could because creatively, it's much more stimulating. In a pre-cable world, we ran into a lot of flak. This show *now*, compared to some shows that are on network, wouldn't raise an eyebrow!

FRED SILVERMAN:

We got flak from everybody. We didn't have Martians yet on the show, so we didn't hear from the Martians yet . . . we heard from the Martians the third season.

But it was a feeding frenzy. I remember that the man who was in charge of the Group W stations, Don McGannon—who had a couple of affiliates at ABC—led the charge against the show, and he was a very distinguished broadcaster. He had never even *seen* it. And here was somebody who was a pillar of the broadcast establishment just leading the charge against this poor little show.

JAY SANDRICH:

The biggest problem, I always felt, more than anything: Katherine Helmond's character has an affair because her husband has been cheating on her. And she's having an affair with a tennis pro who's also having an affair with her daughter, and she doesn't know about it. But it was the idea of a woman going out and having an affair.

PAUL JUNGER WITT:

We had a very interesting screening for the O&Os[8] and for the station owners. Some guys got up and walked out. Now, whether that was because they had already been sensitized by what they had read or whether they were unable to deal with the fact that traditional sexual comedy and innuendo—such as the philandering husband, which has always been a comedic device—was turned on its head. We had a *wife* being unfaithful as a result of her husband's infidelity. Cuckoldry somehow wasn't nearly as funny to these guys . . .

SUSAN HARRIS:

. . . as food fights!

PAUL JUNGER WITT:

Exactly. So that's what we were facing. Y'know, we had affiliates in the South who weren't running the show at all, or were running it Thursday night at

---

[8] *Network "owned and operated" TV stations across the country, as opposed to affiliates, which are owned privately and pay for programming from the big three networks.*

1:00 in the morning. We had a peculiar lineup. The O&Os ran us where we supposed to be—the network was very happy creatively. And the network supported us as long as they could afford it.

Four years, ninety-nine episodes.

SUSAN HARRIS:

And they lost money. But they stuck with us for quite a long time, losing money.

FRED SILVERMAN:

But it was nice, because it went on the air and it was a big hit.

PAUL JUNGER WITT:

And it's been very successful in syndication. We get mail from young fans who are exposed to it for the first time when whichever cable outlet happens to own it at the time runs it. Very often they'll run as marathons. And we'll get mail. We also became an icon to the gay community.

Billy Crystal as Jodie Dallas, one of the first openly gay characters to regularly appear on a network TV series.[9]
© ABC Television Network

SUSAN HARRIS:

Well, we told them, when there was a reaction—and it was a premature reaction—to just wait until they saw the Jodie character develop. It's very hard, in one episode or two episodes, when you're faced with fourteen characters, to paint three-dimensional ones. So, we said, "Wait until we have a few more episodes, and you'll see." And he did become a human being.

In the very beginning, because of the time constraints in television, you have to paint in broad strokes. It's short; you don't have much time. And in a pilot, there's a lot you have to do . . . you have to give the backstory, you have to bring everyone up to date, you have many characters who are all new. There's nothing you can do except paint with the broadest possible strokes—and so the characters *were* a bit cartoon-like.

[9] *In an earlier attempt, Vincent Schiavelli played a gay set designer named Peter Panama in ABC's short-lived (and barely noticed) sitcom,* The Corner Bar *(1972).*

But once a show is on three or four times, then you can have a more nuanced approach . . . and the characters become more three-dimensional. That's what happened to Jodie. It wasn't that we shifted in our approach. The show evolved on its own, and it was not a reflection of the kind of feedback we were getting, unless it was people loving characters we were about to kill—and then, of course, we wouldn't do that.

ALFRED SCHNEIDER:

The key is viewer expectation. When you put something on for the first time as an individual program—where the viewer doesn't know what to expect—you get a lot of concerns raised, as distinguished from those who see your program week after week and know what the program is all about. And therefore, you have that audience who comes to it knowing that that's what they want to see.

PAUL JUNGER WITT:

Y'know, we did meet with gay groups who were concerned that the first openly gay character on television would be seen as wildly effeminate. We told them that other gay characters who we planned to introduce would be the antithesis of that. And we also explained that, you know, there *was* going to be an evolution.

ALFRED SCHNEIDER:

The whole question of balancing Billy Crystal's portrayal of homosexuality . . . that was the toughest. The homosexuals were saying, "You're stereotyping!" and the religious community said, "You're proselytizing!"

And we said, "We're doing neither. We're showing this man in a satirical, humorous vein, and hopefully in a fair way." Well, there were those who never agreed with us.

PAUL JUNGER WITT:

When we say that this was the most fun creatively we ever had, it was because first of all, we were working with an incredible cast! Billy Crystal has a level of humanity and warmth in him that took this character that most of America had never seen before—and might very well be shocked by—and ingratiated himself with the audience almost immediately.

FRED SILVERMAN:

I think you just got to know him better. The character initially seemed very, very, very flamboyant and bizarre. But then you really got to know and

On the set with most of the original Soap ensemble. Seated (l-r): Diana Canova, Robert Mandan, Katherine Helmond, and Cathryn Damon. Standing (l-r): Arthur Peterson, Jennifer Salt, Robert Guillaume, Ted Wass, Richard Mulligan, Bob Seagren, and Billy Crystal. © ABC Television Network

understand the character, 'cause she really did write very dimensional characters. These weren't caricatures.

PAUL JUNGER WITT:
We had an extraordinary ensemble . . . and it really allowed Susan to reach even further creatively, because they could do *anything* she wrote for them.

SUSAN HARRIS:
It was truly [a great] ensemble. And everyone eventually had their moments, and had their stories.

JAY SANDRICH:
It was the most challenging, interesting thing for a director, 'cause you had one very dramatic scene, one broad scene, one very literate scene, you know? It had everything, and a cast that was so good. And some weeks they'd be so under-used . . . I mean, you just couldn't service everyone! Everybody was unhappy sometime or another.

PAUL JUNGER WITT:

Compared to what I read about ensembles on current shows, we had a walk in the park. Our people were highly professional. They knew that it was an ensemble show, they knew there were gonna be weeks that they were light, and weeks that they were heavy. They knew that, y'know, stories would ebb and flow. Sure, there was some frustration—but it never got ugly, and they always had great mutual respect for one another. If you're a good actor, and this is what you're doing for a living most of the year and you felt you haven't had a lot to do for a few weeks, it's frustrating! But it wasn't competitive. It was just that good actors want to work as much as possible.

All by Myself: A One-Woman Writing Staff

JAY SANDRICH:

Susan Harris is brilliant—she's just amazing. She wrote every word the first few seasons, every single word . . . and I don't think it's ever been done, before or since, on a comedy show. There was no staff. There was Susan.

Paul, Tony, and Susan would work on stories. The big advantage for a writer was that you didn't have to tell a beginning, middle, and end story, because it was episodic scenes of stories. So, Susan and Paul and Tony would break the scenes with me. They'd come up with how the situations would develop—and then she would sit and write 'em.

FRED SILVERMAN:

You know, it was originally conceived as a twice a week show. But it would've been too difficult, 'cause she wrote all the scripts.

SUSAN HARRIS:

Believe me, it was not a decision we made. I couldn't find anybody else who could write it! It was our baby—and once it's your baby, nothing is good enough except *perfect*. So, I found myself, whenever we'd hire a writer, rewriting them. And then we'd fire them.

PAUL JUNGER WITT:

What happened was—to make Susan sound a little less difficult—we were breaking two forms. We were breaking storytelling form, and we were also breaking the *setup, joke, setup, joke, setup, joke* rhythm of situation comedy, which Norman Lear had done to a large degree, but we may have taken this even a step further.

Soap, at times, stopped dead and played serious, legitimate moments. And it was the juxtaposition of real drama—of moving, very real moments—with bizarre and unique comedy, that made it difficult for us to find staff that *got* the show. And we didn't have enough time or enough money to raise a staff, to bring them along with us.

SUSAN HARRIS:
Because we had to have a show on the table every week!

PAUL JUNGER WITT:
We were living hand to mouth.

SUSAN HARRIS:
That was the *worst* part of it. But fortunately, it was an ongoing story. That helped enormously, when you don't have to meet that criteria every week. You just *do* it—when you have to do it, you do it. I didn't get a cold that year. I couldn't afford to. The three of us were working constantly.

And then we got—thank God—a really fine writer on board, Stu Silver. Stu caught on very quickly, and he was wonderful. So then we could divide the show up.

PAUL JUNGER WITT:
Yeah, Stu really got the show, and was a godsend. Because I think it would've destroyed Susan, ultimately.

SUSAN HARRIS:
So it got a little bit easier.

PAUL JUNGER WITT:
Considering what we were doing, considering the ground we broke, the network really worked with us. Again, there were times we were frustrated . . . there were times we were heartbroken . . . there were times an *absolutely* hysterical moment or joke or whatever *had* to go. And there simply was no winning. What we learned was not to die every time that happened, but to get 'em back.

And it was never a contentious relationship. I must say, we just revere Al Schneider's work during that period with us, because we could've made him miserable. [laughing] I'm sure we did, at times. But he was always fair, and always supportive.

ALFRED SCHNEIDER:

It wasn't contentious. They're bright, intelligent people. I respected what they had to do, and I guess they respected what I had to do. I never looked at censorship as saying you had to say *no* all the time. In order to be able to go forward and be successful in this industry, you have to find a way to say yes. And the way to find a way to say yes is to work with the production community to make the material *acceptable*.

FRED SILVERMAN:

The entire top management loved the show. 'Cause, y'know, you have to remember that a couple of years earlier, the network was a disaster! And all of a sudden, we had some shows that were really defining shows. *Family* was a great drama. And we had a lot of very successful *popular* shows. *Happy Days*, and *Laverne & Shirley*, and *Three's Company* were super hits—they were top-five shows. But *Soap* had some real style and sophistication. This was a much smarter show, and everybody was very proud of it. And we were proud of our association with Susan, who is a giant.

ALFRED SCHNEIDER:

It was a wonderful time! *Soap* was a provocative program . . . it was very well done. The medium was alive at that point.

PAUL JUNGER WITT:

All we remember is that we received tremendous support from Freddie, from Marcy Carsey and Tom Werner, up and down the line. Everybody liked the show, everybody felt the show had been treated unfairly . . . and I think everyone saw that this emerging organized religious watchdog thing was an imminent threat in that television has always had the best of all possible safeguards. Which is: Change channels. Turn it off. Children shouldn't be watching by themselves anyway. And television is not a babysitter—especially not for a show that's on at 9:00 or 9:30 in the evening. Some of the same people who scream the loudest about the content of television abandon their children to television, because they're either too busy, or don't care enough to watch what they're watching.

ALFRED SCHNEIDER:

Parents certainly have a shared responsibility with the broadcaster. We were careful on what we did, we put disclaimers on, but the parent would have to make their individual judgment as to whether they want their children to watch or not.

SUSAN HARRIS:

I like to think that we were tasteful people and that whatever we did was done with good taste. It wasn't so much to shock as it was to present different points of view.

PAUL JUNGER WITT:

Also, quite frankly—and this is in no way a recommendation of censorship on any level, but—there were limitations that forced us to sometimes go the extra mile in terms of subtlety . . . to find even more clever ways to articulate what it was we wanted to say. But bottom line, we wanted to do a comedy that said something. And Susan is the kind of writer whose strength has always been reality. She doesn't write jokes. She writes people who are funny.

And that's what we wanted to do without the shackles of traditional sitcom storytelling. We would be doing the same thing today, it just would reflect a much more evolved and different society. I mean, feminism was just gaining traction. The gay movement was barely a movement at that time. So we were dealing with the world as we found it at that time . . . and if we were doing it now, we'd be dealing with it as it is now.

SUSAN HARRIS:

Like the zeitgeist.

PAUL JUNGER WITT:

But I would hope we would still piss somebody off . . . I think it's always a good feeling when hypocrites and poseurs and the pompous are upset by creative work. That's always a rewarding feeling.

SUSAN HARRIS:

You're having some impact when you do that.

PAUL JUNGER WITT:

The last part of our final year, they tried us at 10:00—as basically an hour show; they were playing two episodes back to back—and we were successful doing that. The numbers were very, very solid. What it really came down to was a meeting in which the network very apologetically showed us that they could no longer afford to carry us.

And we understood. We had not only had a great creative experience, and one that we hoped ultimately would be financially rewarding—but we also had *Benson*, which was spun out of it. And *Benson*, at the time, was already on its feet and quite successful, so we were able to walk away sadly but with our heads up.

And we weren't killed by a fearful network. The network had been incredibly supportive. We had been doing it long enough to understand that they were in a business, and they sat down and showed us—dollar for dollar—why they couldn't afford to do it anymore.

SUSAN HARRIS:

They had been operating in the red for years with our show. I think at the end, we had one pickle company as just about our only advertiser.

PAUL JUNGER WITT:

Vlasic pickles, the only brand we allow into our house.

FRED SILVERMAN:

I think that after a while, they really started to get too outlandish for their own sake. And it's like anything else . . . you know, a show gets older. The novelty value kind of wore out, and it got increasingly difficult to top themselves. So, therefore, they created these outrageous storylines. When it first when on

Some rather silly-looking aliens hold Burt captive aboard their mother ship, prior to cloning him. © ABC Television Network

the air, there were no Martians in there. It was reality-based, initially. And then, a couple of years in, they started going for the *really* absurd.

See, initially, the Billy Crystal character was an outlandish character, but it was still based in reality. I mean, there are people like that. And the Richard Mulligan character . . . very nervous. That's a very, very real character. Funny, but nevertheless very real—who didn't understand the Billy Crystal character? These are very solid comedic relationships that sustained the show. And the characters were a little bit out there, but they were nevertheless grounded in reality. But the moment you start getting into Martians and talking ventriloquist dummies, I think you're in trouble.

I think ultimately the ratings started to go down, and that's what killed it. That's what kills any show. And I think, also, that she got very, very tired. It just took its toll on her.

A (Densely Plotted, Intricately Layered, Tightly Structured, Smartly Written) Show about Nothing

9

It's rare when a half-hour TV comedy comes along that changes the face of television. It's even rarer when one comes along that changes the way society thinks and talks. For nine years and 169 episodes, NBC's *Seinfeld* did both, holding a magnifying glass to the mundane ordinariness of life in New York City as lived by four very neurotic, eccentric friends.

The show sprang from the brains of two very different standup comics, Jerry Seinfeld and Larry David, neither of whom had any experience creating a situation comedy. Seinfeld's style is keenly observational and aloof, yet engaging. David's style is keenly observational and aloof—and misanthropic and cantankerous. The result of the pairing was a sitcom like no other. The country called it "water-cooler television"—a series that had much of the workplace talking about what had happened on TV the night before. *Seinfeld* tapped into the psyches of young and older viewers alike who recognized themselves and their friends in affable Jerry (playing a fictionalized version of himself), obsessive loser George Costanza (Jason Alexander), plucky, aggressive Elaine Benes (Julia Louis-Dreyfus), Jerry's enterprising hipster goofball neighbor, Cosmo Kramer (Michael Richards), and George's and Jerry's parents and relatives. Kramer's chubby pal Newman (Wayne Knight) also appeared frequently to taunt his archenemy, Jerry (whom Seinfeld would greet with a disdainful, "Hello, *Newman*").

If most comedy series tend to depict events that are larger than life, *Seinfeld* was as *small* as life. The show's inside joke, which soon became an enormously famous outside joke, was that this was a show about "nothing." In fact, it was about everything, all at once—the tiny day-to-day minutiae, petty annoyances, and obsessions that we all cope with and complain about—an outgrowth of comedian/star Jerry Seinfeld's standup act.

Though television was changed forever by *All in the Family, Maude, M*A*S*H*, and some of the other series discussed in this book, there were still a few taboos in place; human foibles and functions that remained verboten, not to be depicted on primetime network TV. *Seinfeld* pulled that last cork out of the bottle. They created—and NBC ran—episodes featuring oral sex, flatulence, masturbation, penis size, and "man-boobs," among other things. Illnesses and infirmities like mental retardation, deafness, and cancer were made fun of. And all of it was executed with style and wit.

More than any prior show, *Seinfeld* exposed the artifice of the sitcom form and stripped it away. Anything deemed remotely warm and fuzzy was quickly tossed and replaced with cold and clammy. Characters growing and learning from their mistakes? Forget it. The show's mantra: "No Hugging, No Learning." They were so resolute about it they even made up jackets for the staff, bearing that motto. *Seinfeld*'s main characters shamelessly lied, schemed, cheated, and backstabbed other characters on the show, as well as each other. Romantic partners and potential suitors were dumped mercilessly, capriciously, and often, for the shallowest of reasons—like being too nice, having a big nose, or wanting to share a toothbrush—or absurd reasons, like having "man hands," eating peas one at a time, or having breasts that were too perfect (they *had* to be implants . . . or were they?).

Selfishness, indifference, and bad behavior were celebrated: Jerry admits that funerals are great for dates ("She's crying, you put your arms around her, you console her."). George, sitting with Jerry and Elaine in Monk's Diner, thinks he's having a heart attack—yet Jerry and Elaine continue to casually banter. Kramer, trying to help Jerry get even with a laundromat owner they believe has found and purposely not returned Jerry's money, dumps sixty pounds of cement powder into a washing machine. At a bakery, Jerry wants to buy their last marble rye bread, but a frail old lady ahead of him in line buys it first. No problem: Jerry mugs her, snatches the bread out of her hands, and dashes away with it tucked under his arm. Kramer and Jerry, munching candy while observing a surgical procedure, accidentally drop a Junior Mint into the open body cavity . . . and say nothing.

No TV show in history was as dark at its core as *Seinfeld*, which absolutely dared its audience to laugh at its callousness and lack of heart. In perhaps the most celebrated (and controversial) instance of bad behavior rewarded, George—a victim of cold feet on the eve of his marriage to fiancée Susan Ross—is actually relieved when she dies from licking too much of the toxic glue from the envelopes of their wedding invitations, which he had chosen because they were the cheapest.

Ironically, the series that's now hailed far and wide as one of the greatest sitcoms of all time—*the* greatest, to many—didn't begin as a series at all, but as a one-time NBC special called *The Seinfeld Chronicles*. "The essence of the show, originally, was my desire to transplant the tone and subjects of my conversations with Larry to television," Seinfeld has said. "At first, the idea was to have two comedians walking around in New York, making fun of things, and in between you'd have standup bits." NBC was fine with the idea, although not particularly enamored of Larry David initially. "Well, they liked *him* enough that they figured it was worth a pilot. I think they would've gotten rid of me in a split second if they could've," David told *The New Yorker* magazine. "They would have gotten rid of me without even thinking about it."

The show was born with very little fanfare and without any great expectations . . .

The Early Chronicles

RICK LUDWIN, V.P. of Late-Night and Primetime Series at NBC:

We had been using Jerry Seinfeld on about every show that we had on the air. He had been on *The Tonight Show*, he had been on the *Letterman* show as a guest, we had used him as the host of a show called *Spy Magazine: How to Be Famous* . . . we even used him on the *Bloopers and Practical Jokes* series. So, we knew him well.

My mandate from Brandon Tartikoff was to try to find the next Jay Leno, [someone who] had the potential to break open to a much wider audience. We thought Jerry was a potential person who could do that.

When we had our first meeting with Jerry and George Shapiro—I was there with Brandon Tartikoff, and Warren Littlefield, in my office—we said to him, "Jerry, what would you like to do in television? Would you like to do a late-night talk show? Would you like to do primetime specials? Primetime series? What is it that you would like to do? We'd like to do it with you."

GEORGE SHAPIRO, manager and executive producer:

Jerry said, "One thing is, I don't wanna play like an accountant or a shoe salesman. I'd like to be myself." That's pretty much what he came out of the meeting with.

He went back to New York three days later, and met with his friend Larry David at Catch a Rising Star,[10] 'cause Larry was doing standup. They knew each other from the standup circuit. And then they went out for a walk, to a Korean deli, and started talking and making fun of stuff on the shelves . . . and said, "*This* is what we should do. Just two guys talking and making fun of things."

GLENN PADNICK, president of Castle Rock Television:
The very first week we started Castle Rock, one of our film executives said to me, "Would you like to read a really funny script?" It was *Prognosis Negative* by Larry David, one of those legendary never-produced screenplays. And then it was only a year later that Jerry said the man he'd brought in to work with him was Larry David. And I'd actually read *Prognosis Negative*. So I had no objection to him, certainly. The network didn't know who he was—well, some of them *did* know who he was, 'cause he'd had a very tempestuous year on *Saturday Night Live*.

RICK LUDWIN:
We found out later that Jerry had returned to New York and met with his friend Larry David—who I did not know at that point. He'd been a writer on *Saturday Night Live* . . . and although I was at NBC at the time, that was before I was in

A younger Larry David in a publicity pose from Friday, *one of ABC's failed attempts to compete with NBC's late-night juggernaut,* Saturday Night Live. *Michael Richards was a fellow cast member.* © *ABC Television Network*

charge of late night. He'd also been a regular on the ABC late-night show called *Fridays*, and though I'd seen that show, I didn't know Larry specifically from it.

---

[10] *An extremely popular comedy club at the time, located on Manhattan's Upper East Side.*

GEORGE SHAPIRO:

I knew Larry from *Fridays*, which my client Andy Kaufman hosted a couple of times. It was like *Saturday Night Live*. Larry David was in it—and I loved him. He played Larry from the Three Stooges . . . and he played the valet for Howdy Doody: "This way, Mr. Doody! Oh, the door's open here, Mr. Doody! Right this way, Mr. Doody!"

I used to have long talks with Larry, so I knew he was very funny. And anyone that could stimulate Jerry into getting interested in doing a show like that was good. I felt great about Larry David.

RICK LUDWIN:

So, they had their legendary meeting in a Korean deli in New York, and then came back to us and suggested a show. That phrase, "a show about nothing," was never used. At least *I* don't remember it ever being used in the pitch meeting. The pitch was that it was to be a show about what a comedian does when he's not on stage and where a comedian gets his material. And based on that pitch, we agreed to a pilot script.

GEORGE SHAPIRO:

At the time we met with NBC, my mind said, "Well, we have to have a production company." Howard West and I would be executive producers, but we're not capable of deficit financing millions of dollars.

So, I called Rob Reiner—who is my cousin—and I said, "Look, NBC is interested in doing something with Jerry. You think Castle Rock is interested?" Castle Rock was young, like only a couple of years old. He said, "I love Jerry." And then I called Jerry and told him our feelings—Howard and I both agreed that Castle Rock would be good 'cause the executives there were young, creative guys that Jerry could relate to. Then NBC said, "You've got to have someone that's experienced, to help them write the script." Gary Gilbert was under contract to Castle Rock. So Gary Gilbert started working with Larry and Jerry . . . but they saw things so differently that Larry and Jerry said, "*We* have to write our script. We can't do it his way."

GLENN PADNICK:

Jerry and Larry were so strongwilled about what they had done. Gary did sit in on the writing sessions and contribute a few thoughts . . . but there was very little for him to do, because truly Jerry and Larry were executive producing this. He bowed out gracefully. He knew there was no role for him to grow in once it went forth to a series.

GEORGE SHAPIRO:

Gary Gilbert wrote a script, and Jerry and Larry wrote a script—and it went to the Writers Guild. And "created by" went to Larry and Jerry. 'Cause they're just not the normal sitcom beats—they're just so different, as history has showed.

GLENN PADNICK:

We loved the material from day one. We had creative input, but I loved the script from the moment it was written, and any notes or comments we had were very peripheral. I remember one of them was that *on the page*, before anyone was cast in a part; I felt that the characters—especially George and Jerry—spoke alike. They were very similar on the page, and shouldn't there be some distinction among the characters in the series?

And Larry said, "Why would I be friends with somebody who wasn't like me?"

Which of course went to the heart of all sitcoms. If we were that different, why would we be friends? And he really stumped me when he said that. But if you think about it—of course it's hard, 'cause the casting is so indelible now—but the characters, including Elaine, are written very, very similar to each other. They can almost exchange lines. But in the end, they *were* different from each other, 'cause the casting made 'em different.

MARC HIRSCHFELD, casting director:

We needed Jerry's kind of nebbishy best friend . . . a neurotic best friend based on Larry David. Jerry wanted Larry Miller, and he was really the front-runner. And then we had Jason Alexander go on tape in New York. I knew Jason from the days when I did this half-hour comedy called *E/R* starring Elliott Gould, George Clooney, and Mary McDonnell. Jason Alexander played this kind of snooty administrator.

When we put Jason on tape, he was the guy! He did it very much like Woody Allen, in a way, but he just had the cadence . . . the neuroses they were looking for. So I showed his tape to Larry and Jerry—and they were very enthusiastic about the audition. But still, it was between him and Larry Miller down to the end. I think Jerry was convinced that Larry was the guy, and Larry was convinced that it was Jason. It was difficult to make that decision.

Kramer was a whole other thing. When we started casting it, he was really envisioned as this sort of bathrobe wearing, shuffling neighbor who never left the apartment building. We were looking for someone funny but not particularly physical. And it really came down to two actors: Michael Richards and Steve Vinovich. In fact, Steve was a lot closer to the original conception of the character. He has kind of a hangdog face. But it became very clear . . . I mean, Michael sort of exploded into the room. He was *extremely* physical, and that was not at all part of what this character was—but he was just so much funnier. Michael really sort of brought it to a whole other level.

NBC Shoots the Pilot . . . Down

RICK LUDWIN:

I thought the pilot was good. Did I know that it was going to ultimately be a series that would be called the defining comedy of the 1990s? No. No one involved had that foresight. We thought we had a good little show on our hands.

GLENN PADNICK:

We loved the pilot. And so did NBC. Everything was great until the testing came in. I'd just been through this so many times, so it wasn't like I was dumbfounded. Anything that's really interesting, research is tough on. The general rule of thumb is—and this was said to me by no less a person than Brandon Tartikoff, who nevertheless was a slave to research—that research will always favor the familiar.

GEORGE SHAPIRO:

The research report? It said, "Pilot Performance: Weak."

It said, "Who cares about people going to a laundromat?" and "None of the supports were particularly liked, and viewers felt that Jerry needed a better backup ensemble. George was negatively viewed as a wimp who was only mildly amusing—viewers said he whined and did not like his relationship with Jerry . . . Despite the slice-of-life approach, the program was considered only mildly realistic and believable, and many did not identify with the things with which Jerry was involved."

MARC HIRSCHFELD:

The testing was very bad. The audience sort of rejected these people as not lovable, not likable, that sort of thing. And there was no Elaine.

RICK LUDWIN:

The guy who wrote that research report always felt badly about it. 'Cause he felt it should've been categorized as a "moderate"—that it was on the borderline between "moderate" and "weak" . . . but the call was made by whoever was in charge of research at the time that it needs to be called "weak."

GEORGE SHAPIRO:

That was *The Seinfeld Chronicles* . . . which was telecast, I think, in July. Anyhow, it looked like we weren't going to be picked up. And then I got a call from Brandon saying it's not on the schedule.

GLENN PADNICK:

The show was dead. And it was burnt off that summer. They showed the pilot, y'know, which is the kiss of death usually. And we were dead. In fact, we took it to another network, and pitched it there. To Fox. They passed, too.

GEORGE SHAPIRO:

But I knew Rick was a great supporter, so I called Rick and said, "Is there any way we can do *some* episodes? Even if it's like four episodes?"

RICK LUDWIN:

I thought it was funny. I thought people could relate to this. I felt *I* could relate to it. It was different than what was already on the air. And I felt it was something we shouldn't give up on. By the way, I wasn't alone in that. There were people at NBC, my colleagues, executives here, who came up to me after the pilot originally screened and said, "You've got something there." So it's not like I was the lone voice. Because it got laughs at the screening—believe me, you *know* when you've got a bomb pilot. The lights come up and there's this death-defying silence. And that was not the case with the *Seinfeld* pilot.

So what I did was, I went to Brandon and just said, "I'll take two hours of my specials budget."

I was doing primetime specials at that point, and we always had uncommitted hours in our budget—just because, in the specials area, sometimes things will walk through the door at the last minute, and you don't want to have every single hour of your budget committed already. So I said to Brandon, "I'll take two hours that are not committed to anything else, and we'll cut those two hours into four half hours."

And Brandon said, "Okay, alright. Go."

GEORGE SHAPIRO:

One thing they were very insistent on was adding a regular female cast member. The guys said that makes sense—and then they came up with the concept of an ex-girlfriend. But during those first episodes, NBC wanted Jerry to have a relationship with Elaine, and Jerry really fought that. The fact is, Larry and

Jerry admit that that was a good idea, having a recurring female role, but they stood up to the idea that Jerry get married or engaged to her.

MARC HIRSCHFELD:

The network wanted to add a woman who was very comfortable hanging out with guys. Could sort of *be* one of the guys. The scenes for the role were not that developed . . . they were really looking for a woman to come in the room and kind of own it and feel like she was comfortable hanging with these guys.

We saw pretty much everyone who was available. We had Megan Mullally audition—she was great. Rosie O'Donnell auditioned for it. She was terrific, very funny . . . but they just didn't feel like they wanted to hang out with her. But she was hilarious. At the time, Julia Louis-Dreyfus was tied to another series. I kept calling her manager to try to at least get her in the room for a meeting. He was like, "Well, we can't do that yet" . . . so the *day* that her option expired on the series, she came in for a meeting with the guys.

And that was it. They were like, "She's the one!"

RICK LUDWIN:

The famous quote from Brandon Tartikoff, which—obviously before he passed away—he was good enough to acknowledge and admit to, when he was explaining to me why we weren't going to go forward with *Seinfeld*, was, "It's too New York and it's too Jewish." Now, I have to put that in context: He was from New York and he was Jewish. But he felt that it was only going to appeal to someone like him; he felt it wasn't going to be appealing to a wide enough audience that you have to have in network television to make a living.

GEORGE SHAPIRO:

Yeah. When Brandon was first mulling it around, he once said, "Who would care about four Jews running around New York?" Even though they weren't all Jews . . . but it had that feeling. George Costanza is an Italian name, but his mannerisms—and Jerry Stiller's—were Jewish. Michael Richards and Julia Louis-Dreyfus are far from Jewish. But you have to give Brandon credit, because he went with his gut.

RICK LUDWIN:

I'm not Jewish, and I thought it was funny! It didn't strike me as being too Jewish. I thought it was funny enough not to give up on, and that's why I came up with this plan: Okay, we won't buy nine, we won't buy thirteen—okay, if you're concerned that it's going to be too expensive a commitment, then fine. We'll just back off.

And as Jerry has commented over the years, "An order for six is a slap in the face. NBC ordered four." To my knowledge, it's the lowest number of episodes ever ordered for a series.

We'll Take Just Four More, Please

GEORGE SHAPIRO:

At a meeting that we had right after we met with Warren Littlefield—it was Rob Reiner, Jerry, Larry, me, and Howard in the parking lot right outside of NBC—Jerry and Larry said, "Look. We can do four episodes. We'll be proud of the episodes we did, and we can move on, feeling good about it, doing it the way we wanted to do."

GLENN PADNICK:

Well, four episodes is a very tiny order. Some people might consider it an insult. But I was not insulted. We took the order. So, that's how we got the initial four episodes. That's all that was being ordered, but we seized on it as a breath of life, and we obviously hoped that there'd be more after that. We hoped that four would lead to more, which, as it turns out, it did.

GEORGE SHAPIRO:

The great part is that it didn't go through the regular comedy department, where they have a bunch of people that give a lot of notes. This was Rick Ludwin, who'd never worked on a situation comedy! So it was a blessing, the greatest thing that ever happened, that the whole thing went through the variety department.

MARC HIRSCHFELD:

There wasn't a lot of network interference. There wasn't a lot of contact between myself and the head of casting at the network on it. They didn't really see our choices until we had 'em approved! A lot of times, y'know, you go in and the network will see the choices and reject them, and you have to start over again. We got both choices—George and Kramer—approved at the same session. They said, "Go!" And then with Julia, they approved that—she didn't even have to audition.

TOM CHERONES, director and supervising producer:

After the pilot, Castle Rock and the network decided that Larry and Jerry hadn't had enough experience running a show, so they hired Fred Barron to be the executive producer. I had worked with Fred at MTM and at Warner Bros., and he called me and asked if I'd like to direct two episodes. I said, "Yes, I would."

I hadn't seen it yet, but I'd heard that it was a good show . . . and then, when I got there, the line producer had a better offer for more shows, so she left—and Fred said, "Will you produce it, too?" And I said, "Okay." So I was supervising producer of the show: postproduction, casting, hiring the crew, and maintaining the budget, for five years. And after we'd done a couple of episodes, they asked me to direct the other two.

RICK LUDWIN:

When we did the four episodes—if you look at even that first one, "The Stake Out," which is where George and Jerry are standing in the lobby of a building, waiting for the girl that Jerry has met to come down in the elevator. They know she works in the building. You see, even in that first episode, the sort of style that the show would become. So, we filmed those four episodes . . . and it didn't make the fall schedule for the second year in a row. Once again, it was deemed not strong enough to make the fall schedule.

GLENN PADNICK:

They were made around December and January of the following season, with the thought that they go on the air in the spring. But then they didn't, 'cause they tested badly again!

But the four episodes were terrific. And Brandon called me in March and actually said he'd give us a "Sophie's Choice." The choice was this: He said, "You can either go on next month, April, in a not great time slot after *Dear John* . . . but you'd be eligible then to be on my fall schedule if you do well. Or . . . you can hold off and not go on till the summertime—in which case you'll have missed the fall schedule—but I'll put you on after *Cheers*."

I said, "I like the *Cheers* spot." So we went on that summer in the good time slot.

RICK LUDWIN:

I thought we were on track. I thought we were getting there. And even though it didn't make the fall schedule, those four episodes played after *Cheers* on Thursday nights in late May into June of 1990. And the ratings were pretty good. There was a feeling we were onto something there . . . so based on the performance after *Cheers* on that Thursday night run, NBC ordered thirteen more episodes.

Let's put it this way: I thought we were being fair to the show at that point. And if it made it beyond that, great—but even if it didn't, I felt we were being fair to the people involved. That they were getting their shot.

TOM CHERONES:

Seinfeld was different, from the beginning. The stories, as seemingly insignificant as they were, had very little gentle emotion. I think Larry had said early on, "No hugging, no learning," as a policy. They just felt different. And I was directing every week—I would've been happy doing that most anywhere, but this one was special. And even though they didn't let Larry David run it the first four episodes, the series was always his voice.

Probing the Human Psyche, Just for Laughs

LARRY CHARLES, writer and producer:

We had never done a sitcom before, and people would say to us, "Well, do you have a bible?" Sitcoms usually create a bible, where they'd have all the characters broken down, and their traits, and their characteristics, and their motives, and their personalities. And we were like, "A bible? We don't know what the hell you're talking about!" We would just do what we thought was funny, y'know? And almost wish that it would get canceled in some ways. Because we really didn't know what we were doing. And we didn't wanna really work that hard, and all that stuff—but we got kind of trapped.

The way it often got written was, it was just Jerry and Larry and myself, and eventually Peter Mehlman . . . we would just sit and kind of examine, and talk, and think about things and themes and ideas and dilemmas and morality and ethics. And in doing that, it was almost like a Talmudic examination of these ideas. So, it was a very intellectual process that seemed to come from that Talmudic tradition of the commentaries . . . of turning an idea around, and examining it and shining a light on it, and getting kind of a dialectic going about it. And then, eventually, those discussions turned into episode ideas.

DAVID STEINBERG, freelance *Seinfeld* director:

Besides Larry and Jerry, Larry Charles was the most important voice on that show, because he is an exceptional writer. He and Larry David had been friends since they worked on *Fridays* together. Larry was able to find someone else's voice and still not lose his own writing style. That's very rare when you're a young writer.

LARRY CHARLES:

In some ways, working with Larry and Jerry, I felt like George Harrison working with Lennon and McCartney. They were totally in synch, and dominated, and I would just try to get a good song on the album, y'know? But what I was able to do was shore up certain kind of weaker sides of the show.

What I was able to contribute was, first of all, I was really able to almost be like the devil on Larry's shoulder when Jerry was the angel—and kind of push him to go darker, which he had the instinct and intuition to do. And also, I felt very connected to Kramer, so I would push to make sure he got developed and expanded.

And just in terms of breaking the stories, Larry and I used to take these hikes in Fryman Canyon in Studio City, near where the show was done, and see if we could get these plot twists and turns in such a way that they would be endlessly surprising and fascinating, and almost, in a way, like you'd be able to go back and watch them again and again the way we saw the shows that we sort of liked.

We all shared an affinity for the *Abbott & Costello* TV show, we all shared an affinity for Superman, we all shared an affinity for the 1950s sitcoms that were on in reruns when we were growing up . . . like *Honeymooners* or *Bilko* and shows like that that were on WPIX in New York. And we all have watched those shows again and again and again, until they were ingrained in our brains. Even things like *Jack Benny*—shows where

Seinfeld's *creators and writers were strongly influenced by* 1950s *sitcoms like* The Abbott & Costello Show, *in which famous comedians portrayed fictionalized versions of themselves.* © *CBS Television Network*

there was a blurry line between reality and fiction—or *Burns & Allen . . . Danny Thomas . . .* or *Joey Bishop Show.*

Y'know, all those shows were about comedians who played themselves, and it was always sort of provocative in some way. It's like, is it supposed to be real? Is it fiction? And the line was even being blurred back then. They're very avant-garde shows that don't get their due.

PETER MEHLMAN, writer and producer:

I wrote the first freelance script that got on the air. I had met Larry in New York a couple of times, and bumped into him out here in L.A. He said, "I'm doing this little TV show with Jerry Seinfeld. Maybe you can give me a writing sample." And what I gave him was an "About Men" column from the *New York Times.*

It's so funny, because so many people who I know—who knew Larry better than I did—got the same offer. And they would turn in their writing sample, and he would pass it on to Jerry. Y'know, Jerry always played the heavy. He never had any problem going, "Yeah, just say I wasn't into it."

Like a week later, I got a call from Larry saying, "Jerry loved your stuff and said sign him up." Which meant, y'know, coming in to pitch an idea. So I pitched an idea, and Larry Charles happened to be in the room when I pitched it, and he gave it a nudge in a really good direction. Really, all I had was one storyline with basically two beats.

And they go, "Okay, go ahead."

The great thing about them is they didn't know anything. No other show in the history of the world would've sent me off to just write at that point. I mean, I remember going into that office, and it was in the afternoon . . . and Jerry is on the couch, going, "Y'know, I haven't done anything all day. I don't know why I'm so tired."

So, I was thinking now, "This is the place for me!"

TOM CHERONES:

Larry and Jerry are both very bright guys. They were smart, and willing to do what they had to do to make the show work. They knew what they were doing—they just didn't know *how* to do it. I knew how to do it. I said to them right away, "If you can think of it, we can do it. I'll shoot it if you write it." And they did, and we did.

And we changed the way sitcoms looked. I had a note, in each of the first two seasons from the network executives: "Can you make it look more like a sitcom?" I said no . . . and they shook their heads and walked away.

The first four were particularly fun for me, because we were doing it in a way that you hadn't seen before . . . and I was gettin' away with it! I was the only one that knew what was going on. [laughing] Making it look different—not like a sitcom. And because we had the variety department at NBC running the show, they didn't mess with us. So I was able to do some things I probably wouldn't have been able to do had the comedy guys been there. I was shooting it—although with multiple cameras—and planning the shots as if it were a single-camera show, so it looked better.

DAVID STEINBERG:

The thing about comedy directing—and comedy *anything*—is there is a shorthand. It's like jazz. You either hear the music or you don't. So, for Larry David *and* Jerry, but Larry especially, when people outside who don't hear the music and just don't know it—network executives, managers, agents, all these other people—started giving input into the show, it drove them nuts! I remember Warren Littlefield at one point coming in and saying, "Y'know, I just thought of a wonderful line in the car on the way in" . . . and you'd see smoke go out of Larry David's ears.

And he'd say, "See? That's what I'm talking about! That's what I mean! That drives me nuts!" Because what he's saying is, they've examined the script like a piece of Talmud! They've gone through every cul-de-sac, every corner. I mean, yes, anyone can contribute a line. *That* isn't what it's about.

That's where the frustration was. And they didn't think much of the show at that time. It wasn't doing well. Hadn't hit its stride. But you could see where it was headed. And you know, the way in which they worked out to have three stories converge—they all meet at some point in a Larry David script—that was an invention of his and Jerry's, and Larry Charles, and whoever else.

LARRY CHARLES:

The shows became so densely packed with story . . . I mean, even in great sitcoms like *All in the Family*, there were basically three scenes. Four scenes. An amazingly ambitious *All in the Family* might have six scenes or something. And we would have shows with like thirty-five scenes in them!

People were going, "You can't do a show like this. We don't have the sets!" We'd go, "They can just stand against the wall!"

Y'know, we didn't care. And, kind of inadvertently, a style emerged out of that that was very densely packed. It just sort of evolved—because we didn't know what we were doing on a certain level. We didn't know how to write a sitcom, so we just tried to write a funny show.

PETER MEHLMAN:

People who got to create shows were always people who had been on *other* shows. And they maintained the same system of doing things. Larry and Jerry didn't. Larry had never run a sitcom . . . so they just did it their way. There's really no jokes in it. That's what's so great, there're no jokes. It's just people talking, and funny conversation. Especially, like, the conversation early on about Magellan:

George says, "*That's* who you like? Magellan?"

And Jerry goes, "Sure. All around the world! Who do you like?"

And he goes, "DeSoto."

"What did he do?"

"He discovered the Mississippi."

"Oh, like they wouldn't have found *that*."

It's all these little snippets of life. There's a lot of importance placed on being observant and informed . . . and yet, they also talk about themselves— like in my first episode, there was this run in there. We had Jerry and George arguing about who's a bigger idiot between the two of them, and each of them arguing for themselves! Y'know:

"I'm a much bigger idiot than you."

And George going, "With all due respect, no one's a bigger idiot than me."

The fact that we could get away with something like that was so great.

DAVID STEINBERG:

The most *personal* comedy will get the widest audience, always, because the audience can accept a personal opinion about anything. It's the way in which news that's subjective—even if it's contrary to your opinion—is more valuable than phony *objective* news. It's the same thing with comedy. Just give me your personal version—you don't have to be black to appreciate Richie Pryor's anger about the white/black world. You're getting the humor of it. Cause you're relating to the emotion, and the emotion is: "I'm pissed about something. And I'm gonna get myself heard about this."

Same thing with *Seinfeld*: You've got very much Larry David's sort of misanthropic view of relationships in the world . . . and you've got Jerry's sort of centrist version of that, moving him back to the center. And that combination was exhilarating to an audience who'd never seen anything like that! They might not be able to *define* it, but they could just say, "Wait a second. This is genuinely funny, and everything else feels like *fake* funny."

LARRY CHARLES:

I think that was just very much Larry's sensibility. He didn't believe in the false morality of most TV shows, and I agree with him. And Jerry agreed with him, too. It was fake. And one of the things that I think was a breakthrough about *Seinfeld* was we did not traffic in that false morality, or happy endings, or contrivances of most sitcoms. We were willing to examine the darker side of the human psyche, and let it sort of flow wherever it might go.

DAVID STEINBERG:

I would describe those characters as a small community of outsiders that are just like you and me . . . they embody all of the sorts of emotional traits that everyone does—a little bit of larceny, a little bit of deception. And, at a particular age, I would say: They were thirtysomething. That group at forty-five or fifty would be very different.

PETER MEHLMAN:

One of the great things about the show is that it not only dealt with the world as it is, but it dealt with the world as the characters wished it would be. They were always looking for a perfect world.

I wasn't on staff yet, but when they shot "The Deal"—when Jerry and Elaine try to make that deal where they can sleep together and still be friends—I was going to every episode, 'cause I was going to be on the show next year. So I was at that taping, and in the first scene, where they're talking about how *this* can't get in the way of *that*, I remember sitting there thinking, "This is the greatest single scene in the history of sitcoms." The most beautiful, perfect, funny, real thing. 'Cause here are these two people just trying to succeed at something that people have been trying to do *forever*. That was a big theme, trying to make the world perfect. That, to me, was the best episode the show ever did.

LARRY CHARLES:

Another Talmudic aspect of the show—and one of the ways that these issues and ideas and themes and conflicts could be explored—was our love of language. We always tried to find a way of talking about things that sort of had a flavor unto itself. Almost like a Noam Chomsky examination of how language works, and how we perceive and listen and hear and process those ideas, depending on how they're written out and how they're spoken.

Dancing a Nimble Verbal Tango

One of the defining characteristics of *Seinfeld* was indeed its wordplay. Jerry Seinfeld, Larry David, and the others they brought in were wordsmiths of the highest order. These were writers who loved words, who adored them, and took sheer delight in turning a clever phrase and crafting dialogue that crackled. In "The Deal," close pals Jerry and Elaine—former lovers suddenly finding themselves attracted again—attempt to negotiate terms that would allow them to resume sleeping together without compromising their friendship. The word "this" quickly becomes a euphemism for friendship, with "that" meaning sex:

Jerry: I mean if anything happened and we couldn't be friends the way we are now, that would really be bad.
Elaine: Devastating.
Jerry: Because this is very good.
Elaine: And *that* would be good.
Jerry: *That* would be good, too. The idea is to combine the *this* and the *that*. But *this* cannot be disturbed.
Elaine: Yeah. We just wanna take *this*, and add *that*.

A second season episode, "The Chinese Restaurant," was in fact nothing more than Jerry, Elaine, and George standing around for the length of the show, talking, joking, starving, suffering, and unsuccessfully attempting to bribe an inscrutable maître d' into seating them for dinner. Though *Seinfeld* eventually grew quicker paced and more densely plotted, it remained dialogue-driven throughout, with so much of the series' witty repartee becoming part of the national lexicon. People everywhere began parroting what they'd heard on the show, and referring to "Seinfeldian" moments in their own lives.

In "The Outing," Jerry and George are mistaken for gay lovers . . . "not that there's anything wrong with that." Learning that store supplies of her favored method of birth control are running low, Elaine must decide in "The Sponge" if her current boyfriend is "sponge-worthy." George emerges from a cold swimming pool in "The Hamptons" and is instantly mortified when Jerry's girlfriend briefly glimpses him naked and later dishes on the goods to the woman George has just begun to date—without taking "shrinkage" into account. And, most famously, Kramer, Elaine, Jerry, and George square off in "The Contest" to see who can abstain from doing "that" to themselves the longest, thereby remaining "master of their domain." More than any other episode, that one showed how far network TV standards had evolved.

GLENN PADNICK:

In the early years, we didn't have any content that would be problematic. The only thing we ever heard from NBC was about "The Chinese Restaurant" episode—they didn't want us to do it because it had no plot. We got a lot of static from NBC about doing that episode . . . that was our famous argument during the second season.

TOM CHERONES:

"The Chinese Restaurant" was a major departure for any sitcom. A sitcom generally doesn't leave its own set for more than a scene or two—and this was the entire episode. Plus, Michael Richards wasn't in it, because this is what happened to these guys in reality, and there was no Kramer there.

These shows came from things that had actually happened to them, like the masturbation contest. There *was* a contest. Larry was in a contest.

RICK LUDWIN:

For reasons that are obvious, they didn't let us know what the story for the following week's script was. Normally, we'd sort of have an inkling of what the storylines are that were coming up . . . and for some reason, we were in the dark on that one.

One night, a bunch of the writers, Jerry, Julia, and I, a bunch of us went to the Tiffany Theater on Hollywood Boulevard, because Jason Alexander was doing a one-man show called *Give 'Em Hell, Harry*. And at the act break or at the end of the show, a guy who worked for me, Todd Schwartz, said, "I just found out what the storyline for tomorrow's table read is."

I said, "What is it?"

He said, "Masturbation."

"Oh, man. Oh, *man!*"

Because that was unheard of, to do a topic like that!

TOM CHERONES:

Larry wouldn't share the scripts any sooner than he had to, so I don't think I saw it more than a week ahead of time. I was thinking, "Are they gonna let us do it?" There was some concern at the network.

RICK LUDWIN:

I thought, "This is gonna be a rough week." And so the next day was the table read. We read the script . . . and it was so clever and so *funny*—and the word "masturbation" was never used. I thought to myself, "Any viewer of this show is not gonna be offended by this."

Y'know, I've learned over the years from the Standards department that one of the ways they look at broadcast standards is the audience's expectation. When the audience knows what they're going to get up front—what kind of a show it is—then you are more likely to be able to handle topics that might be considered over the line. And the manner in which the show was written, and the cleverness of it, made me think we're going to be okay with this. I didn't think this was gonna be a huge firestorm.

PETER MEHLMAN:

I remember reading it. Just before that I had written "The Virgin" episode, which went extremely well, and I was feeling fairly good about things. And then I read Larry's script . . . and I walked in and said, "I just read 'The Contest.' I'm so depressed."

And Larry goes, "That's the highest compliment you can pay me." Then he said, "You think they're gonna let me do this?"

I said, "I don't know . . . it's very deftly done . . . you don't use the word. It's suitably subtle. And to answer your question, I don't *know* if they're gonna let you do this!"

RICK LUDWIN:

I found out subsequently that Larry was prepared to quit. That Larry thought the network would not allow this episode to run—or be produced, for that matter—and that he was prepared to quit the show if that's what happened.

GLENN PADNICK:

That was the first episode that had anything in it to make you say, "Holy smoke!" in terms of content. It raised my eyebrows—but it was funny! And they dealt with it so well. Jerry and Larry were just operating at a much higher level than any sitcom I'd ever been involved in. Just turning out consistently strong scripts every week . . . frankly I'd never experienced it before. They worked their asses off. And it was a pleasure picking up a script—other scripts from other shows I'd sort of wince as I picked 'em up. Sort of, "Oh, brother." But you always looked forward to a new *Seinfeld* script.

LARRY CHARLES:

One of the things that I've always admired about Larry, and it's a trait that I don't particularly possess, is that he has a kind of intuitive sense of tone.

He knows how far to take something, and how far not to take it—he knows where that line is, essentially, just intuitively.

RICK LUDWIN:

It also had to do with the fact that Jerry is interested in being delicate with language. I'm told this was more Jerry than it was Larry. He took it as a challenge—and a fun sort of exercise—how to get over, around, or under this wall. And he did it for the sport! He wanted to find a way to do this in a clever, funny way, as opposed to just using the word as sort of a sledgehammer.

GEORGE SHAPIRO:

Larry and Jerry were very careful. Every single script that was done was completely rewritten . . . the last pass of the script was Larry and Jerry in the room together. They had this partners' desk, where they looked at each other and went over every script. They read every line—'cause they're both good actors, and every word passed through them.

LARRY CHARLES:

Amazingly enough, if you can believe this, there were no notes from the network on "The Contest"! There's not even close to a single bad word uttered. It's done so discreetly, so brilliantly. But the network, at first, was like, "We don't want to do this episode."

At Castle Rock, we were discouraged. Y'know, those ideas—for "The Outing" and "The Contest"—had been knocking around for a year or two before we actually got a chance to do them. We were discouraged from doing those kinds of episodes. When we finally had a little bit more of the confidence of the network behind us, and we did them, they wound up being classic episodes.

But also, they were done in such a way that they didn't offend anybody! They wound up being completely embraced, and even the censors were not disturbed by it.

RICK LUDWIN:

If there were any changes at all, they were minor. As I recall, one sponsor dropped out of the show after we screened it, before it aired. But the show was then getting hot, and we were able to replace that sponsor rather quickly.

With "The Outing," I think Broadcast Standards gave them the note that "you've gotta add some sort of line." The issue was just the thought that the script could come across suggesting that being gay was an aberration, or that it was socially unacceptable . . . and that's when Jerry added the line, "Not that there's anything wrong with that." That was a Standards note for some sort of line, which is what led to what's now sort of a catchphrase.

GLENN PADNICK:

By the time the show started doing storylines involving content that you might consider iffy, the show had reached a level of success in the history of dealing with stuff that we kept going along hand in hand—like the season of the masturbation episode. Warren Littlefield said that by then it was *Seinfeld*, and even though it seemed outrageous, he and the Broadcast Standards guy decided to let it go.

At the height of Seinfeld's *popularity, press coverage was all-encompassing. This 1998 caricature of the cast appeared in* TV Guide, *depicting (standing from l-r): Kramer (Michael Richards), Elaine (Julia Louis-Dreyfus), and Jerry (Jerry Seinfeld). Seated on the sofa: George (Jason Alexander).* © *Glen Hanson*

PETER MEHLMAN:

It really kind of went up in increments about what we could get away with. And things that would redefine the characters in a little way. Like in "The Junior Mint," when Kramer was bugging Jerry to come watch this guy get an operation, Jerry—during a run-through—just happened to ad-lib a line. He said, "All right, all right, just lemme finish my coffee and we'll go watch the doctors slice the fat bastard up."

He said it kind of as a joke during the run-through, and everybody laughed so loud, we said, "Eh, let's leave that in!" I think from that point on, Jerry became a little bit of a prick as a character. That really opened up another whole avenue.

LARRY CHARLES:

I think that's true. Jerry was very smart and very brilliant on many levels, and was also very courageous—which was against his managers' and the network's advice—when he finally embraced the idea that he didn't have to come out smelling like a rose in every episode. That people would still love him because he had innate lovability—like Tony Soprano[11], in a way. Look, Tony Soprano is a murderer, but people love him. Why? Again, it's the "X" factors, it's the variables. Love the actor, the way the actor projects that character.

And it was the same thing with Jerry. People loved Jerry, even when he was being evil . . . even when he became very dark. And once that was established, we were able to delve much deeper into these ideas. Look, he was the guy that was on camera, and he was willing to do that—and that was very courageous.

MARC HIRSCHFELD:

That sort of evolved. Really, George was the only self-centered one of the group in the pilot . . . and all these other people sort of evolved over time. They found what was really funny was the fact that they all had their own agendas—that they were friends, but they would happily backstab each other and be self-absorbed.

It was also a very unusual show in that Jerry was very generous in letting other people be funny around him. I'm not talking just the series regulars, but also, y'know, the Newmans and the parents . . . he would allow the other people to be the funny ones. The more outrageous ones. I think that's really smart.

GEORGE SHAPIRO:

Jerry has that Jack Benny mentality. I was in writing sessions sometimes, and he'd say, "Give that one to Jason," or "That'll be good for Julia"—funny stuff that was written for him. I call him the Magic Johnson of the comedy world, 'cause he would pass off so great. Jack Benny was known for that. His cast got so many laughs. And Jerry loved that. Some stars want all the laughs—Jerry was never that way, and I saw it, even in the writing sessions.

PETER MEHLMAN:

There are four or five episodes Larry David wrote—some of them were just, like, I would never even think of something like that. But there were certain storylines that I either should have thought of, or I *wished* I thought of.

---

[11] *Character portrayed by actor James Gandolfini on HBO's hit series about a New Jersey crime family,* The Sopranos.

One that I wished I'd thought of was Jerry and his girlfriend being caught making out during *Schindler's List*. Y'know, that's a perfect story. Unbelievably funny, and it maps out the second you think about it. Because you think: Okay, they do that . . . that's funny. Who would be offended most by that? Jerry's parents. You can't have them in the same movie theater, so how would they find out? Somebody would have to drop a dime on them. Who would drop a dime on them? Newman. It was the most perfect story.

The only one that kind of fell out of the sky for me, the closest I came to the *Schindler's List* one, was "The Sponge." Because I heard on the radio that the sponge was going out of business, and immediately I thought to myself if Elaine is a big sponge user and she hears about this, let's say she tries to buy out as many as she can. So she buys out the entire Web site but she's still got a limited number . . . that would have to change her whole screening process for who she sleeps with. So right there, boom boom boom. That one was very gratifying.

Larry and I were talking about it . . . and I remember saying, "They have to be worth the sponge."

And Larry goes, "Yeah. They have to be sponge-worthy." It was like a perfect creative process. Which is the exact reverse of "shrinkage." Because Larry had the idea of, what if George goes in the pool and it's cold. And I said, "Oh, you mean, he gets shrinkage?"

And Larry's genius was saying, "Yes. Shrinkage. And use that word. Use it a lot!"

Running Out of Nothing

For seven seasons, *Seinfeld* flourished under the guidance of the Larry David/Jerry Seinfeld creative tandem. Throughout this period the show kept growing and evolving, adding unforgettable new characters to the mix, like George's quirky father, Frank Costanza. Jerry Stiller, whose hilariously fevered shouting matches with Estelle Harris as George's shrill mother threatened to steal every episode the pair appeared in, doesn't even show up until the fifth season's "The Puffy Shirt." Jerry's parents, Helen and Morty Seinfeld (Liz Sheridan and Barney Martin, taking over for Phil Bruns), had been seen as regular characters from very early on, but gradually grew more involved in storylines. Because *Seinfeld* took so long to make NBC's regular schedule, and for its audience to find it, after seven years the show hadn't grown tired yet . . . but one of its two creators surely did.

RICK LUDWIN:

Larry David left after the seventh season. I think he was just exhausted. He wasn't so sure they were going to be able to do the *four* after the first episode! He was always concerned about the quality of the show, and about making it the best it could be.

He had a notebook filled with little notes that he would make about something that happened in his own life, or just observations, and he would constantly go to that notebook for storylines or ideas. I think he really wanted the show to end after seven seasons, because he felt that they had done all the permutations they could do. And Larry was just tired.

GLENN PADNICK:

Without Larry there, the types of shows started altering . . . the show got more postmodern. But there were some incredible episodes in those last two seasons.

PETER MEHLMAN:

It just got harder and harder to come up with really small stories. Stories based on tiny little observations of life. Those were the kinds of stories I always liked. So, you'd get to the point where you'd come up with an idea, and you'd tell somebody about it. And they'd say, "That's so great!"—and then, "Oh, wait a minute . . . y'know, we kind of did that back in episode two. Remember that 'B' story about blah blah blah?" So it got harder and harder, in a way.

That's why "The Yada Yada" was so gratifying, because all the stories in there were just really tiny. I loved the idea of somebody converting to Judaism just for the jokes! Because my best friend is a converted Jew. And as we were driving off the golf course one day, he made some Jewish joke . . . and for some reason, I'd never even thought of him as being not Jewish—but then I was thinking to myself, "I wonder how long it took him to feel comfortable making that kind of joke?"

And then I thought it would be funny if someone converted, and then like a day later they're making those kinds of jokes. That's such a small, little idea, and I just love that. Those are real hard.

LARRY CHARLES:

It's weird. What *Seinfeld* did was effectively kill the sitcom, in a way. Which was great. I mean, it went so against the prevailing wisdom, I think a lot of executives resented that and wanted to prove that the formula they had been using worked. And, in a way, they've continued to try to push that formula . . . and effectively have destroyed that genre, in a sense.

Out of that have come things like *Curb Your Enthusiasm*. I think that's the direction that sitcoms took, almost inadvertently, as a result of *Seinfeld*. It was like, when you could no longer tell that kind of story in that sort of format, there'd have to be a new format to discuss these things. And in a sense, even *Seinfeld*, to some degree, is rendered quaint by *Curb Your Enthusiasm*.

DAVID STEINBERG:

Of course, Larry couldn't have done a show like *Curb* had he not done *Seinfeld* first and had the clout. And HBO had the foresight, unlike a network, where they just said, "Okay, let's let him do what he does." And in fact, this improv form is *written* by Larry. It's ironic that everybody keeps on talking about how it's all ad lib. It's all written except for the dialogue, which is the easiest thing to write once you've got your story broken. Now, *Curb Your Enthusiasm* is a very bold show, because it's almost a Jewish W.C. Fields character that he's playing. And what's courageous about it is he plays rich—he plays that he has money! He goes against every single rule of what you do on television: endear yourself to the audience, make yourself likable, cuddly and all of that. Larry does the opposite.

GLENN PADNICK:

While we were making *Seinfeld*, Larry, of course, was the mystery. People didn't appreciate—as they never do—the writers. And I always felt that for a long time people didn't appreciate Larry David's incredible contribution, which was amazing. But now, everybody credits Larry—and I think they don't appreciate how much Jerry did!

I mean, not only did he co-rewrite most of the episodes, but he acted in the show. *And* he wrote and performed all the standup himself. He was the hardest working man in show business during those years he was doing the show. It's amazing what he did, in terms of writing, acting, and producing. He was incredible. I don't know how he did it, but he was always calm and relaxed . . . an incredible force. And he could not have been nicer—he set the tone for the whole show.

TOM CHERONES:

Seinfeld changed the face of comedy. It opened the doors for other people to do things they never thought *possible* in multi-camera comedy. And now you see other shows doing things that we did first. I think that Larry and Jerry gave the world of comedy another way to do it. I think they were pioneers—and I helped 'em do that.

GLENN PADNICK:

The show added phrases to the national vocabulary. People talk about a "*Seinfeld* moment"—and you know exactly what they mean. The show's been off the air now for quite a number of years, though it's still in reruns, yet you see it referenced in sports shows and everything. Sometimes, people don't even know what they're referencing anymore!

There's a beer commercial where a girl says, "They're real, and they're spectacular." Which is just a direct lift from our show. I assume the writers knew they're lifting it from *Seinfeld* . . . but maybe not.

RICK LUDWIN:

It was as wonderful an experience as anything I've ever experienced in television, from start to finish. And as *unlikely*, from the aspect of it not coming from the comedy development department, the fact that neither Jerry or Larry had ever written a sitcom before, the fact that our department had never developed a sitcom before, the order pattern in terms of the pilot, then four, then thirteen, and then the fact that it didn't make the regular schedule until its third year out. And that it just flew under the radar for such a long period of time.

Every aspect of it, from start to finish, was as unlikely as anything I expect ever to be involved with in television. But what a wonderful, unlikely ride! There's no question, if you're lucky enough to be involved with a primetime show that turns into a *Seinfeld*—that becomes a landmark show, that *TV Guide* votes as the greatest show of all time—if you're lucky enough to get involved with *one* of those shows in your career, you're way ahead of the curve.

Bibliography

BOOKS

Akass, Kim, and Janet McCabe. *Reading Sex and the City*. London: I.B. Tauris, 2004.

Brooks, Tim, and Earle Marsh. *The Complete Directory to Prime Time Network TV Shows*. New York: Random House, 1992.

Caesar, Sid, with Eddy Friedfeld. *Caesar's Hours: My Life in Comedy, with Love and Laughter*. New York: Public Affairs, 2003

Chunovic, Louis. *One Foot on the Floor: The Curious Evolution of Sex on Television from "I Love Lucy" to "South Park."* New York: TV Books, L.L.C., 2000.

Lear, Norman. *Meet the Bunkers*. Belmont, Cali.: Pitman Learning, Inc., 1981.

Marc, David, and Robert J. Thompson. *Prime Time, Prime Movers*. Boston: Little, Brown and Company, 1992.

McCrohan, Donna. *Archie & Edith, Mike & Gloria*. New York: Workman Publishing, 1987.

Meadows, Audrey, with Joe Daly. *Love, Alice: My Life as a Honeymooner*. New York: Crown Publishers, Inc., 1994.

Moore, Mary Tyler. *After All*. New York: G.P. Putnam's Sons, 1995.

Schneider, Alfred R., and Kaye Pullen. *The Gatekeeper: My Thirty Years as a TV Censor*. New York: Syracuse University Press, 2001

Stern, Leonard B., and Diane L. Robison. *A Martian Wouldn't Say That: Confidential Memos TV Executives Wish They Hadn't Written*. New York: Price Stern Sloan, Inc., 1994.

Tinker, Grant, and Bud Rukeyser. *Tinker in Television: From General Sarnoff to General Electric*. New York: Simon & Schuster, 1994

ARTICLES

Kaplan, James. "Angry Middle-Aged Man," *The New Yorker* (January 19, 2004).

"Is Prime Time Ready for Sex?." *Time* 110, no. 2 (July 11, 1977).

"Special Seinfeld Issue." *Entertainment Weekly* 430 (May 4, 1998).

SPECIAL PUBLICATIONS

Muldaur Media Ltd.,"*Smothered: The Censorship Struggles of the Smothers Brothers Comedy Hour.*" New Video, 2002.

Academy of Television Arts & Sciences Foundation's Archive of American Television, *Excerpts from a Carroll O'Connor interview*, conducted by Charles Davis, August 8, 1999

Academy of Television Arts & Sciences Foundation's Archive of American Television, *Excerpts from a Jean Stapleton interview*, conducted by Karen L. Herman, November 28, 2000

Academy of Television Arts & Sciences Foundation's Archive of American Television, *Excerpts from a Beatrice Arthur interview*, conducted by Karen L. Herman, March 15, 2001

THE STARS OF OUR SHOW

BEA ARTHUR:

Actress, singer. (TV) *Caesar's Hour, All in the Family, Maude, Golden Girls;* (stage) *The Shoestring Revue, The Threepenny Opera, Fiddler on the Roof, Mame, And Then There's Bea*

CHRIS BEARDE:

Comedy writer, producer, director. Staff writer, *Rowan & Martin's Laugh-In;* executive producer, *The Sonny & Cher Comedy Hour, Cos;* creator, *The Gong Show, Sherman Oaks*

ALLAN BLYE:

Writer, producer, singer, cantor. Writer and producer, *The Smothers Brothers Comedy Hour, The Andy Williams Show, The Sonny and Cher Comedy Hour;* performer, *GE Showtime*

ALLAN BURNS:

Writer, producer. Co-creator, writer, producer, *The Mary Tyler Moore Show, Rhoda, Lou Grant, Friends and Lovers;* creator, *The Duck Factory;* writer, *Get Smart, He & She, Room 222*

PAT CARROLL:

Actress, singer. Cast member, *The Danny Thomas Show, Caesar's Hour, The Bobby Sherman Show, The Ted Knight Show,* Rodgers & Hammerstein's *Cinderella;* (film) *The Little Mermaid*

ERNEST CHAMBERS:

Writer, producer. Co-creator, producer, *The Smothers Brother Comedy Hour;* head writer, *The Danny Kaye Show,* writer, *As Caesar Sees It, The Dick Van Dyke Show, My Three Sons*

LARRY CHARLES:

Writer, producer, director. Writer, *Fridays;* writer, supervising producer, *Seinfeld, Mad About You; The Tick, Dilbert;* director, executive producer, *Curb Your Enthusiasm, Entourage*

TOM CHERONES:

Director, producer. Supervising producer and director, *Seinfeld;* director, *My Sister Sam, Ellen, NewsRadio, Caroline in the City, Boston Common, Men Behaving Badly, The Pitts*

STEPHEN COX:

Television and film historian. Author, *The Beverly Hillbillies, The Addams Chronicles, Here's Johnny!, The Munchkins of Oz, Dreaming of Jeannie: TV's Prime Time in a Bottle*

MIKE DANN:

V.P. of Programming at CBS (1963–1970). Series include *Mission: Impossible, Mannix, Hawaii Five-0, The Smothers Brothers Comedy Hour, 60 Minutes, The Carol Burnett Show*

SAM DENOFF:

Writer, producer. Writer, producer (with Bill Persky), *The Dick Van Dyke Show;* co-creator, executive producer, writer, *That Girl, Lotsa Luck, The Montefuscos, Big Eddie*

LARRY GELBART:
Writer, producer, developer, *M*A*S*H*. Writer (TV) *Caesar's Hour*; (film) *The Wrong Box, Tootsie, Oh, God!, Movie Movie*; (stage) *A Funny Thing Happened on the Way to the Forum, City of Angels*

LEONARD GOLDBERG:
Former Head of Programming at ABC. Producer (with Aaron Spelling), *Charlie's Angels, T.J. Hooker, Starsky and Hutch, The Rookies, Fantasy Island, Hart to Hart, Family*

BARRY HARMAN:
Writer. (TV) *All in the Family, The Jeffersons, The Carol Burnett Show, How Do You Spell God?*; (stage) *Romance/Romance, Olympus on My Mind*

VALERIE HARPER:
Actress. (TV) *The Mary Tyler Moore Show, Rhoda, Valerie, Sex and the City, That '70s Show, Touched by an Angel*; (stage) *Tale of the Allergist's Wife, Golda's Balcony*

SUSAN HARRIS:
Writer, producer (with Paul Junger Witt and Tony Thomas). Writer, *All in the Family, Maude*; creator, writer, producer, *Soap, Fay, Benson, The Golden Girls, Empty Nest, Good & Evil*

CHARLIE HAUCK:
Writer, producer. Writer, *Maude, One Day At a Time*; executive producer, *Home Improvement*; consulting producer, *Frasier*; author (novel), *Artistic Differences*

MARC HIRSCHFELD:
Executive V.P. of Casting at NBC. Casting director, *Seinfeld, 3rd Rock from the Sun, NewsRadio, The Larry Sanders Show* (HBO), *The Nanny* (CBS), *Married with Children, Mad TV* (Fox)

ARTE JOHNSON:
Actor, comedian. Original cast member, *Rowan & Martin's Laugh-In*; performer, (TV) *The Bobby Vinton Show, The Love Boat, The Gong Show, Fame*; (film) *Love at First Bite*

COSLOUGH JOHNSON:
Writer. Staff writer, *Rowan & Martin's Laugh-In*; writer, *Bewitched, The Partridge Family, Good Times, The Sonny & Cher Comedy Hour, The Glen Campbell Goodtime Hour*

KEN KRAGEN:
Producer, manager. Producer, *The Smothers Brothers Comedy Hour*; creator, *We Are The World*; clients include Kenny Rogers, Lionel Richie, Olivia Newton John, the Bee Gees

PERRY LAFFERTY:
Former V.P. of Programming, CBS. Series include *The Beverly Hillbillies, The Smothers Brothers Comedy Hour, The Mary Tyler Moore Show, All in the Family, M*A*S*H*; director, *The Twilight Zone*

NORMAN LEAR:
Writer, producer. Developer, producer, *All in the Family*; creator, producer, *Maude, The Jeffersons, Sanford & Son, Good Times, Mary Hartman, Mary Hartman*; founder, People for the American Way

RICK LUDWIN:
Senior VP of Late Night & Primetime Series at NBC. Producer, *Seinfeld, The Tonight Show with Jay Leno, Saturday Night Live, Late Night with Conan O'Brien, Last Call with Carson Daly*

DICK MARTIN:
Comedian, producer, director. Creator, co-star, *Rowan & Martin's Laugh-In*; performer, *Dean Martin Summer Show, The Lucy Show*; director, *The Bob Newhart Show, Archie Bunker's Place*

PETER MEHLMAN:
Writer, producer, journalist. Writer, executive producer, *Seinfeld, It's Like, You Know, Father of the Pride*; writer, producer, *SportsBeat with Howard Cosell*

BURT METCALFE:
Writer, executive producer, director, M*A*S*H, AfterM*A*S*H; casting director, Bewitched Anna and the King; performer (TV) Father of the Bride, (film) Diamonds Are Forever

CARROLL O'CONNOR:
Actor. (TV) All in the Family, Archie Bunker's Place, In the Heat of the Night; (film) Cleopatra, Kelly's Heroes, Marlowe, For Love of Ivy, What Did You Do in the War, Daddy?

GARY OWENS:
Actor, comedian, radio announcer. Original cast member, Rowan & Martin's Laugh-In; (cartoon voices) Roger Ramjet, Space Ghost, The Blue Falcon, The Ren & Stimpy Show

GLENN PADNICK:
President of Castle Rock Television. Production supervisor, Seinfeld, Boston Common, The Single Guy, Movie Stars, Mission Hill, Married with Children, Who's the Boss?, 227

ROD PARKER:
Writer, producer. Writer, The Honeymooners, All in the Family; executive producer, Maude, Love, Sidney, All's Fair, The Nancy Walker Show, Gimme A Break, Empty Nest, Dear John

BILL PERSKY:
Writer, producer, director. Writer, producer, The Dick Van Dyke Show; co-creator, executive producer, writer, That Girl; director, The Bill Cosby Show, Kate and Allie

JOYCE RANDOLPH:
Actress. (TV) The Honeymooners, Cavalcade of Stars, The Jackie Gleason Show, Everything's Jake; (stage) No, No, Nanette, Stage Door, A Goose for the Gander

CARL REINER:
Actor, writer, producer, director. Creator, The Dick Van Dyke Show; actor, Your Show of Shows, Caesar's Hour; director, Where's Poppa?, Oh, God!, The Jerk, All of Me, Dead Men Don't Wear Plaid

GENE REYNOLDS:
Director, producer, actor. Director, producer, M*A*S*H, The Ghost and Mrs. Muir; co-creator, producer, Room 222, Lou Grant; actor, Our Gang comedies, Babes in Toyland

MICHAEL ROSS:
Writer, producer (with Bernie West and Don Nicholl). Writer, All in the Family, Chico and the Man, Designing Women; developer, writer, The Jeffersons, Three's Company

JAY SANDRICH:
Director. He & She, The Mary Tyler Moore Show, Soap, The Cosby Show, Lou Grant, WKRP in Cincinnati, The Tony Danza Show, The Golden Girls, Two and a Half Men

BOB SCHILLER:
Writer (with Bob Weiskopf). Series include The Abbott and Costello Show, I Love Lucy, The Lucy Show, Make Room For Daddy, All in the Family, Maude, The Carol Burnett Show, The Flip Wilson Show

GEORGE SCHLATTER:
Producer, director, writer. Creator, executive producer, Rowan & Martin's Laugh-In, Turn-On, Real People, The American Comedy Awards, Sinatra: 80 Years My Way, Next Big Star

ALFRED SCHNEIDER:
Head of Program Practices at ABC (1960–1990). Series include Roots, Soap, Charlie's Angels, Three's Company, Thirtysomething, Moonlighting

GEORGE SHAPIRO:
Agent, manager, producer. Packaging agent, The Steve Allen Show, That Girl, Gomer Pyle, U.S.M.C.; executive producer (with Howard West), Seinfeld

ELLIOT SHOENMAN:
Writer, producer, playwright. Writer, story editor, *Maude*; co-executive producer, show runner, *The Cosby Show*, executive producer, *Home Improvement*, author (book), *Nobody's Business*

FRED SILVERMAN:
Head of Programming at CBS, ABC, and NBC. Series include *The Mary Tyler Moore Show, All in the Family, M*A*S*H, Maude, Three's Company, Charlie's Angels, Soap, The Waltons, Hill Street Blues*

TREVA SILVERMAN:
Writer. Writer, script consultant, *The Mary Tyler Moore Show*; writer (TV) *Get Smart, The Monkees, Room 222, Captain Nice*; (stage) *Heart's Desire, Scandal*

TOM SMOTHERS:
Comedian, writer, producer. Co-star (with Dick Smothers), producer, *The Smothers Brothers Comedy Hour*; performer, *The Smothers Brothers Show*

JEAN STAPLETON:
Actress. (TV) *All in the Family*; (stage) *The Corn Is Green, Damn Yankees, Bells Are Ringing, Rhinoceros, Funny Girl, Arsenic and Old Lace, Eleanor: Her Secret Journey*

MARTIN STARGER:
Former President of ABC Entertainment. *Movie of the Week, The Odd Couple, Happy Days, Barney Miller, Roots, Rich Man, Poor Man*; producer (film), *Nashville, Sophie's Choice, Mask*

DAVID STEINBERG:
Comedian, director. Performer, *The Smothers Brothers Comedy Hour, The Tonight Show, Sit Down Comedy with David Steinberg*; director, *Seinfeld, Curb Your Enthusiasm, Mad About You*

LEONARD STERN:
Writer, producer, director. Writer, *The Honeymooners, The Phil Silvers Show*; writer, producer, *The Steve Allen Show, Get Smart, McMillan and Wife, He & She, The Snoop Sisters*

DON TAFFNER:
Sales agent, buyer, producer. Executive producer, *Three's Company, The Ropers, Three's a Crowd, Too Close for Comfort, As Time Goes By*

WILLIAM TANKERSLEY:
Announcer, program director, producer, network executive. Director of Program Practices at CBS (1955–1972); President, CEO, Council of Better Business Bureaus (1975–1988)

GRANT TINKER:
Ad agency program executive, producer, former Head of Programs, CEO of NBC. Producer, *The Mary Tyler Moore Show, The Bob Newhart Show, Rhoda, Phyllis, Lou Grant, Hill Street Blues*

ALAN WAGNER:
Producer, former V.P. of Primetime Development at CBS. Series include *The Dick Van Dyke Show, The Mary Tyler Moore Show, All in the Family, M*A*S*H, Maude, Kojak, The Waltons*

MASON WILLIAMS:
Writer, performer, composer. Writer, *The Roger Miller Show, The Smothers Brothers Comedy Hour, Saturday Night Live*; composer, *Classical Gas*

PAUL JUNGER WITT:
Producer. (TV) *The Partridge Family, Soap, Benson, The Golden Girls, Blossom, Empty Nest, Beauty and the Beast*; (film) *Brian's Song, Dead Poet's Society, Three Kings, Insomnia*

ALAN BUD YORKIN:
Director, producer. Producer (TV) *All in the Family, Sanford & Son, Maude, Good Times, The Jeffersons*; director (film) *Come Blow Your Horn, Divorce American Style, Start The Revolution Without Me*

Photograph and Illustration Credits

Photograph of Dick Van Dyke and Larry Mathews on page 6
 courtesy of Stephen Cox

Album cover for *That Was the Week That Was* on page 30
 courtesy of Jeffrey Abraham

Photograph of the Smothers Brothers and Mason Williams on page 41
 courtesy of Mason Williams

Photograph of *Laugh-In* cast on page 69 courtesy of Stephen Cox

Photograph of Rowan and Martin on page 73 courtesy of Stephen Cox

Photograph of Ted Bessell and Marlo Thomas on page 92
 courtesy of Stephen Cox

Photograph of *The Mary Tyler Moore Show* cast on page 99
 courtesy of Stephen Cox

Photograph of *Till Death Us Do Part* cast on page 127 courtesy of BBC

Photograph of Norman Lear, Jean Stapleton, and Carroll O'Connor on
 page 146 courtesy of Act III Communications

Photograph of the Bunkers and the Jeffersons on page 150
 courtesy of Stephen Cox

Photograph of *M*A*S*H* ensemble on page 164 courtesy of Stephen Cox

Photograph of Bea Arthur on page 188 courtesy of Stephen Cox

Photographs of *Maude* cast on pages 191 and 196 courtesy of Stephen Cox

Photograph of *Soap* ensemble on page 211 courtesy of Stephen Cox

Illustration of *Seinfeld* cast on page 240 by Glen Hanson

All other photographs courtesy of the author's personal collection

Index

Books from Allworth Press

Allworth Press is an imprint of Allworth Communications, Inc. Selected titles are listed below.

Makin' Toons: Inside the Most Popular Animated TV Shows and Movies
by Allan Neuwirth (paperback, 6 × 9, 288 pages, 75 b&w illus., $21.95)

Get the Picture? The Movie Lover's Guide to Watching Films
by Jim Piper (paperback, 6 × 9, 240 pages, 91 b&w illus., $18.95)

Animation: The Whole Story
by Howard Beckerman (paperback, 6 ⅞ × 9 ¾, 336 pages, $24.95)

The Best Things Ever Said in the Dark: The Wisest, Wittiest, Most Provocative Quotations from the Movies
by Bruce Adamson (hardcover, 7 ½ × 7 ½, 144 pages, $14.95)

Making It on Broadway: Actor's Tales of Climbing to the Top
by David Wiener and Jodie Langel (paperback, 6 × 9, 288 pages, $19.95)

Letters from Backstage: The Adventures of a Touring Stage Actor
by Michael Kostroff (paperback, 6 × 9, 224 pages, $16.95)

The Quotable Artist
by Peggy Hadden (hardcover, 7 ½ × 7 ½, 224 pages, $19.95)

The Quotable Musician: From Bach to Tupac
by Sheila E. Anderson (hardcover, 7 ½ × 7 ½, 224 pages, $19.95)

Documentary Filmmakers Speak
by Liz Stubbs (paperback, 6 × 9, 240 pages, $19.95)

So You Wannabe on Reality TV
by Jack Benza (paperback, 6 × 9, 224 pages, $19.95)

Please write to request our free catalog. To order by credit card, call 1-800-491-2808 or send a check or money order to Allworth Press, 10 East 23rd Street, Suite 510, New York, NY 10010. Include $6 for shipping and handling for the first book ordered and $1 for each additional book. Ten dollars plus $1 for each additional book if ordering from Canada. New York State residents must add sales tax.

To see our complete catalog on the World Wide Web, or to order online, you can find us at ***www.allworth.com.***

Neuwirth, a prolific writer, producer, director, and (*The Boys*), is clearly fascinated with American television's contentious evolution from the 1960s to today, a time which took us from married couples shown sleeping in separate beds, and forbidden words like *pregnant*, to the nearly anything-goes-outrageousness of today's on-air antics.

"It was just a small group of groundbreaking primetime comedy series that caused TV to grow up, with Norman Lear's *All in the Family* (CBS, 1971) as the main dividing point," Neuwirth points out. "We really have to view television in terms of B.L. or A.L.— Before Lear and After Lear." Or as the great comedy writer Larry Gelbart observes in the book, "With that first (toilet) flush, you know, all of television's inhibitions and ridiculous rules went down the drain, literally."

While researching and writing ***They'll Never Put That On The Air***, the author quickly realized that it would be smarter to let the voices of the famed TV creators tell their behind-the-scenes stories themselves. So the book became an oral history, filled with firsthand tales of determination and defiance, legendary battles with censors, and great showbiz anecdotes. Still, Neuwirth's wry voice and cogent observations are very much on hand to guide us throughout.

The voices of many of the brightest lights behind these landmark shows, like Lear, Reiner, Gelbart, Tom Smothers, George Schlatter, Dick Martin, Susan Harris, Allan Burns, Jay Sandrich, Valerie Harper, Carroll O'Connor, Jean Stapleton, Grant Tinker, Fred Silverman, Larry Charles, and scores of others—as well as their

ALLWORTH PRESS
10 East 23rd Street
Suite 510
New York, NY 10010

For more information visit our Web site at:
www.allworth.com

Distributed to the trade by Watson-Guptill Publications: 1-800-451-1741.

Allan Neuwirth is a producer, director, and comedy writer of TV shows, comic books, animation, and music videos. In addition to his award-winning work for Nickelodeon, Cartoon Network, and Fox Family, he has written comedy screenplays, stand-up material for performers like Regis Philbin, scripts for cartoon TV series like "Courage the Cowardly Dog," and much more. His syndicated comic strip, "Chelsea Boys," appears bi-weekly in dozens of publications across the U.S., Canada, and the UK. He has lectured on writing for television at New York University and the School of Visual Arts, and is the owner of a production company, Neuwirth Design. The author of *Makin' Toons* (Allworth Press), he lives in New York City.

<u>Applause for THEY'LL NEVER PUT THAT ON THE AIR</u>

"Reading–or should I say, devouring–this wonderfully (and literally) outspoken book is nearly as much fun as watching the shows themselves. This is a great read, and essential for anyone who desires a first-hand account of how TV grew up while making us laugh. As it chronicles legendary censorship battles and landmark breakthroughs, this book is at heart a celebration of the creative process in a medium that could certainly use another wake-up call." –Matt Roush, Senior Critic, *TV Guide*

"A fascinating read. Allan Neuwirth has deepened my appreciation of television's most daring and successful comedies. It's a miracle that anything good has ever gotten on the air, let alone stayed there!" –Susie Essman, Comedian and Actress, *Curb Your Enthusiasm*

then-adversaries, legendary chief censors Bill Tankersley and Alfred Schneider—are present and accounted for in the book. Filled with dozens of photos and distinctive black & white line drawings by artist Glen Hanson, *They'll Never Put That On The Air* is both a visual and verbal treat, and reads as a terrific documentary on how TV grew up while making us laugh.

At present, however, with a federal government in place that continues to push an aggressively conservative agenda, Neuwirth wonders which direction the medium is headed. "Much has changed since the '60s, of course... but there's no denying that we've been backsliding lately," he notes. "The sad truth is, many of TV's most daring shows—and ultimately the greatest successes—would never make it today. Religious organizations lobby harder than ever, threatening boycotts which cause affiliates to turn away series like the recently cancelled *The Book of Daniel* because they perceive them as anti-Christian—without even looking at them. All this chatter about red states vs. blue states... what's 'appropriate' for audiences to view... whether conservative private interest groups are still using Janet Jackson's brief flashing of her nipple on national TV two years ago to further their own aims... the massive fines the FCC continues to levy against TV and radio networks for language and content deemed vulgar—most recently it's the 'S-word' on cable... well, the subject matter of *They'll Never Put That On The Air* has never been more topical or relevant."

They'll Never Put That on the Air can be found in better bookstores, or it can be ordered directly from the publisher by calling 1-800-491-2808, or by

News

from

Allworth

Press

Contact:
Nana Greller
Tel: 212-777-8395 x13
Fax: 212-777-8261
E-mail
Ngreller@allworth.com

They'll Never Put That On the Air
by Allan Neuwirth

$19.95, 6 x 9, 272 pages, 55
Paperback, ISBN: 1-58115-417-8
Publication Date: April 2006

Timely New Book Looks at Taboo-Breaking TV Comedies
First-hand Accounts from the Voices Who Made TV Comedy Grow Up

"We were doing a war thing, and we were in the trenches. And somebody said, 'War is hell.' The censor said, 'You can't say that. Can't say hell.' So, the line was, 'Oh, war is heck!' We actually said that. We knew we were making a comment, though, on the stupidity of it," recalls TV and film legend Carl Reiner in Allan Neuwirth's entertaining and illuminating new book *They'll Never Put That On The Air*.